Women in American Religious History

an annotated bibliography and guide to sources

G. K. Hall

WOMEN'S STUDIES

Publications

Barbara Haber
Editor

Women in American Religious History

an annotated bibliography and guide to sources

DOROTHY C. BASS

SANDRA HUGHES BOYD

G.K.HALL &CO.

70 LINCOLN STREET, BOSTON, MASS.

Library of Congress Cataloging-in-Publication Data

Bass, Dorothy C.
  Women in American religious history.

  (A Reference publication in women's studies)
  Includes index.
  1. Women and religion—United States—Bibliography.
2. United States—Religion—Bibliography.   I. Boyd,
Sandra Hughes.   II. Title   III. Series.
Z7963.R45B37 1986   [BL458]   016.291′088042   86-22397
ISBN 0-8161-8151-9

This publication is printed on permanent/durable acid-free paper
MANUFACTURED IN THE UNITED STATES OF AMERICA

Contents

The Authors

Dorothy C. Bass is assistant professor of church history at the Chicago Theological Seminary, where she teaches courses on American religion, history of Christian thought, and women's studies. Her previous teaching positions include service as a Harper Fellow in the Humanities at the University of Chicago and as an associate for research in women's studies and church history at the Harvard Divinity School. A graduate of Wellesley College, Union Theological Seminary, and Brown University, she has published several articles on the religious history of American women.

Sandra Hughes Boyd is assistant librarian for public services at Princeton Theological Seminary. Prior to her recent appointment to that post, she was for eight years reference librarian and adjunct member of the faculty at Episcopal Divinity School in Cambridge, Massachusetts. She serves as vice-president of the Episcopal Women's History Project and director of the Episcopal Deaconess History Project. A graduate of Colorado College, the University of Minnesota, and the Episcopal Divinity School, she has published several articles on women and religion and has edited a guide to gathering church women's history.

Foreword

   This fine volume will quickly become one of the most indispensable
reference works in American women's history. Its appeal will not be
limited to scholars of religious history per se, since it embraces
social, economic, political, and regional issues as well as denominational, doctrinal, and devotional themes.

   From the Puritans to the present the history of American women
has been closely intertwined with American religious history, but
until now scholars have lacked a systematic means of exploring that
connection. This volume provides the means. Its publication makes
possible the exploration of a wide variety of new questions. How
has women's religious culture differed from that of men? What part
did women play in the evolution of institutional and cultural change
in American religious life? How does the full inclusion of women in
American religious history change our understanding of that history?

   Given the central importance of religion in the lives of American
women, the task of completing this richly annotated bibliography
might at first glance seem impossible. The magnitude of this under-
taking has demanded dedication and resourcefulness of its compilers.
Historians and students of history will be in their debt for genera-
tions to come.

Kathryn Kish Sklar

Preface

More than a decade ago, as students in two different theological seminaries, each of us was seized by a set of questions that still engages us: Who were the religious women who preceded us? How did they believe and minister and agitate and pray--or did they? Why were they absent from the histories we had read? Unknown to one another at that time, each of us set out in search of answers. We did so with little guidance: sources were hard to find, few excellent scholarly works on the subjects that most interested us had been published, and even the general outlines of a religious history of American women were difficult to discern. Even so, each of us learned that with diligence and imagination we could discover a great deal of material for the study of women in American religious history. We began to make lists, to teach courses, and to do further research.

Several years later, we met and decided to collaborate on this volume. The years since each of us first took up the study of American women's religious history have been extraordinarily productive for researchers on this topic. Now there are some excellent scholarly works, though many more are needed. The literature taken as a whole begins to suggest some general outlines of a religious history of American women. And sources are becoming relatively more available. This bibliography aims to gather together and make more accessible the work that has been done thus far, thereby both recording the current state of knowledge and preparing the way for future work.

To study women in American religious history, one must draw upon the literature and methods of several fields of inquiry. Chapter 1 presents general works in the fields that surround and define our topic. Its first two sections are devoted to specializations within the field of American history: the history of women and the history of religion. Although authors in each of these areas too often overlook the importance of the other, our readers need to be aware of both. The third section of chapter 1 introduces works on the methodology of feminist studies in religion and lists some anthologized examples of their practice. Scholarship in this relatively new area of inquiry is appearing at such a rapid rate that this section may well be the first to be rendered obsolete; when that happens readers are advised to receive the material listed here as historical evidence from an important period in the religious history of American women. Chapter 1 concludes with a section on general histories

and anthologies on our own topic. In this first chapter and throughout the bibliography, we have also provided readers with resources
that will lead them to other material not listed here. The reference
works included in chapter 1 will repay the attention of those doing
research on topics covered in our later chapters, while the indexes
and periodicals listed there will keep readers informed of material
published after 1985.

Each successive chapter is devoted to the history of women in a
particular religious tradition or family of traditions. Yet rarely
are the sources narrowly tied to specific religious institutions or
denominations. Women's religious history, these sources collectively
demonstrate, has been intertwined with the other important matters in
women's lives. In some minority groups, for example, religious
identity has infused a variety of cultural expressions; thus fiction
and poetry are important sources for understanding the religious history of black women, and guides to locating and interpreting such
literature are included here. Similarly, many sources on the history
of Jewish or Roman Catholic women reach far beyond the bounds of
synagogue and church (where women have been in a subordinate position)
to consider experiences of immigration or family life in which religion played a part. And material in the longest chapter, chapter 2,
on Protestantism, demonstrates the importance of religion in many
aspects of women's lives, from domestic arrangements to participation
in movements of social reform.

In adopting an understanding of religion that permits us to
discern its manifestations in a wide range of cultural locations, we
share a perspective that is coming to prominence among historians of
American religion, though sufficient attention to women is still not
the rule in this field. Scholarship in women's history also supports
this perspective, as historians at first uninterested in religion
have discovered (often to their surprise) just how important religion
has been as an arena for women's activities. We hope and expect that
the interaction between these two fields will be increasingly fruitful in coming years.

This bibliography is, in part, a report on the current state of
research. In arranging the large number of sources listed here, it
seemed best to follow the contours of the literature itself. This
has not always resulted in ethically or aesthetically pleasing
divisions. Some chapters are very long, and others are woefully
short, and there is meaning in the imbalance. One cannot help but
think that the dominance in this bibliography of white Protestantism
over Native American religion exemplifies dominance of a more significant and tragic kind. And the segregation of sources on black
women in chapter 5 reflects the fact that almost none of the works in
the chapter on Protestantism, into which this topic might have been
integrated, pays substantial attention to black women's history. We
hope that this bibliography will contribute to the correction of
these and other imbalances by helping to disclose the fact of their
existence.

Preface

For those who diligently seek them, resources for the study of women in American religious history are beyond number. This bibliography concentrates its attention on secondary sources (works by scholars about history) rather than primary sources (material written by the historical figures themselves), although a small number of landmark primary sources are included. Since our emphasis is historical, we have not included most of the works being produced by religious women in our own time, such as feminist theology and ethics or reports on current events in the churches and synagogues. However, for those who wish to explore these topics, entry can be gained through the section on feminist studies in religion in the first chapter of this volume, as well as through the many works in each chapter that treat both historical and contemporary material.

We encourage our readers to be resourceful in their use of this book and the many other books listed here. Our format combines features of several reference genres, including the annotated bibliography, the bibliographical essay, and the research manual. Cross-references within the bibliography point to relationships among topics. Guides to further information at the end of each chapter or section point to the wide range of primary sources required for advanced research, since a complete catalog of primary sources is far beyond our means. (Researchers should also be aware that the footnotes and bibliographies of scholarly works on particular subjects are often excellent guides to primary sources.) The arrangement of topics displayed in the table of contents serves both to lead readers to their interests and to outline this field. The index lists all references to proper names, including authors, editors, and the historical figures who are our subjects.

We cannot claim that our lists are exhaustive, though we have tried to include as many appropriate entries as possible. Some articles have been intentionally omitted because they are insubstantial or seriously inaccessible; in all probability, others are not here because they simply (and regrettably) escaped our attention. Sources on Canadian history are not included. Nor are works published after 1985. These last, which will someday require a new edition of this bibliography or one like it, are to be eagerly anticipated.

We offer this volume in the hope that it will prove useful to several kinds of readers. We hope that it will ease and support the efforts of those whose research and teaching will continue to expand our collective understanding of the religious history of American women. We also hope that it will help to persuade scholars in related fields of the extent and importance of research in women's religious history, as well as directing them to sources that will be helpful in their work. And we hope that, at least occasionally, students like we once were will find this book and recognize in it an invitation to study some aspect of this complex, challenging, and fascinating topic.

Many people assisted in the preparation of this volume. The staffs of the Episcopal Divinity School/Weston School of Theology Libraries and the Hammond Library of Chicago Theological Seminary, where most of the work was accomplished, deserve special thanks. Support for early phases of research came from the Episcopal Divinity School and from the Program on Women's Studies in Religion at the Harvard Divinity School and its gifted director, Constance Buchanan. Numerous individuals suggested items for inclusion; consulted on specific topics were Carolyn DeSwarte Gifford, Kathryn Hellerstein, Christa Ressmeyer Klein, Marilyn Richardson, Rosemary Radford Ruether, and Arlene Swidler, though we retain responsibility for all shortcomings. Valuable clerical assistance was provided by Jane Boyd. We also express gratitude to the Lilly Endowment for financial support of this project, and especially to Robert W. Lynn, senior vice president for religion, for his conviction that historical study is an indispensable part of sound reflection on the important issues of our own time.

I. General Works

I.A. AMERICAN HISTORY AND AMERICAN RELIGIOUS HISTORY

Even though most works on American history and American religion have
neglected the contributions of women, several resources in this area
are useful as supportive material, research guides, and background
for research on women in American religion. A select list of such
resources is included here.

I.A.1 AMERICAN HISTORY

1   America: History and Life. 1964-.
        A guide to periodical literature that abstracts articles on
    the history of America contained in approximately 2,000 serial
    publications, issued quarterly and available as a computerized
    data base. Robert deV. Brunkow's Religion and Society in North
    America: An Annotated Bibliography (entry 6) and Cynthia
    Harrison's Women in American History: A Bibliography (entry 40)
    are based on this resource.

2   Freidel, Frank, ed. Harvard Guide to American History. Rev.
    ed. 2 vols. in 1. Cambridge, Mass.: Harvard University
    Press, 1974. xxx, 1290 pp.
        A basic reference bibliography for American history. Vol. 1
    includes helpful introductory material in "Research Methods and
    Materials" and topical materials under "Biographies and Personal
    Records," "Comprehensive and Area Histories," and "Histories of
    Special Subjects" (with one subtopic on women). Vol. 2 is
    arranged chronologically and then by subject areas within histori-
    cal periods (with one subtopic on women). There is a complete
    name index and a subject index.

3   Frick, Elizabeth. Library Research Guide to History: Illus-
    trated Search Strategy and Sources. Ann Arbor, Mich.: Pierian
    Press, 1980. x, 84 pp.
        This guide is intended to aid advanced college or graduate
    students in selecting topics and collecting information for pre-
    paring term or research papers in history. It is one of a number
    of such guides (several of which are noted by Frick), but it is
    unique in that a topic of concern to women's history, "Women's
    Suffrage," is used as an example throughout its illustrated search

strategy. The guide highlights several specialized reference
sources in women's history in addition to traditional American
history reference works.

I.A.2. AMERICAN RELIGIOUS HISTORY

4   Ahlstrom, Sydney E. A Religious History of the American People.
New Haven, Conn.: Yale University Press, 1973. 2d ed. 2 vols.
Garden City, N.Y.: Image Books, 1975. 697, 701 pp.
      Less than five percent of the names appearing in the index
to this monumental and comprehensive work are those of women.
Ahlstrom, in his preface to the 1975 edition, recognized "the need
to expand the account in several areas," one of which was "diverse
matters on women in religious history" (p. 18). Nevertheless,
this work remains the most comprehensive on American religious
history.

5   Alexander, Jon, ed. American Personal Religious Accounts,
1600-1980: Toward An Inner History of America's Faiths. New
York: Edwin Mellen Press, 1983. xiii, 503 pp.
      This anthology of excerpts from 100 personal documents
illustrating American religious experience from the seventeenth
century to the present represents most fully Protestant evangelical conversion experiences but endeavors to be inclusive of women,
blacks, and Native Americans in its coverage. A general introduction, bibliography of references to 500 other personal religious
accounts, and biographical information about the writer of each
account are included.

6   Brunkow, Robert deV., ed. Religion and Society in North
America: An Annotated Bibliography. Santa Barbara, Calif.:
ABC-CLIO, 1983. xi, 515 pp.
      The abstracts of 4,304 articles published from approximately
1973 to 1980 in about 600 periodicals are assembled here, indexed
by author and subject. The detailed subject index aims to alert
readers to multiple subjects within each entry, and researchers
on women in religious history will readily find much that is useful, beginning with some 200 abstracts listed under the subject
heading "Women" and continuing to listings under individual,
organizational, and topical headings. The abstracts here were
compiled from the index to America: History and Life (entry 1),
and for articles published since 1980 see that publication's
quarterly indexes and annual cumulations.

7   Burr, Nelson Rollin. A Critical Bibliography of Religion in
America. 2 vols. Princeton: Princeton University Press,
1961. xx, 1-541 pp.; xv, 545-1219 pp.
      This comprehensive bibliography and commentary in a classi-
fied arrangement includes works in the following categories:
bibliographical guides; general surveys and histories; the evolution of American religion; religion and society; religion in the
arts and literature; and intellectual history, theology, philosophy, and science. An author index is included. An abridged and
updated version containing brief annotations was published under

the title <u>Religion in American Life</u> (New York: Appleton-Century-
Crofts, 1971). Sandeen and Hale's <u>American Religion and Philosophy: A Guide to Information Sources</u> (entry 11) serves as a sequel
to this monumental bibliography.

8   Gaustad, Edwin S., ed. <u>A Documentary History of Religion in
    America</u>. 2 vols. Grand Rapids, Mich.: Eerdmans, 1982-83.
    Vol. 1, to the Civil War, xviii, 535 pp.; vol. 2, since 1865,
    xx, 610 pp.
        Gaustad presents hundreds of short selections from histori-
cal documents, introducing them with brief remarks. Since he has
cast his net widely, the volumes include material on groups often
overlooked. Bibliographical essays at the conclusion of each
chapter are helpfully selective, providing useful resources for
further reading in many areas of American religious history. Although selections focus on women only infrequently, the volumes as
a whole provide a vivid background for students of women or any
other particular topic within American religious history.

9   Melton, J. Gordon. <u>Encyclopedia of American Religions</u>. 2 vols.
    Wilmington, N.C.: McGrath, 1978. xiv, 608 pp.; 595 pp.
        Believing that American religions are too complex to be
categorized as "churches" or "sects" or "cults," Melton has
organized 1,200 religious bodies extant in the United States in
1976 into seventeen "families." The member bodies in each family,
Melton says, each "share a common heritage, thought world, and
life style" (p. ix). Beginning with "The Liturgical Family"
(Western and Eastern), the work moves to "Lutheran," "Reformed-
Presbyterian," etc. Unlike Piepkorn's work (entry 10), which
focuses on traditional Christian religious groups, this one includes Mormons, communalists, New Thought and Christian Science
groups, psychic, occult and witchcraft groups, Jewish groups,
Muslims, Hindus, Buddhists, and "New Unaffiliated Religious
Bodies" (including "Jesus People," "Gay Religion," "Mail-Order
Denominations," "Politically and Socially Oriented Bodies," etc.).

10   Piepkorn, Arthur Carl. <u>Profiles in Belief: The Religious
    Bodies of the United States and Canada</u>. 4 vols. in 3. New
    York: Harper & Row, 1978. xix, 324 pp.; xx, 721 pp.; xvii,
    262 pp.; xviii, 191 pp.
        The religious beliefs of the members of more than 700 Ameri-
can and Canadian religious bodies are portrayed and interpreted
in this encyclopedic work. The history and theological development
of each tradition is told and the current status of each is described. Although Christian Scientists, Latter-day Saints, and
Spiritualists are omitted, this work provides helpful and concise
background information on most of the traditional religious groups
in this country. Vol. 1, Roman Catholic, Old Catholic, and Eastern Orthodox; vol. 2, Protestant Denominations; vol. 3, Holiness
and Pentecostal; vol. 4, Evangelical, Fundamentalist, and Other
Christian Bodies.

11   Sandeen, Ernest R., and Hale, Frederick. <u>American Religion and</u>
      <u>Philosophy: A Guide to Information Sources</u>. Detroit: Gale
      Research Co., 1978. xvi, 377 pp.
            Designed to take up where Burr's work (entry 7) ended, this
      work is a guide to the recent literature and key primary documents
      that have appeared since 1961. Although it is reflective of the
      scarcity of resources on women in religion published before the
      mid-1970s and lists only about a dozen such works, it is otherwise
      comprehensive and contains helpful annotations. Full author,
      title, and subject indexes are included.

                    I.A.3. BIBLIOGRAPHIES AND INDEXES

12   <u>Catholic Periodical and Literature Index</u>. Vol. 14 (1967/68)-.
      (Combines <u>Catholic Periodical Index</u>, 1939-67, and <u>Guide to</u>
      <u>Catholic Literature</u>, 1888-1967.)
            Published bimonthly by the Catholic Library Association,
      this work indexes the material in approximately 150 Catholic
      periodicals by author and subject. Each year about 2,500 books by
      Catholics or of Catholic interest are listed by author, title, and
      subject. Book reviews are also included. There is a listing of
      papal documents and commentary in chronological order under the
      name of the appropriate pope.

13   <u>Index to Jewish Periodicals</u>. Vol. 1 (1963)-.
            This index to "selected English language journals of general
      and scholarly interest" indexes about 40 periodicals by author and
      subject. Citations to book reviews are listed under the author's
      name with a title listing under the general heading "Book Reviews."

14   <u>Religion Index One: Periodicals</u>. Vol. 13 (1977/78)-. (Former
      title: <u>Index to Religious Periodical Literature</u>, 1949-77.)
            Published semiannually by the American Theological Library
      Association, this work indexes articles and book reviews from
      about 200 primarily, but not exclusively, Protestant-oriented
      journals. The items are arranged in alphabetical subject order
      with (since 1975) an author index including abstracts. A com-
      panion volume, <u>Religion Index Two: Multi-Author Works</u>, indexing
      by subject and author composite works by various authors published
      during the year, has been published beginning coverage with the
      year 1976.

15   <u>Women and Religion: A Bibliography Selected from the ATLA</u>
      <u>Religion Database</u>. 3d rev. ed. Chicago, Ill.: American
      Theological Library Association, 1983. 660 pp.
            Produced by a computer search of the American Theological
      Library Association's religion index database, this bibliography
      includes citations to more than 3,800 articles and books that
      appeared from 1949 through September 1983. The citations appear
      in over 11,000 subject categories and are indexed by author or
      editor. Although periodical entries are missing for the period
      1960-74, there is coverage from festschriften and multiauthor
      works for that period. About 1,100 of the entries have abstracts
      or tables of contents. See <u>Index to Religious Periodical</u>

Literature, 1960-1974 for the period missing from this bibliography and Religion Index One: Periodicals (entry 14) and Religion
Index Two: Multi-Author Works for material published since late
1983.

I.B. AMERICAN WOMEN'S HISTORY

The rapidly expanding field of women's history is providing students
and researchers with a considerable variety of new resources. What
follows is a selective list of those resources which provide useful
background and reference information for the study of women in American religion. (A fuller annotation for a particular essay will be
found in a later chapter under the number indicated in parentheses.)

I.B.1. SURVEYS AND ANTHOLOGIES

16   Berkin, Carol Ruth, and Norton, Mary Beth, eds. Women of
      America: A History. Boston: Houghton Mifflin, 1979. xv,
      442 pp.
         Original essays and documents organized to present "a
chronologically and topically balanced picture of the lives of
American women throughout the history of European settlement on
the North American continent" (p. xv). The essays represent a
variety of approaches to the history of women: biography, legal
analysis, quantitative data, organizational studies, and examina-
tions of role prescriptions. Of particular interest are "Women of
Light (Quaker Women)," by Mary Maples Dunn (entry 318); "Women
Founding of Mount Holyoke College," by Kathryn Kish Sklar (entry
138); and "'A Truly Subversive Affair': Women Against Lynching in
the Twentieth-Century South," by Jacquelyn Dowd Hall (entry 209).

17   Conway, Jill K. The Female Experience in Eighteenth- and
      Nineteenth-Century America: A Guide to the History of American
      Women. New York: Garland Publishing, Inc., 1982. xxiv,
      290 pp.
         By means of short essays and unannotated bibliographies,
Conway surveys the traditional and secondary sources published
before the mid-1970s for ways of approaching women's experience.
The chapter on women's religious life and the reform tradition
covers women in the antislavery movement, reform communities, and
Unitarianism, serving as a supplementary guide to older sources
in selected areas of religious concern.

18   Cott, Nancy R., and Pleck, Elizabeth H., eds. A Heritage of
      Her Own: Toward a New Social History of American Women. New
      York: Simon & Schuster, 1979. 608 pp.
         Gathering together many of the best articles in women's his-
tory to appear in the first decade of the late twentieth-century
American women's movement, the editors' introductory essay provides a context within which to read the essays, presented in historical period chronological order. Of particular interest are
"Vertuous Women Found: New England Ministerial Literature, 1668-
1735," by Laurel Thatcher Ulrich (entry 95) ; "Passionlessness: An
Interpretation of Victorian Sexual Ideology, 1790-1850," by Nancy

F. Cott (entry 122); and "Beauty, The Beast and The Militant
Woman: A Case Study in Sex Roles and Social Stress in Jacksonian
America" (entry 165), and "The Female World of Love and Ritual:
Relations Between Women in Nineteenth-Century America" (entry
140), by Carroll Smith-Rosenberg.

19   Friedman, Jean E., and Shade, William G., eds. Our American
      Sisters: Women in American Life and Thought. 3d ed. Lexing-
      ton, Mass.: D.C. Heath, 1982. ix, 593 pp.
         This sizeable collection of essays is arranged into four
chronological periods, each one preceded by an introduction to the
major unifying themes. Of particular interest are the following
essays: "Husbands and Wives," by John Demos (entry 84); "The
Liberation of Black Women," by Pauli Murray (entry 443); and
"Religion and the Bonds of Womanhood," by Nancy Cott (entry 121).

20   Katz, Esther, and Rapone, Anita, eds. Women's Experience in
      America: An Historical Anthology. New Brunswick, N.J.:
      Transaction Books, 1980. 414 pp.
         Dissenting from the opinion that economic roles have dic-
tated women's status in American history, the editors propose an
alternative approach based on the examination of social structures
that govern the interaction of women with their society (pp. 4-5).
Among the essays of most direct interest to a study of women in
American religion are "The Case of the American Jezebels: Anne
Hutchinson and Female Agitation During the Years of the Antinomian
Turmoil, 1636-1640," by Lyle W. Koehler (entry 109); "Ladies
Bountiful: Organized Women's Benevolence in Early Nineteenth-
Century America," by Keith Melder (entry 132); and "The Spiritual-
ist Medium: A Study of Female Professionalism in Victorian
America," by R. Laurence Moore (entry 556).

21   Kelly, Mary, ed. Woman's Being, Woman's Place: Female Iden-
      tity and Vocation in American History. Boston: G.K. Hall,
      1979. 372 pp.
         The essays, most of which were presented at a conference
on the history of women in St. Paul (1977), address historiographical questions of sources and methodology, socialization as a
process, the ways wifehood and motherhood served as identity and
vocation, and the variety of women's responses to this "calling."
Of particular interest are the essays in the section entitled "A
Woman's Place: The Halls of Domesticity," which present "four
glimpses of a powerful spiritual and moral ambition grounded in
the bedrock of mundane domesticity" (p. 197).

22   Kerber, Linda K., and Mathews, Jane DeHart, eds. Women's
      America: Refocusing the Past. New York: Oxford University
      Press, 1982. xi, 478 pp.
         The editors have collected into one volume about sixty docu-
ments and articles covering a wide range of American women's history, providing an excellent survey of the field, from the early

seventeenth century to contemporary feminism, including both
unknown and famous women in American history. A bibliography
provides information for further exploration into the field.

23 Lerner, Gerda, ed. Black Women in White America: A Docu-
    mentary History. New York: Pantheon, 1972. xxvi, 630 pp.
        In this collection of primary documents (letters, speeches,
    memoirs, periodical articles, oral history transcripts) by black
    women, Lerner focuses on the family and work experiences of black
    women in the nineteenth and early twentieth centuries. Each topic
    and selection of sources is introduced briefly. The subjects
    covered are slavery; education; sexual oppression; domestic
    service and factory work; the struggle for survival of the family;
    government work and political life; racism and resistance strug-
    gles; and black women's views on womanhood and women's liberation.

24 Lerner, Gerda, ed. The Female Experience: An American Docu-
    mentary. Indianapolis: Bobbs Merrill, 1977. xxxvi, 509 pp.
        This work was written and edited in response to the question
    "what would history be like if it were seen through the eyes of
    women and ordered by values they define?" (p. xxi). Lerner
    approaches the task first by providing a large number of primary
    resources, many of them the writings of unknown women and never
    printed before. The material is then organized thematically in
    three sections: the life stages and turning points in women's
    lives, women's experiences in male-defined institutions, and the
    developmental stages of feminist consciousness. Many of the
    selections reflect religious beliefs of the women, among them
    those of preacher Salome Lincoln, heretic Anne Hutchinson, Quaker
    martyr Mary Dyer, frontier feminist Marian Louise Moore, and
    abolitionist Sarah Grimke.

25 Ryan, Mary P. Womanhood in America: From Colonial Times to
    the Present. 3d ed. New York: Franklin Watts, 1983. 392 pp.
        In this comprehensive survey of women's actual experiences,
    Ryan describes "the creation and transformation of womanhood in
    America." She sees that process expressing itself in three dis-
    tinct patterns: "first, the integral position of women in the
    patriarchal household economy of the seventeenth century; second,
    the segregated woman's sphere under industrial capitalism; and
    finally, the more integrated and balanced, but still unequal
    relations of the sexes during the twentieth century" (p. 15). The
    work is very helpful background to the study of women's religious
    history in America.

I.B.2. HISTORIOGRAPHY AND METHODOLOGY

26 Carroll, Berenice A., ed. Liberating Women's History:
    Theoretical and Critical Essays. Urbana: University of
    Illinois Press, 1976. xiv, 434 pp.
        These essays were collected in an initial attempt to remedy
    three deficiencies in the traditional historical approaches to
    history as applied to and identified by the new field of women's

7

history; the need for a critical historiography of women's history, the need "to test a variety of old and new theories or assumptions against the evidence of women's historical experience," and the need "to find greater conceptual clarity and define new directions for research in women's history" (p. v). Among the important contributions toward addressing questions which should arise fairly early in a venture into women's history are "The Problem of Women's History," by Ann D. Gordon, Mari Jo Buhle, and Nancy Schrom Dye, and "Sex and Class in Colonial and Nineteenth-Century America," by Anne D. Gordon and Mari Jo Buhle.

27   Frontiers 2, no. 2 (Summer 1977):1-101.
       This special issue on women's oral history, in its second edition with an updated resource section, contains introductions to the subject, "how-to" articles, narrative accounts of doing oral history with women, and examples of oral history transcripts. The women interviewed range from union women to black women to Chinese women immigrants to suffragists. The resource section includes interview guides, release forms, a state-by-state listing of women's oral history projects and collections, and a bibliography of guides, oral history collections, publications, and published oral histories of women. A second special issue, "Women's Oral History Two," appeared in vol. 7, no. 1 (1983) and included, in addition to a bibliography, an 8-page "Directory of Women's Oral History Projects and Collections" arranged by state. Frontiers is published in association with the Women's Studies Program, University of Colorado, Boulder, CO 80309.

28   Hunter College Women's Studies Collective. Women's Realities, Women's Choices: An Introduction to Women's Studies. New York: Oxford University Press, 1983. 656 pp.
       This ambitious textbook by eight scholars in the humanities, social sciences, and health care surveys information and perceptions about women and raises provocative questions about women's "realities and choices" in numerous aspects of family and society, including religion. Intended as a textbook, it is a useful and genuinely interdisciplinary introduction to some of the basic concepts and sources of women's studies.

29   Kelly, Joan. Women, History, and Theory: The Essays of Joan Kelly. Chicago: University of Chicago Press, 1984. xxvi, 163 pp.
       Gathered together here are essays by the late Joan Kelly, one of the founders of the new scholarship about women. Her work approached women's history from a Marxist feminist perspective and provided a unique view of the field ranging from the Middle Ages to the middle of the twentieth century.

30   Lerner, Gerda. The Majority Finds Its Past: Placing Women in History. New York: Oxford University Press, 1979. xxxii, 217 pp.
       This is the first collection of Lerner's essays, written over a period of eleven years as part of her efforts to develop a theory of women's history. The essays reflect the evolution

of historical thinking in women's studies, as well as Lerner's own
scholarly development. Her introduction specifically addresses
the latter in its "Autobiographical Notes." The essays range from
her early and influential "The Lady and the Mill Girl: Changes in
the Status of Women in the Age of Jackson" through a series of
pieces on historiographical issues in black women's history to a
summary of the ways in which women's history challenges traditional scholarship.

31   Mathews, Donald G. "Women's History/Everyone's History." In
     Women in New Worlds, vol. 1 (entry 81), pp. 29-47.
          In this keynote address delivered at a major denominational
     meeting on women's history, Mathews reflects upon the loss of
     memory of women's history and the importance of its recovery.
     Without the new perspective it brings to historical study, no
     understanding of the "total ethos" of the past can be attained.

32   Norton, Mary Beth. "Review Essay: American History." Signs:
     Journal of Women in Culture and Society 5 (Winter 1979):324-37.
          Noting the dramatic advance in the understanding of women's
     history by its students since 1975, Norton focuses on new areas of
     inquiry represented in the "cutting-edge" literature of journal
     articles. She sees these in three categories: amplifications and
     modifications of previously identified themes having to do with
     nineteenth-century white middle-class women, aspects of the lives
     of nineteenth- and twentieth-century women newly come to the at-
     tention of scholars, and significant breakthroughs in the study of
     colonial women.

33   Sicherman, Barbara. "Review Essay: American History." Signs:
     Journal of Women in Culture and Society 1 (Winter 1975):461-86.
          Sicherman and Mary Beth Norton (entry 32) in their review
     essays survey recent publications from a feminist perspective,
     describing the general trends of scholarship, recommending par-
     ticularly valuable material, and calling into question research
     that fails to take women's issues into consideration. Sicherman
     looks at changing life cycles and family patterns in the eigh-
     teenth century, the doctrine of spheres in the nineteenth century,
     and trends and prospects for future research.

34   Sklar, Kathryn Kish. "The Last Fifteen Years: Historians'
     Changing Views of American Women in Religion and Society." In
     Women in New Worlds, vol. 1 (entry 81), pp. 48-65.
          Sklar perceives four stages of interpretation in twentieth-
     century historical writing about women; her depiction and analysis
     of them constitute a useful overview of research and a clarifica-
     tion of methodology.

I.B.3. BIOGRAPHIES

35   James, Edward T.; James, Janet Wilson; and Boyer, Paul S., eds.
     Notable American Women 1607-1950: A Biographical Dictionary.
     3 vols. Cambridge, Mass.: Harvard University Press, 1971.
     xlix, 687 pp.; 659 pp.; 729 pp.

This is the definitive biographical resource on American women and should be in every library. The readable and authoritative biographical sketches of 1,300 women are accompanied by excellent bibliographies (many of which have already been happily outdated by the flow of recent scholarship). The introduction by Janet Wilson James serves as a historical survey of women in the period. A "Classified List of Selected Biographies" at the end of vol. 3 leads one to the biographies of a number of women in the following categories: ministers and evangelists, missionaries, missionary society leaders, Mormon women, religious educators, and religious founders and leaders. See also its companion volume (entry 36).

36   Sicherman, Barbara, and Green, Carol Hurd, eds. Notable American Women, The Modern Period: A Biographical Dictionary. Cambridge, Mass.: Harvard University Press, 1980. xxii, 773 pp.
    This supplemental work to the original three-volume set (entry 35) includes biographical sketches with bibliographies for 442 women who died between 1 January 1951 and 31 December 1975. The introduction analyzes the biographical data as collective information to provide a description of women in twentieth-century America. The classified list of biographies at the end of the volume reflects prominent women's changing priorities in that it includes fewer explicitly religious categories than its predecessor, recording 18 women in the category "Religion."

37   Willard, Frances E., and Livermore, Mary A., eds. A Woman of the Century. 1893. Reprints. Detroit: Gale Research Co., 1967; New York: Gordon Press, 1975 (2 vols.). 2d ed. as American Women: Fifteen Hundred Biographies. 2 vols. 1897. Reprint. Detroit: Gale Research Co., 1973.
    The first edition is subtitled "biographical sketches accompanied by portraits of leading American women in all walks of life . . ." and contains 1,470 biographies. The second edition has more sketches and, at the end of its second volume, a classified list of biographies, which includes women under the following categories: Christian Scientists, church and religious workers, evangelists, hymn writers, ministers, and missionaries.

I.B.4.   BIBLIOGRAPHIES AND GUIDES

38   Addis, Patricia K. Through A Woman's I: An Annotated Bibliography of American Women's Autobiographical Writings, 1946-1976. Metuchen, N.J.: Scarecrow Press, 1983. xiv, 607 pp.
    Over 2,000 autobiographies published in the mid-twentieth century by American women are found in this bibliography arranged by their authors. An "Index of Authors by Profession or Salient Characteristic" and an "Index of Narratives by Subject Matter" allow one to locate, for example, missionaries, ministers, and ministers' wives as well as spiritual autobiographies. An index of titles is also included.

39   Haber, Barbara. <u>Women in America: A Guide to Books, 1963–</u>
      <u>1975</u>. With an appendix on books published 1976–1979. Urbana:
      University of Illinois Press, 1981. xv, 262 pp.
          An annotated bibliography of current books on American women
      compiled by the curator of printed books at Radcliffe College's
      Schlesinger Library on the History of Women in America. Active in
      developing the Library's collection since 1968, Haber has synthe-
      sized a great deal of information to provide a selective guide to
      books in a broad range of subjects. The original edition, pub-
      lished in 1978 by G.K. Hall, covered 450 books published through
      1975; this edition provides, in an appendix, a bibliographical
      essay covering more than 200 additional works.

40   Harrison, Cynthia E. <u>Women in American History: A Bibliog-</u>
      <u>raphy</u>. 2 vols. Santa Barbara, Calif.: ABC-CLIO, 1979–85.
          Compiled primarily from the index <u>America: History and Life</u>
      (entry 1), this work provides abstracts and annotations of more
      than 7,000 articles published from 1964 to 1984. The first volume
      is arranged in broad chronological divisions with topical head-
      ings, including "Religion and Ethnicity," within each period cate-
      gory. The second volume is organized topically, including a chap-
      ter on "Women and Religion." Both volumes include detailed sub-
      ject and author indexes. For articles published after 1984, see
      <u>America: History and Life</u> (entry 1) quarterly indexes and annual
      cumulations.

41   Hinding, Andrea, ed. <u>Women's History Sources: A Guide to</u>
      <u>Archives and Manuscript Collections in the United States</u>.
      2 vols. New York: Bowker, 1979. xix, 1114 pp.; x, 391 pp.
          Nearly three quarters of the more than 18,000 collections
      described in this invaluable resource had never before been listed
      in a national publication. Collections of individual, family,
      and institutional papers, records, photographs, and oral histories
      are described in the first volume. In the second volume is found
      a complete index providing name, subject, and geographic access to
      items in the first volume. This resource should be supplemented
      by consulting the <u>Directory of Archives and Manuscript Reposi-</u>
      <u>tories</u> (Washington, D.C.: Government Printing Office, 1978) and
      the periodical publication <u>National Union Catalog of Manuscript</u>
      <u>Collections</u> (Hamden, Conn.: Shoe String Press, 1962–). See
      <u>Women Religious History Sources: A Guide to Repositories</u> (entry
      370) for source materials about women in religious orders.

42   Stineman, Esther. <u>Women's Studies: A Recommended Core</u>
      <u>Bibliography</u>. Littleton, Colo.: Libraries Unlimited, Inc.,
      1979. 670 pp.
          Out of Stineman's work as women's studies librarian for the
      University of Wisconsin system came this monumental selective
      bibliography of 1,763 items ranging from anthropology to sports
      and including several chapters on literature and reference mate-
      rials (including published guides to large library, microform, and
      archival collections) as well as a listing of feminist periodicals.
      Intended to serve as a selection tool for the development of
      women's studies collections in undergraduate libraries, it is of

equal value to researchers in the individual subject areas and for
reference because of its broad scope and complete author, title,
and subject indexes.

I.B.5. PERIODICALS

43   Feminist Studies. Vols. 1-3 (1971-[74?]; vol. 4 (1978)-.
      Independently published three times a year "to encourage
analytic responses to feminist issues and to open new areas of
research, criticism, and speculation," this journal should be
consulted by researchers wishing to be kept up-to-date in contemporary women's history research. Direct inquiries to Women's
Studies Program, University of Maryland, College Park, MD 20742.

44   Signs: Journal of Women in Culture and Society. Vol. 1
      (1975)-.
      The most influential journal publishing the new scholarship
on women, this quarterly has published review essays on women and
American history (entries 32-33) and on women and religion (entries
50 and 55), as well as many other articles separately annotated in
this bibliography. With Feminist Studies, this journal is a "must"
for researchers in women's history. It is published by the
University of Chicago Press, 5801 Ellis Ave., Chicago, IL 60637.

45   Women's Review of Books. Vol. 1 (1983)-.
      Coming from the Wellesley College Center for Research on
Women, Wellesley, MA 02181, this monthly publication provides
reviews and information about a wide range of current research in
women's studies.

I.C. FEMINIST STUDIES IN RELIGION

In recent years, feminist scholars have introduced new perspectives
in virtually every field of theological and religious studies. The
methodology of their enterprise is the subject of continuing reflection; entries in the first section below address methodological concerns relevant to all students of women and religion. Subsequent
entries are meant to guide readers in locating the products of this
feminist scholarship, both in its early expressions in anthologies
and in its continuing development in current periodicals.

I.C.1. METHODOLOGY

46   Buchanan, Constance H. "Women and Religion: Feminist Scholar-
      ship in Theology." In The Women's Annual: The Year in Review,
      1980, edited by Barbara Haber. Boston: G.K. Hall, 1981,
      pp. 231-43.
      Buchanan surveys the work of recent feminist theologians who
believe either that the core prophetic vision and message of liberation in Judaism and Christianity will provide the tools against
the oppression of women and other subordinate groups or that the
irredeemably sexist core of these traditions leads to their re-
jection in favor of the construction of new feminist religious

forms and traditions. The work of Mary Daly, Rosemary Ruether, Phyllis Trible, Elaine Pagels, Carol Christ, Judith Plaskow, Naomi Goldenberg and others is examined.

47 Buchanan, Constance H. "Women and Religion: Feminist Scholarship in Theology." In The Women's Annual: The Year in Review, 1981, edited by Barbara Haber. Boston: G.K. Hall, 1982, pp. 236-47.

Buchanan here surveys the most recent work of Dorothee Sölle and Rosemary Ruether as they reject patriarchal concepts of the divine and messiah in favor of new theoretical frameworks. She also discusses feminism and process thought, concepts of the feminine and masculine expressed in myth, and female spirituality arising out of the experience of women.

48 Christ, Carol. "New Feminist Theology: A Review of the Literature." Religious Studies Review 3 (October 1977):203-12.

Christ introduces this concise survey and critique of feminist theology by warning that because the feminist challenge calls not only for a change in the understanding of the core symbolism of Western religion but for a change in the core symbolism itself, readers must face squarely the emotional threat it engenders in order to understand and take it seriously. She includes here discussion of the work of Elizabeth Cady Stanton, Valerie Saiving Goldstein, Plaskow, Daly, Ruether, Letty Russell, Rita Gross, Elisabeth Schüssler Fiorenza, Sheila Collins, and Penelope Washbourn, as well as her own work.

49 Christ, Carol P., and Plaskow, Judith. "Introduction: Womanspirit Rising" and "The Essential Challenge: Does Theology Speak to Women's Experience?" In Womanspirit Rising: A Feminist Reader in Religion (entry 59), pp. 1-24.

Christ and Plaskow agree that while the traditional religions of the West have consistently taught the inferiority of women, this "does not invalidate human need for ritual, symbol, and myth." They and their volume's contributors "are convinced that religion must be reformed or reconstructed to support the full human dignity of women" (p. 1).

50 Driver, Anne Barstow. "Review Essay: Religion." Signs: Journal of Women in Culture and Society 2 (Winter 1976): 434-42.

Eschewing the "steady flow of religious writings in praise of women as virgin or wife or mother," Driver focuses instead on "those materials that criticize the religious traditions and find them to be our most deep-seated cause of patriarchy" (p. 434). These range from a positive defense of biblical tradition to a "post-Christian" exploration of new theological concepts. For a sequel review of the literature see entry 55.

51   Fiorenza, Elisabeth Schüssler. In Memory of Her: A Feminist
      Theological Reconstruction of Christian Origins. New York:
      Crossroad, 1983. xxv, 351 pp.
          Fiorenza, a New Testament scholar, here reconstructs early
      Christian history and theology from the "discipleship of equals"
      in the early Jesus movement through the dominance of patriarchal
      models of the church in the second century. This is an important
      work of biblical scholarship and Christian feminist theology; it
      also provides, in the first three chapters, substantial discussion
      of the methodological problems confronting all historians of women
      in religion. These chapters provide both Fiorenza's assessment of
      the methods of other feminist scholars and her own proposal for
      how to recover the history of women's experience and agency even
      from textual sources dominated by patriarchal attitudes.

52   "Roundtable Discussion: On Feminist Methodology." Journal of
      Feminist Studies in Religion 1 (Fall 1985):73-88.
          Five eminent scholars of varying disciplines and persuasions
      contribute to this illuminating inquiry: Elisabeth Schüssler
      Fiorenza (New Testament), Karen McCarthy Brown (sociology), Anne
      Llewellyn Barstow (history), Cheryl Townsend Gilkes (sociology),
      and Mary E. Hunt (theology).

53   Ruether, Rosemary Radford. Sexism and God-Talk: Toward a
      Feminist Theology. Boston: Beacon Press, 1983. xi, 289 pp.
          Like all good books of feminist theology--including the many
      by Ruether and the works of other authors--this one employs a
      method by which women's experiences interact with tradition.
      Here, especially in chapter 1, Reuther is openly reflective upon
      her method, exploring the role of women's experience as both con-
      tent and criterion of theology and discussing whether and how
      feminists can legitimately "use" the "sexist . . . dominant theo-
      logical traditions." Later chapters subject dominant understand-
      ings of classical themes--such as creation, Christology, and
      eschatology--to feminist criticism, leading up to Ruether's own
      interpretation, sometimes in imaginative forms.

54   Ruether, Rosemary Radford. Womanguides: Readings Toward a
      Feminist Theology. Boston: Beacon Press, 1985. xii, 274 pp.
          Ruether, aiming to provide "a springboard for construct-
      ing . . . a new expression of theology from the perspective of the
      full personhood of women" (p. ix), presents a number of historical
      documents centered on particular issues of Western theology, set
      into context by introductory essays. The themes are creation;
      images of the divine; humanity; evil; redemption; repentance;
      community; scriptural and early church foremothers; and visions
      for new community and theology.

55   Yates, Gayle Graham. "Spirituality and the American Feminist
      Experience." Signs: Journal of Women in Culture and Society
      9 (Autumn 1983):59-72.
          This essay considers the emerging "experiential theology" of
      feminist scholarship in religion, through a review of the most
      important publications in this field from 1976 to 1981. Yates

suggests useful connections among diverse works; her essay also
provides, in effect, a bibliography of works in the period under
consideration. This sequel to Driver's review essay (entry 50)
shows the development of feminist methodology over time.

I.C.2. ANTHOLOGIES

56   Agonito, Rosemary, ed. History of Ideas on Woman: A Source
     Book. New York: Paragon Books, 1977. 414 pp.
     To remedy the lack of availability in a single collection of
primary sources on women, Agonito presents in chronological order
"the most significant and representative thinking in the history
of Western civilization on all aspects of the Woman Question"
(p. 9). A brief introduction precedes each selection, among which
are excerpts from Genesis, Paul, Augustine, Thomas Aquinas, Hobbes,
Locke, Kant, Darwin, Nietzsche, Freud, and Friedan.

57   Atkinson, Clarissa W.; Buchanan, Constance H.; and Miles,
     Margaret R., eds. Immaculate and Powerful: The Female in
     Sacred Image and Social Reality. Harvard Women's Studies in
     Religion Series. Boston: Beacon Press, 1985. viii, 330 pp.
     Eleven articles on a wide range of topics explore the reli-
gious symbolism associated with women in various cultures in
relationship to the social arrangements of women's lives. After
a helpful introduction by Miles, the articles collectively depict
a fascinating variety of ways in which ideals and reality can
interact to shape the lives of women, oppressively or transforma-
tively, but always with an element of ambiguity. Contents include
articles on the Old and New Testaments, women in Indian and
Tibetan religions, Saint Monica, Simone Weil, the Marian Revival
in nineteenth-century Europe, women and Jews in theology, the
sociology of blood sacrifice, and two that are directly concerned
with women in American religious history: Delores S. Williams,
"Black Women's Literature and the Task of Feminist Theology"
(entry 448), and Dorothy C. Bass, "'In Christian Firmness and
Christian Meekness': Feminism and Pacifism in Antebellum
America" (entry 152).

58   Burghardt, Walter J., ed. Women: New Dimensions. New York:
     Paulist Press, 1977. viii, 189 pp.
     The essays presented here first appeared as a special theme
issue of Theological Studies 36 (December 1975), and are aimed at
an interdisciplinary exploration of women's struggle for freedom,
equality, and personhood in the Christian church. The material
presented ranges from cross-cultural exploration of women's current status to women in the fourth Gospel to a survey of significant literature on women and religion. Of particular interest are
"Feminist Theology as a Critical Theology of Liberation," by
Elisabeth Schüssler Fiorenza; "New Patterns of Relationship:
Beginnings of a Moral Revolution," by Margaret A. Farley; "Women
and Ministry," by Elizabeth Carroll; "Toward a Renewed Anthropol-
ogy," by Mary Aquin O'Neill; and "Women and Religion: A Survey
of Significant Literature, 1965-1974" (entry 350).

59   Christ, Carol P., and Plaskow, Judith, eds. <u>Womanspirit Ris-</u>
     <u>ing: A Feminist Reader in Religion</u>. San Francisco: Harper
     & Row, 1979. xi, 287 pp.
         Following the editors' introduction to schools of feminist
     thought in religion (entry 49), the essays range from feminist
     theologizing and evaluation of the past to reconstructing tradi-
     tion and creating new traditions. The work of most of the mid-
     twentieth century's notable feminist religious scholars is
     represented here: Zsuzsanna E. Budapest, Aviva Cantor, Carol P.
     Christ, Sheila Collins, Mary Daly, Elisabeth Schüssler Fiorenza,
     Naomi R. Goldenberg, Rita Gross, Eleanor McLaughlin, Nelle Morton,
     Elaine Pagels, Judith Plaskow, Rosemary Radford Ruether, Valerie
     Saiving, Starhawk, Merlin Stone, Phyllis Trible, and Penelope
     Washburn.

60   Clark, Elizabeth, and Richardson, Herbert, eds. <u>Women and</u>
     <u>Religion: A Feminist Sourcebook of Christian Thought</u>. New
     York: Harper & Row, 1977. viii, 296 pp.
         The editors have provided introductory essays and primary
     source texts that epitomize both negative and positive attitudes
     toward women in Western religious traditions. Selections from
     Aeschylus, the Old and New Testaments, Clement of Alexandria,
     Jerome, Augustine, Thomas Aquinas, Julian of Norwich and Margery
     Kempe, the <u>Malleus Maleficarum</u>, Luther, Milton, Ann Lee, Schleier-
     macher and Baader, John Humphrey Noyes, Sarah Grimké, Elizabeth
     Cady Stanton, the <u>Casti Connubii</u>, Karl Barth, and Mary Daly are
     included.

61   Doely, Sarah Bentley, ed. <u>Women's Liberation and the Church:</u>
     <u>The New Demand for Freedom in the Life of the Christian Church</u>.
     New York: Association Press, 1970. 154 pp.
         The essays in this early collection reflect their writers'
     deep disappointment, disillusionment, and criticism of a religious
     community that is "not true to its own teachings of full humanity
     and new life for all" (p. 13). At the same time, however, these
     women "bear a witness of love in demanding . . . passionately that
     the church take [them] seriously" (p. 12). Of particular interest
     are "Women's Liberation in Historical and Theological Perspective,"
     by Rosemary Radford Ruether; "A Christian Perspective on Feminism,"
     by Sidney Cornelia Callahan; and "An Authority of Possibility for
     Women in the Church," by Peggy Ann Way.

62   Fischer, Clare; Benedicks, Betsy Brenneman; and Bennett, Anne
     McGrew, eds. <u>Women in a Strange Land: Search for a New</u>
     <u>Image</u>. Philadelphia: Fortress Press, 1975. x, 133 pp.
         This anthology, which came out relatively early in the late
     twentieth-century movement, includes essays by a number of women
     struggling with the application of feminist ideas to religion.
     Represented are Dorothee Sölle, Dorothy Donnelly, and Nelle
     Morton, as well as editors Fischer and Bennett.

63   Gross, Rita M., ed. Beyond Androcentrism: New Essays on Women
      and Religion. Missoula, Mont.: Scholars Press for the Ameri-
      can Academy of Religion, 1977. vi, 347 pp.
           This wide-ranging group of essays reflects a paradigm shift
      "from an androcentric model of humanity, which views males as
      carriers and embodiers of the human norm, and women as alien or
      'other' to that central normative version of humanity," to a new
      model of humanity (p. 1). Of particular interest are "The Sacra-
      ment of Serpent Handling," by Mary Lee Daugherty; "From Mother-
      hood to Sisterhood: The Search for Female Religious Imagery in
      Nineteenth- and Twentieth-Century Theology," by Gayle Kimball;
      "Feminists on Christianity: Some Nineteenth-Century Parallels,"
      by Marilyn Chapin Massey and James A. Massey; and "Denial of the
      Female--Affirmation of the Feminine: The Father-Mother God of
      Mary Baker Eddy," by Susan M. Setta.

64   Haddad, Yvonne Yazbeck, and Findly, Ellison Banks, eds. Women,
      Religion, and Social Change. Albany: State University of New
      York Press, 1985. xxi, 508 pp.
           This valuable collection of essays is a vivid reminder of
      the importance of a cross-cultural perspective for any field of
      study and that women and religion is no exception. The essays are
      arranged in three broad theme categories: women and the formation
      of religious tradition (Rabbinic Judaism, early Islam, pre-Buddhist
      India, East Indian and Chinese Buddhism); social transformation,
      the role of women and traditional religious institutions (Chris-
      tian and Islamic art, Hindu and early East Indian imagery,
      Nigeria); and women, religion, and revolution in the modern world
      (Islam, Iran, Nicaragua, India, China). Articles on women and
      religion in North America are "Spirits Defend the Rights of Women:
      Spiritualism and Changing Sex Roles in Nineteenth-Century America,"
      by Ann D. Braude (entry 550); "From Shackles to Liberation: The
      Grimké Sisters and Dissent," by Frank G. Kirkpatrick (entry 167);
      "The American Catholic Bishops and Woman: From the Nineteenth
      Amendment to ERA," by Antoinette Iadarola (entry 344); and
      "Feminism and the Reevaluation of Women's Roles within American
      Jewish Life," by Ellen M. Umansky (entry 415).

65   Hageman, Alice L., ed. Sexist Religion and Women in the
      Church: No More Silence! New York: Association Press, 1974.
      221 pp.
           This volume came out of the earliest efforts of a student
      women's caucus at Harvard Divinity School to redress the de facto
      sexism of their institution. The texts of the 1972-73 Lentz Lec-
      tures on women and religion and a paper written for a seminar on
      women and religion in a sexist society comprise the essays here.
      Among them are "Preaching the Word," by Nelle Morton; "Black Women
      and the Churches: Triple Jeopardy," by Theressa Hoover (entry
      453); "Enrichment or Threat: When the Eves Come Marching In," by
      Krister Stendahl; "Theology After the Demise of God the Father:
      A Call for the Castration of Sexist Religion," by Mary Daly;
      "Women and Missions: The Cost of Liberation," by Alice L. Hageman
      (entry 179); and "Sexism and the Contemporary Church: When

Evasion Becomes Complicity," by Beverly Wildung Harrison (entry
223).

66   Plaskow, Judith, and Romero, Joan Arnold, eds. Women and
      Religion: Papers of the Working Group on Women and Religion,
      1972-1973. Rev. ed. Missoula, Mont.: Scholars Press for the
      American Academy of Religion, 1974. v, 210 pp.
          This selection of papers represents a variety of approaches.
      The papers are arranged under the following topics: "The Women's
      Revolution and Theological Development"; "Image, Myth, and Stereo-
      type"; "The Transvaluation of Values"; and "New Views of History."
      Of most general interest are "Theology After the Demise of God the
      Father: A Call for the Castration of Sexist Religion," by Mary
      Daly; "Phallic Worship: The Ultimate Idolatry," by Elizabeth
      Farians; "Methodological Remarks on the Study of Women in Reli-
      gion: Review, Criticism, and Redefinition," by Rita Gross; and
      "Is Sexism a Sign of Decadence in Religion?," by Leonard Swidler.

67   Ruether, Rosemary Radford, ed. Religion and Sexism: Images of
      Woman in the Jewish and Christian Traditions. New York: Simon
      & Schuster, 1974. 356 pp.
          This collection of essays rests on the belief that religion
      has been "undoubtedly the single most important shaper and en-
      forcer of the image and role of women in culture and society" and
      that even if one believes the causes of misogynism to rest in
      economics or psychology, it still remains that religion has been
      "the ideological reflection of . . . sexual domination and subju-
      gation" and, as a social institution, religion "has been its cul-
      tural sanctifier" (pp. 9-10). Among the essays are "Images of
      Women in the Old Testament," by Phyllis Bird; "The Theology and
      Leadership of Women in the New Testament," by Constance F. Parvey;
      "Misogynism and Virginal Feminism in the Fathers of the Church,"
      by Rosemary Radford Ruether; "Equality of Souls, Inequality of
      Sexes: Woman in Medieval Theology," by Eleanor Commo McLaughlin;
      "Canon Law and the Battle of the Sexes," by Clara Maria Henning
      (entry 381); "Women and the Continental Reformation," by Jane
      Dempsey Douglass; "The Protestant Principle: A Woman's Eye View
      of Barth and Tillich," by Joan Arnold Romero; and "Epilogue: The
      Coming of Lilith," by Judith Plaskow Goldberg.

68   Spretnak, Charlene, ed. The Politics of Women's Spirituality:
      Essays on the Rise of Spiritual Power within the Feminist Move-
      ment. Garden City, N.Y.: Anchor Press, 1982. xxx, 590 pp.
          Defining the title as referring "to our attitude toward life
      on Earth (i.e., spirituality) and the perception, manifestation,
      and use of power (i.e., politics) that stem from that attitude"
      (p. xxiii), Spretnak has gathered more than 50 essays and excerpts
      from larger works that illustrate a "postpatriarchal, holistic,
      and integrative" feminist spirituality. In this volume, the
      reader may sample the thought of many feminist thinkers whose work
      moves beyond urging reforms within patriarchal religion to re-
      claiming "prepatriarchal" religions and creating new ones. Among
      the authors represented are Margot Adler, Z. Budapest, Judy

Chicago, Mary Daly, Sally Gearheart, Naomi Goldenberg, Robin
Morgan, Adrienne Rich, Starhawk, and Merlin Stone. Notes and a
10-page bibliography lead the reader to fuller treatments of this
subject.

69   Weidman, Judith L. Christian Feminism: Visions of a New
      Humanity. San Francisco: Harper & Row, 1984. 196 pp.
      Noting that Christianity reflects, contributes to, and pro-
vides justification in the culture for a male-dominated, hierarch-
ical world view, Weidman has collected a sampling of the systematic works of Christian feminist theologians and ethicists that
counter those pervasive attitudes. Unifying themes for the essays
are women's experience, feminist community, language and imagery,
and change. Represented in the collection are Rosemary Radford
Ruether, Elisabeth Schüssler Fiorenza, Rita Nakashima Brock, Letty
M. Russell, Nanette M. Roberts, Clare B. Fischer, Beverly Wildung
Harrison, and Constance F. Parvey.

I.C.3. BIBLIOGRAPHIES

70   Fischer, Clare B. Breaking Through: A Bibliography of Women
      and Religion. Berkeley, Calif.: Graduate Theological Union
      Library, 1980. x, 65 pp.
      This bibliography is designed to challenge orthodox pedagogy
in which women's concerns are presented as peripheral and to
offer works by and about women as new models for research. The
items are presented in the following categories: "Resources";
"Traditional Approaches"; "Women: As Subjects, As Scholars";
"Feminist Perspectives"; and "Selected Periodicals." Entries are
not annotated and there is no index. The bibliography, however,
is comprehensive and up-to-date at the time of its publication,
making it useful for anyone seeking complete lists of resources.

71   Richardson, Marilyn. Black Women and Religion: A Bibliogra-
      phy (entry 426).
      Noting that bibliographies about black women seldom provide
resources on their religious experiences and that bibliographies
on women and religion usually deal superficially with black women,
Richardson has remedied those deficiencies in this comprehensive,
annotated bibliography. She covers not only primary and secondary
materials usually seen as directly related to the subject matter
but also materials on black women's religious experience as expressed in literature and the arts. Also listed are audiovisual
materials, reference sources, and autobiographical and biographical resources. An author-title-subject index completes this exceedingly useful bibliography.

72   Warren, Mary Anne. The Nature of Woman: An Encyclopedia and
      Guide to the Literature. Inverness, Calif.: Edgepress, 1980.
      xvii, 708 pp.
      The "encyclopedia" part of Warren's book provides general
essays on topics (such as Christianity, the Bible, spiritual feminism) in a single alphabet with descriptive and analytical

articles on individual scholars whose work has shaped and is
shaping Western thought on the nature of women (such as Augustine,
Kierkegaard, Daly). The "guide" part of the work lists anthologies and sourcebooks in various subjects related to women and
includes an annotated list of feminist and women's studies, periodicals. A bibliography provides in one list the works of individual authors discussed elsewhere in the book. The reader's
diligence in using the book is rewarded by the useful synthesis
and analysis found here. Of particular interest are the articles
on Augustine, Aquinas, the Bible, Christianity, Daly, Gilman,
goddesses, Kierkegaard, Grimké, spiritual feminism, Stanton,
Ruether, and Letty Russell.

For Further Information

73   Journal of Feminist Studies in Religion, a new semiannual journal devoted to feminist research, discussion, and dialogue in all
areas of religious studies, begun early in 1985, published by
Scholars Press, P.O. Box 1608, Decatur, GA 30031. Edited by
Judith Plaskow and Elisabeth Schüssler Fiorenza, this journal can
be expected to include important scholarship of high quality. The
spring 1985 issue includes a major review essay, "An Unfinished
Symphony of Liberation: The Radicalization of Christian Feminism
among White U.S. Women," by Carter Heyward (entry 464); "What Are
the Sources of My Theology," by three feminist theologians; and
several other major articles. The fall 1985 issue includes articles, reviews, poetry by Jewish women, a report of a feminist
experiment in theological education, and "Roundtable Discussion:
On Feminist Methodology" (entry 52).

I.D.   WOMEN IN AMERICAN RELIGIOUS HISTORY

In this section are listed anthologies and compendiums relevant to
our subject matter. The works are briefly and generally described
and the chapters/essays/sections listed. The list thus serves as a
recommended core bibliography of general works on women and American
religion. Many essays found in these works were deemed to be of note
for study in particular subject areas. Where this is the case, an
annotation for the essay will be found in a later chapter by following the number reference in parentheses.

74   Greaves, Richard L., ed. Triumph Over Silence: Women in
Protestant History. Westport, Conn.: Greenwood Press, 1985.
xii, 295 pp.
Following essays on women in the Lutheran, Calvinist, and
Anabaptist reform movements in continental Europe as well as on
women in the early nonconformist and sectarian movements in
England, this collection contains the following essays about the
experience of Protestant women in the United States: "'The Hidden
Ones': Women and Religion in Puritan New England," by Gerald F.
Moran (entry 90); "Expanding Horizons: Women in the Methodist
Movement," by Frederick A. Norwood (entry 292); "To Make the World
Better: Protestant Women in the Abolitionist Movement," by Blanche
Glassman Hersh (entry 157); "Questions of Power and Status:

American Presbyterian Women, 1870–1980," by Lois A. Boyd and
R. Douglas Brackenridge (entry 306); and "Participation of Women
in the Public Life of the Anglican Communion," by V. Nelle Bellamy
(entry 254).

75   James, Janet Wilson, ed. <u>Women in American Religion</u>. Phila-
      delphia University of Pennsylvania Press, 1980. 274 pp.
          Declaring that women's experiences in institutional
      religion "can illumine much of the scene outside the sanctuary in
      past time," the essays in this collection "indicate some avenues
      of research and interpretation" (p. 3). About half of the essays
      first appeared as a special issue of the <u>American Quarterly</u> 20
      (Winter 1978). Of particular interest are "Saints and Sisters:
      Congregational and Quaker Women in the Early Colonial Period," by
      Mary Maples Dunn (entry 96); "'Sisters' in Christ: Women and the
      Church in Seventeenth-Century New England," by Gerald F. Moran
      (entry 91); "Vertuous Women Found: New England Ministerial Lit-
      erature, 1668–1735," by Laurel Thatcher Ulrich (entry 95); "A
      Women's Awakening: Evangelical Religion and the Families of
      Utica, New York, 1800–1840," by Mary P. Ryan (entry 135); "Catho-
      lic Women Religious and Women's History: A Survey of the Litera-
      ture," by Sister Elizabeth Kolmer (entry 366); "Organized Volun-
      tarism: The Catholic Sisters in Massachusetts, 1870–1940," by
      Mary J. Oates (entry 368); "American Women in Ministry: A History
      of Protestant Beginning Points," by Virginia Lieson Brereton and
      Christa Ressmeyer Klein (entry 193); "Eve, Mary, and the Histo-
      rians," by James J. Kenneally (entry 346); "Transitions in Judaism:
      The Jewish American Woman through the 1930's," by Norma Fain Pratt
      (entry 410); and "Minister's Wife, Widow, Reluctant Feminist:
      Catherine Marshall in the 1950's," by Paul Boyer.

76   Keller, Rosemary Skinner; Queen, Louise L.; and Thomas,
      Hilah F., eds. <u>Women in New Worlds: Historical Perspectives
      on the Wesleyan Tradition</u>. Vol. 2. Nashville: Abingdon
      Press, 1982. 445 pp.
          With its companion volume (entry 81), these essays are the
      first to celebrate the history of women in one denomination in
      this country. The essays, however, speak broadly to the status of
      women in American religious history. In this volume, the first
      group of essays analyzes prescriptive attitudes about women's role
      in religion, and the second, larger, group describes the actual
      life experience of women. Covered in the second category are
      clergy wives, national missions and social reform, foreign mis-
      sions and cultural imperialism, and professions in the church.
      See especially "Subversion of the Feminine Ideal: The <u>Southern
      Lady's Companion</u> and White Male Morality in the Antebellum South,
      1847–1854," by James L. LeLoudis (entry 210); "Civil Rights, 1920–
      1970: Three Southern Methodist Women," by Arnold M. Shankman
      (entry 215); "Three Afro-American Women: Missionaries in Africa,
      1882–1904," by Sylvia M. Jacobs (entry 438); and "The Legacy of
      Georgia Harkness," by Joan Chambers Engelsman (entry 199). Com-
      plete notes and a name/subject index for the volume are included.

77   Mason, Mary Grimley, and Green, Carol Hurd, eds. <u>Journeys:</u>
      <u>Autobiographical Writings by Women</u>. Boston: G.K. Hall, 1979.
      228 pp.
          This volume of selections from women's autobiographical
      writings focuses on the decision of each "to make a journey . . .
      beyond individual concerns toward involvement or commitment, to a
      creed, to an institution, to a leader, to another culture"
      (p. vii). The journeys range from a medieval religious pilgrimage
      to a twentieth-century political pilgrimage. Each selection is
      preceded by a biographical/historical introduction, including a
      short list of suggested readings. Of interest to American women's
      religious history are chapters on Ann Bradstreet (entry 107),
      Jarena Lee (entry 459), Anna Julia Haywood Cooper (entry 457),
      Vida Scudder (entry 169), Dorothy Day (entry 388), and Denise
      Levertov and Susan Sontag.

78   Ruether, Rosemary Radford, and Keller, Rosemary Skinner, eds.
      <u>Women and Religion in America</u>. Vol. 1, <u>The Nineteenth Century</u>.
      New York: Harper & Row, 1981. xiv, 353 pp.
          This work, the first of three volumes (for vol. 2, see
      entry 79; vol. 3 to be published 1986), consists of primary docu-
      ments with introductions providing historical context. It not
      only makes primary material readily accessible but serves as a
      survey of the field. Topics covered in this volume are "Women and
      Revivalism," by Martha Tomhave Blauvelt (entry 117); "Women in
      Utopian Movements," by Rosemary Radford Ruether (entry 502); "The
      Leadership of Nuns in Immigrant Catholicism," by Mary Ewens
      (entry 365); "The Jewish Woman's Encounter with American Culture,"
      by Ann Braude (entry 395); "The Struggle for the Right to Preach,"
      by Barbara Brown Zikmund (entry 202); "Lay Women in the Protestant
      Tradition," by Rosemary Skinner Keller (entry 184); and "Women in
      Social Reform Movements," by Carolyn De Swarte Gifford (entry 155).

79   Ruether, Rosemary Radford, and Keller, Rosemary Skinner, eds.
      <u>Women and Religion in America</u>. Vol. 2, <u>The Colonial and Revo-</u>
      <u>lutionary Periods</u>. San Francisco: Harper & Row, 1983. xxi,
      434 pp.
          From the earliest period of American history, the subjects
      addressed in this second volume of the series are "American Indian
      Women and Religion," by Jacqueline Peterson and Mary Druke (entry
      486); "Women and Religion in Spanish America," by Asuncion Lavrin
      (entry 348); "Women in Colonial French America," by Christine
      Allen (entry 340); "New England Women: Ideology and Experience in
      First-Generation Puritanism (1630-1650)," by Rosemary Skinner
      Keller (entry 86); "The Religious Experience of Southern Women,"
      by Alice E. Mathews (entry 103); "Black Women and Religion in the
      Colonial Period," by Lillian Ashcraft Webb (entry 447); "Women in
      Sectarian and Utopian Groups," by Rosemary Radford Ruether and
      Catherine M. Prelinger (entry 502); "Women and Revivalism: The
      Puritan and Wesleyan Traditions," by Martha Tomhave Blauvelt and
      Rosemary Skinner Keller (entry 101); and "Women, Civil Religion,
      and the American Revolution," by Rosemary Skinner Keller (entry
      102).

80   Ruether, Rosemary, and McLaughlin, Eleanor, eds. <u>Women of</u>
<u>Spirit: Female Leadership in the Jewish and Christian Tradi-</u>
<u>tions</u>. New York: Simon & Schuster, 1979. 400 pp.
     The editors hope in this collection to "make a contribution
both toward the recovery of important chapters of women's history
and toward the charting of the paradigms of female leadership possible within successive theological world views" (p. 16). The
essays range from women in the early Christian communities to the
twentieth-century women's ordination movement. Of interest are
the following: "The Feminist Thrust of Sectarian Christianity,"
by Barbara Brown Zikmund (entry 504); "Women in the Holiness Movement: Feminism in the Evangelical Tradition," by Nancy Hardesty,
Lucille Sider Dayton, and Donald Dayton (entry 127); "Removing the
Veil: The Liberated American Nun," by Mary Ewens (entry 364);
"'Their Prodigious Influence': Women, Religion and Reform in
Antebellum America," by Dorothy C. Bass (entry 114); "American
Women in Ministry: A History of Protestant Beginning Points," by
Virginia Lieson Brereton and Crista Ressmeyer Klein (entry 193);
"Women in Judaism: From the Reform Movement to Contemporary
Jewish Religious Feminism," by Ellen M. Umansky (entry 415); and
"Entering the Sanctuary: The Struggle for Priesthood in Contempo-
rary Episcopalian and Roman Catholic Experience," the Episcopal
story by Norene Carter (entry 258) and the Roman Catholic story by
Rosemary Ruether (entry 378).

81   Thomas, Hilah F., and Keller, Rosemary Skinner, eds. <u>Women in</u>
<u>New Worlds: Historical Perspectives on the Wesleyan Tradition</u>.
Vol. 1. Nashville: Abingdon Press, 1981. 445 pp.
     The first of two volumes (for the second volume, see entry
76) of papers presented at a United Methodist conference in 1980,
this one begins with introductory papers that analyze the larger
context of women in American church history and how that history
has been written. The remainder of the papers use a variety of
approaches to discuss the movement of women into fuller participation in the life of the church and the world. Of particular rele-
vance are "Women's History/Everyone's History," by Donald G.
Mathews (entry 31); "The Last Fifteen Years: Historians' Changing Views of American Women in Religion and Society," by Kathryn
Kish Sklar (entry 34); "Minister As Prophet? or As Mother? Two
Nineteenth-Century Models," by Nancy A. Hardesty (entry 198);
"Georgia Harkness: Social Activist and/or Mystic," by Martha L.
Scott (entry 199); "The Laity Rights Movement, 1906-1918: Woman's
Suffrage in the Methodist Episcopal Church, South," by Virginia
Shadron; "Nineteenth-Century A.M.E. Preaching Women: Cutting Edge
of Women's Inclusion in Church Polity," by Jualynne Dodson (entry
431); "Evangelical Domesticity: The Woman's Temperance Crusade of
1873-74," by Susan Dye Lee (entry 161); and "For God and Home and
Native Land," by Carolyn De Swarte Gifford.

II. Protestantism

II.A.1. NEW ENGLAND: PURITANISM THROUGH
THE GREAT AWAKENING

82   Cowing, Cedric B. "Sex and Preaching in the Great Awakening."
      American Quarterly 20 (1968):624-44.
          Cowing explores the relation of theology and preaching style
      to the sex ratio of church members, arguing that the New Light of
      the Great Awakening increased the proportion of men for a variety
      of social and psychological reasons. Although this article does
      not treat the religious experience of women, the long-term pre-
      ponderance of women as church members frames the discussion, which
      includes serious attention to gender as a clue to religious be-
      havior. For a contrasting treatment of gender differences in the
      Great Awakening, see Epstein, The Politics of Domesticity (entry
      125); chapter 1, "Religious Conversions in the Eighteenth Century:
      The Shared Experience of Men and Women," analyzes the accounts men
      and women gave of their conversions during the Great Awakening and
      finds significant similarities.

83   Demos, John Putnam. Entertaining Satan: Witchcraft and the
      Culture of Early New England. New York: Oxford University
      Press, 1982. xiv, 543 pp.
          Working with evidence painstakingly and exhaustively amassed
      from seventeenth-century documents, Demos offers a multidisciplin-
      ary explanation of why colonial New Englanders legally charged 234
      persons with witchcraft and executed 36 "witches." His attention
      is directed primarily to the 93 cases (leading to 16 executions)
      that were not part of the Salem episode of 1692. A section of
      biography provides a portrait of the accused, while sections on
      psychology, sociology, and history deal also with their "victims"
      and accusers, as well as with the dense local communities in which
      the cases arose and had social meaning. Almost all of the accused
      were women; thus Demos's fascinating narratives of cases provide
      rare glimpses into women's daily lives in seventeenth-century New
      England.

84   Demos, John. <u>A Little Commonwealth: Family Life in Plymouth
      Colony</u>. New York: Oxford University Press, 1970. xvi, 201 pp.
          This early example of the new family history searches physi-
      cal artifacts, wills, inventories, and court records (as well as
      more standard literary sources) in order to explain how one set of
      colonists acted in families, rather than merely what they believed
      about families. Drawing on the methods and theories of various
      social sciences, Demos develops portraits of daily life, relation-
      ships, and the life cycle. Both women and religion are omnipres-
      ent, although neither receives separate treatment. Chapter 5,
      "Husbands and Wives," appears also in <u>Our American Sisters: Women
      in American Life and Thought</u> (entry 19), pp. 41-54.

85   Karlsen, Carol. F., and Crumpacker, Laurie, eds. <u>The Journal
      of Esther Edwards Burr, 1754-1757</u>. New Haven: Yale University
      Press, 1984. xiv, 318 pp.
          Esther Edwards Burr (1732-58) was the daughter of Jonathan
      and Sarah Edwards (see entry 108) and the wife of the clergyman-
      president of the College of New Jersey (now Princeton University).
      This journal, written in epistolary form to a woman friend, offers
      a rare glimpse into the daily life of a colonial woman of deep
      religious sensibility. The editors' extensive introduction pro-
      vides biographical information and also interprets the journal as
      a document in the history of evangelical women, emphasizing the
      importance of sisterhood in their lives.

86   Keller, Rosemary Skinner. "New England Women: Ideology and
      Experience in First-Generation Puritanism (1630-1650)." In
      <u>Women and Religion in America</u>, vol. 2 (entry 79), pp. 132-92.
          Keller's introductory essay traces the Old World roots and
      New World manifestations of Puritan views of women, contrasting
      some favorable images of mutuality with harsh enforcement of sexual
      hierarchies. The fourteen documents that follow include seven
      statements about women by ministers and accounts of five court
      proceedings against rebellious women, including substantial ex-
      cerpts from the trials of Anne Hutchinson and Anne Hibbens.

87   Koehler, Lyle. <u>A Search for Power: The "Weaker Sex" in
      Seventeenth-Century New England</u>. Urbana: University of
      Illinois Press, 1980. viii, 561 pp.
          Critical of both the Puritans and historians who have
      treated them sympathetically, Koehler argues that sexism prevailed
      in seventeenth-century New England. After tracing its sources to
      "a theology of ultimate powerlessness" with disastrous implications
      for child-rearing and, thus, the Puritan psyche, Koehler describes
      repressive attitudes toward sex, violence against women, economic
      and social oppression, and the measures taken against women rebels:
      criminals, heretics, and witches. Chapter 11, "The Rhode Island
      Alternative," casts light on the less well-known colony where
      women fared somewhat better and exemplifies Koehler's exhaustive
      research. Psychological theory and feminist theory shape the lan-
      guage and structure of this ambitious synthesis. A 44-page
      bibliography is included.

88   Malmsheimer, Lonna M. "Daughters of Zion: New England Roots
      of American Feminism." New England Quarterly 50 (1977):484-504.
         In the seventeenth century, ministers' depictions of women
      were based largely on negative attitudes toward Eve, but in the
      next century ministers increasingly emphasized women's distinctive
      contributions to community and church and their superior moral and
      religious attributes. Malmsheimer's interpretation is based
      mostly on funeral sermons published between 1670 and 1790. Cotton
      Mather emerges as an important transitional figure; researchers
      should consult his Ornaments for the Daughters of Zion, or the
      Character and Happiness of a Virtuous Woman (1692 and many re-
      prints).

89   Masson, Margaret W. "The Typology of the Female as a Model for
      the Regenerate: Puritan Preaching, 1690-1730." Signs: Jour-
      nal of Women in Culture and Society 2 (1976):304-15.
         This study of ministerial views argues that "the Puritans
      had not yet arrived at definitions of sex roles or personality
      structure that were as fixed or mutually exclusive as those found
      in the nineteenth century" (p. 305). The fact that ministers
      presented the female role of bride as the model for every believ-
      er's relation to Christ is chief among Masson's several explana-
      tions for this assertion. Amanda Porterfield, in chapter 2
      ("Bridal Passion and New England Puritanism") of her Feminine
      Spirituality in America (entry 234), also considers the implica-
      tions of this imagery for the piety of both men and women.

90   Moran, Gerald F. "'The Hidden Ones': Women and Religion in
      Puritan New England." In Triumph Over Silence: Women in
      Protestant History (entry 74), pp. 125-49.
         Moran's thesis that women began to move into control of the
      moral, religious, and intellectual guidance of children as early
      as the American Revolution is illustrated by means of the examina-
      tion of Puritan sermons, church membership figures, women's roles
      in the household, women's literacy, and women's group activity.

91   Moran, Gerald F. "'Sisters' in Christ: Women and the Church
      in Seventeenth-Century New England." In Women in American
      Religion (entry 75), pp. 47-65.
         Numerical analysis of persons admitted to membership in
      eighteen Massachusetts and Connecticut churches between 1630 and
      1699 shows that a balance between men and women prevailed in the
      first generation but that there was a consistent preponderance of
      women by 1700. Moran's explanation of this shift contrasts the
      religious experiences of men and women as they faced the transi-
      tion to adult life, the normal time for joining the church. Draw-
      ing on some writing by women and more theology and preaching by
      men, he argues that the Puritan model of a regenerate Christian
      was closer to the social experience of married women than to that
      of men in New England's second generation. Richard E. Shiels, in
      "The Feminization of American Congregationalism, 1730-1835"
      (American Quarterly 33 [1981]:46-62), provides a very detailed
      statistical analysis of female church membership over the period.

92   Morgan, Edmund S. The Puritan Family: Religion and Domestic
      Relations in Seventeenth-Century New England. New York:
      Harper & Row, 1966. x, 196 pp.
           Morgan explores how the Puritans sought to order the family,
      which they saw as an indispensable foundation of their Bible
      Commonwealth, in accordance with their theological views and also
      considers, more briefly, the impact of the family on religion.
      Beliefs receive more attention than behavior, although Morgan's
      use of court records offsets this somewhat; considerable informa-
      tion on women is included, especially in chapter 2, "Husbands and
      Wives." One topic is treated further in Morgan's "The Puritans
      and Sex," New England Quarterly 15 (December 1942):592-607, which
      is also found in Our American Sisters: Women in American Life and
      Thought, edited by Jean E. Friedman and William G. Shade, 2d ed.
      (Boston: Allyn & Bacon, 1976), pp. 11-23. Gerald Moran and Maris
      Vinovskis, "The Puritan Family and Religion: A Critical Re-
      appraisal," William and Mary Quarterly 39 (1982):29-63, represents
      more recent research, with emphasis on actual social behavior.

93   Starkey, Marion L. The Devil in Massachusetts: A Modern In-
      quiry into the Salem Witch Trials. New York: Alfred A. Knopf,
      1950. 310 pp.
           Though dated, this is a well-regarded narrative history. An
      account that relies heavily on psychology is Chadwick Hansen,
      Witchcraft at Salem (New York: George Braziller, 1969). Paul
      Boyer and Stephen Nissenbaum, Salem Possessed: The Social Origins
      of Witchcraft (Cambridge, Mass.: Harvard University Press, 1974),
      emphasize tensions related to social change in the Salem area in
      their interpretation. J. Gordon Melton, Magic, Witchcraft, and
      Paganism in America: A Bibliography (New York: Garland Publish-
      ing, 1982), lists 50 books and articles on the events in Salem.
      See also Steven H. Keeney, "Witchcraft in Colonial Connecticut and
      Massachusetts: An Annotated Bibliography," Bulletin of Bibliog-
      raphy and Magazine Notes 33 (1976):61-72.

94   Ulrich, Laurel Thatcher. Good Wives: Image and Reality in the
      Lives of Women in Northern New England, 1650-1750. New York:
      Alfred A. Knopf, 1982. xv, 298 pp.
           Ulrich paints a rich portrait of the lives of ordinary women
      in the colonial period. Seeking ways to discover both what was
      expected of women (roles) and what they actually did (role per-
      formance), she explores women's economic contributions, their
      experiences of sex and reproduction, and the points at which
      aggression became a factor in their lives. Her extensive research
      has produced both a mass of social detail and numerous lively
      anecdotes, and she is sensitive to the role of religion in the
      lives of her subjects. Several maps, 16 pages of photographs of
      needlework, artifacts, and portraits are included as well as ex-
      tensive notes and a short bibliographical essay.

95   Ulrich, Laurel Thatcher. "Vertuous Women Found: New England
      Ministerial Literature, 1668-1735." In Women in American
      Religion (entry 75), pp. 67-87. Also in A Heritage of Her Own:

Toward a New Social History of American Women (entry 18),
pp. 58-80.
    Ulrich identifies the norms of female piety depicted by minis-
ters writing about women in elegies, memorials, funeral sermons,
and works of practical piety, arguing that these norms were based
on beliefs in the "spiritual equality of men and women and the
essentially asexual nature of godliness" (p. 36). This was not
to last, however; consideration of the disjunction between earthly
inequality and spiritual equality and of the appearance of gender-
distinct formulations in the eighteenth century suggests interesting connections between religious norms and changing social
realities.

II.A.2.   OTHER GROUPS AND REGIONS

96   Dunn, Mary Maples. "Saints and Sisters: Congregational and
      Quaker Women in the Early Colonial Period." In Women in Ameri-
      can Religion (entry 75), pp. 27-46. Also in Anne Hutchinson:
      Troubler of Puritan Zion, edited by Francis J. Bremer.
      Huntington, N.Y.: Krieger Publishing Co., 1981, pp. 140-49.
          Dunn's comparison of women's place in the scriptural inter-
      pretation, theological formulations, and church governance of two
      colonial religious bodies concludes that "Quaker women played a
      more forceful role in the Society of Friends than Puritan women
      did in the Congregational church" (p. 601). This depiction of the
      oppression of Puritan women draws much evidence from the harsh
      treatment of Anne Hutchinson and other "aggressive females."

97   Edkins, Carol. "Quest for Community: Spiritual Autobiogra-
      phies of Eighteenth-Century Quaker and Puritan Women in
      America." In Women's Autobiography: Essays in Criticism,
      edited by Estelle Jelinek. Bloomington: University of Indiana
      Press, 1980, pp. 39-52.
          This literary study sees conformity to communal models of
      spirituality, rather than individuality, in the texts under study,
      providing a helpful introduction to some little-known sources.

98   Irwin, Joyce, ed. Womanhood in Radical Protestantism, 1525-
      1675. New York: Edwin Mellen Press, 1979. 298 pp.
          Most of the sources excerpted in this anthology are from the
      left wing of the continental and English Reformations (Anabaptists,
      Puritans, Quakers), but some New World sources are also included.
      This volume is a useful reminder of transatlantic continuities and
      is a good place to encounter the early Quaker defense of women's
      right to preach.

99   Norton, Mary Beth. "The Evolution of White Women's Experience
      in Early America." American Historical Review 89 (1984):
      593-619.
          Countering the "golden age" theory that women in the Ameri-
      can colonies were better off than either their English contempo-
      raries or their nineteenth-century descendants, Norton argues that
      restrictive nineteenth-century ideals were continuous with aspects
      of women's status in the colonial period. In her survey, she
      treats Puritan theology, women in the Society of Friends, the

nurture of the young, patriarchal family ideals and the state, disestablishment of the churches, the growth of voluntary associations, and the separation of public and private spheres.

100   Ruether, Rosemary Radford, and Keller, Rosemary Skinner, eds. Women and Religion in America. Vol. 2, The Colonial and Revolutionary Periods (entry 79).
       This anthology is a good place to begin the study of American women's religious history. Each chapter focuses on one group of women and includes a historical essay, several excepts from historical documents, and a few pictures. The volume as a whole demonstrates the diversity of women's experiences in the colonies, with chapters (annotated in the appropriate chapters of this bibliography) on American Indian women (entry 486); women and religion in Spanish America (entry 348); the French colonies (entries 340); black women (entry 447); and sectarian and utopian groups (entry 502). Chapters on white Protestant women in the seventeenth and eighteenth centuries are by Rosemary Keller, "New England Women: Ideology and Experience in First-Generation Puritanism (1630-1650)" (entry 86), and the following:

101   Blauvelt, Martha Tomhave, and Keller, Rosemary Skinner. "Women and Revivalism: The Puritan and Wesleyan Traditions," pp. 316-67.
       The introductory essay describes and compares the experiences of women as subjects and leaders in two forms of eighteenth-century evangelicalism, concluding that greater scope was permitted to Methodist women. Puritan documents excerpted here are a woman's conversion account, four statements from ministers about pious women, Sarah Osborn's defense of her role in leading revivals (see entry 110) and Jonathan Edwards's treatise on marriage (see entry 108). Methodist documents include letters from pious women to John Wesley and accounts of the early spread of Methodism in the middle and southern colonies.

102   Keller, Rosemary Skinner. "Women, Civil Religion, and the American Revolution," pp. 368-408.
       Keller depicts the impact on American women of the Enlightenment and Revolution, with emphasis on how women participated in the religious patriotism of the era and how this shaped their views of "republican motherhood," women's education, and their own rights. Documents excerpted are a patriotic drama by Mercy Otis Warren; two broadsides by anonymous women; letters of Abigail Adams; Judith Sargent Murray's essay "On the Equality of the Sexes" (1790); and views of female education by Benjamin Rush, the English feminist Mary Wollstonecraft, and a young student.

103   Mathews, Alice E. "The Religious Experience of Southern Women," pp. 193-232.
       Mathews's essay surveys the religious life of the colonial South, where the stability of organized religion and of social life generally was far less than in New England; for

women, she argues, religion was an important source of
security and inner liberation, in spite of their secondary
status. Her emphasis is on the established church (Angli-
canism), with some attention to religious minorities
(Quakers, Jews, Catholics, Moravians), and to the growth of
the evangelical denominations after the Great Awakening.
Among the thirteen documents excerpted here are three on the
relationships of black Christians to whites; three prescriptive statements on womanhood by prominent clergymen; memoirs
of three wealthy ladies; and letters from a Catholic and a
Jewish woman.

104　Spruill, Julia Cherry. Women's Life and Work in the Southern
　　　Colonies. 1938. Reprint. Introduction by Anne Firor Scott.
　　　New York: W.W. Norton, 1972. x, 426 pp.
　　　　　This early work documents the life and status of white women
in the English colonies of the South. Women as upholders of the
church, their activity in the Society of Friends, and witchcraft
are treated along with a study of the prescriptive religious literature read by women. A 27-page bibliography of primary sources
is included.

For Further Information

105　Three histories of women in the late colonial and revolutionary
　　　periods that contain only brief explicit treatments of religion
　　　but are important explications of its social and cultural context
　　　in the lives of women are Mary Sumner Benson's pioneering work,
　　　Woman in Eighteenth-Century America: A Study of Opinion and
　　　Social Usage (1935; reprint, New York: AMS Press, 1976); Linda K.
　　　Kerber, Women of the Republic: Intellect and Ideology in Revolu-
　　　tionary America (Chapel Hill: University of North Carolina Press,
　　　1980); and Mary Beth Norton, Liberty's Daughters: The Revolution-
　　　ary Experience of American Women, 1750-1800 (Boston: Little,
　　　Brown & Co., 1980).

106　An unannotated guide to older sources is Eugenie Andruss Leonard,
　　　Sophie Hutchinson Drinker, and Miriam Young Holden, The American
　　　Woman in Colonial and Revolutionary Times, 1565-1800: A Syllabus
　　　with Bibliography (1962; reprint, Westport, Conn.: Greenwood
　　　Press, 1976), which includes a chapter on religion. An ambitious
　　　researcher could also search through the titles listed in Charles
　　　Evans, American Bibliography: A Chronological Dictionary of All
　　　Books, Pamphlets, and Periodicals Printed in the United States of
　　　America from the Genesis of Printing in 1639 Down To and Including
　　　the Year 1820 (1903; reprint, New York: P. Smith, 1941-59).

II.A.3.　INDIVIDUAL WOMEN

107　Anne Bradstreet (1612?-1672)
　　　　　The John Harvard Library edition of The Works of Anne
Bradstreet (edited by Jeannine Hensley [Cambridge, Mass.: Harvard
University Press, 1967]) contains the complete poetry and prose,
together with a sensitive foreword by the contemporary feminist

poet Adrienne Rich. A critical edition preserving the original
transcription is Joseph R. McElrath, Jr., and Allan P. Robb, eds.,
The Complete Works of Anne Bradstreet (Boston: G.K. Hall, 1981).
Bradstreet's spiritual autobiography is also in Journeys: Auto-
biographical Writings by Women (entry 77), pp. 29-39, together
with two poems and a brief essay by editors Mary Grimley Mason and
Carol Hurd Green. Other important critical and biographical
treatments are Adelaide P. Amore, ed., A Woman's World: Selected
Poetry and Prose of Anne Bradstreet (Lanham, Md.: University
Press of America, 1982); Wendy Martin, An American Triptych
(entry 232), part 1; Josephine Ketcham Piercy, Anne Bradstreet
(New York: Twayne Publishers, Inc., 1965); Anne Stanford, Anne
Bradstreet: The Worldly Puritan, An Introduction to Her Poetry
(New York: Burt Franklin Co., 1974); "Three Puritan Women: Anne
Bradstreet, Mary Rowlandson, and Sarah Kemble Knight," in American
Women Writers: Bibliographical Essays (entry 231), pp. 3-14;
Elizabeth Wade White, Anne Bradstreet, "The Tenth Muse" (New York:
Oxford University Press, 1971); and biographical listing about her
in Notable American Women (entry 35), 1:222-23.

108   Sarah Pierrepont Edwards (1710-58)
       Jonathan Edwards considered his wife's conversion during the
Great Awakening an exemplary instance of evangelical religion and
published excerpts of her first-person account in "Some Thoughts
Concerning the Present Revival of Religion" (in The Works of
Jonathan Edwards, vol. 4, The Great Awakening, edited by Clarence
C. Goen [New Haven: Yale University Press, 1972], pp. 331-41).
Amanda Porterfield, Feminine Spirituality in America: From Sarah
Edwards to Martha Graham (entry 234), draws upon Sarah Edwards's
full account and other sources to paint a provocative portrait of
her piety. Biographies are by Elisabeth D. Dodds, Marriage to a
Difficult Man: The "Uncommon Union" of Jonathan and Sarah Edwards
(Philadelphia: Westminster Press, 1971), and listing about her in
Notable American Women (entry 35), 1:564-65.

109   Anne Hutchinson (1591-1643)
       Hutchinson's theological criticisms of the clergy of Massa-
chusetts led to her expulsion from the colony, though not until
after her intellectual skill and the ministers' views of women's
subordination had become evident. The basic source for studying
the events surrounding Hutchinson are the documents collected in
David D. Hall, ed., The Antinomian Controversy, 1636-1638
(Middletown, Conn.: Wesleyan University Press, 1968). The case
of this brilliant but unfortunate woman has elicited many con-
flicting interpretations; some of the most important are G.J.
Barker-Benfield, "Anne Hutchinson and the Puritan Attitude Toward
Women," Feminist Studies 1 (1972):65-95; Emery Battis, Saints and
Sectaries: Anne Hutchinson and the Antinomian Controversy in the
Massachusetts Bay Colony (Chapel Hill: University of North
Carolina Press, 1962); Elaine C. Huber, Women and the Authority of
Inspiration: A Reexamination of Two Prophetic Movements From a
Contemporary Feminist Perspective (Lanham, Md.: University Press
of America, 1985); and Lyle Koehler, "The Case of the American
Jezebels: Anne Hutchinson and Female Agitation During the Years

of Antinomian Turmoil, 1636-1640," in Women's Experience in
America: An Historical Anthology (entry 20), pp. 21-45. For
biography see listing about her in Notable American Women (entry
35), 2:245-47, and Selma R. Williams, Divine Rebel: The Life of
Anne Marbury Hutchinson (New York: Holt, Rinehart & Winston,
1981). A recent collection of commentary on Hutchinson's case--
including excerpts and abridgments from those by Barker-Benfield,
Battis, Hall, and Koehler noted above, reprint of article by Mary
Maples Dunn (entry 96), and eight others--is by Francis J. Bremer,
ed., Anne Hutchinson: Troubler of the Puritan Zion (Huntington,
N.Y.: Krieger Publishing Co., 1981).

110   Sarah Osborn (1714-96)
        The life and views of this school teacher, mother, and
leader of religious revivals are discussed in Mary Beth Norton,
"'My Resting Reaping Times': Sarah Osborn's Defense of Her 'Un-
feminine' Activities, 1767," Signs: Journal of Women in Culture
and Society 2 (1976):515-29. Osborn led meetings of revived
Christians, including many blacks, in her Newport, Rhode Island,
home; Norton's article includes a long letter from Osborn to a
minister defending this activity. Samuel Hopkins, one of New
England's leading ministers, considered her an exemplary Christian
and after her death published Memoirs of the Life of Mrs. Sarah
Osborn (Worcester, Mass.: Leonard Worcester, 1799), which is
drawn mostly from Osborn's own autobiographical and spiritual
diaries. Hopkins also published a similar volume about Osborn's
close friend, The Life and Character of Miss Susanna Anthony
(Worcester, Mass.: Leonard Worcester, 1796).

111   Phillis Wheatley (1753-84)
        The basic source is Memoir and Poems of Phillis Wheatley, a
native African and a slave, edited, with a memoir, by Margaretta
Matilda Odell (Boston: G.W. Light, 1834). A modern critical edition is The Poems of Phillis Wheatley, edited, with introduction,
by Julian D. Mason, Jr. (Chapel Hill: University of North
Carolina Press, 1966). For a wide range of comments on Wheatley
drawn from the eighteenth to the twentieth centuries, see William
H. Robinson, ed., Critical Essays on Phillis Wheatley (Boston:
G.K. Hall, 1982). Phillis Wheatley: A Bio-Bibliography, by
William H. Robinson (Boston: G.K. Hall, 1981) lists and annotates
hundreds of works about Phillis Wheatley. See also listing in
Notable American Women (entry 35), 3:573-74.

II.B.   THE NINETEENTH AND TWENTIETH CENTURIES

II.B.1.   EVANGELICAL RELIGION, DOMESTICITY,
EDUCATION, AND BENEVOLENCE

112   Altschuler, Glenn C., and Saltzgaber, Jan M. Revivalism,
      Social Conscience, and Community in the Burned-Over District:
      The Trial of Rhoda Bement. Ithaca, N.Y.: Cornell University
      Press, 1983. 184 pp.
        In 1843 the First Presbyterian Church of Seneca Falls, New
York, excommunicated Bement for challenging her pastor's authority

after he had refused to read announcements about abolitionist lectures to the congregation. This case study, which interprets the
transcript of the church disciplinary trial within the context of
the social history of the region, illuminates both the limits of
women's rights in the church and the complex relationship between
evangelical religion, community order, and social reform in the
antebellum period.

113   Bass, Dorothy C. "Sex Roles, Sexual Symbolism, and Social
       Change: A Study in the Religious Popular Culture of Nineteenth-
       Century American Women." Radical Religion 4 (1978):21-27.
       Bass contrasts the theories of gender supported by the cult
of domesticity and by abolitionist feminists, with particular attention to how these views were or were not conducive to social
reform.

114   Bass, Dorothy C. "'Their Prodigious Influence': Women,
       Religion and Reform in Antebellum America." In Women of Spirit:
       Female Leadership in the Jewish and Christian Traditions (entry
       80), pp. 279-300.
       Bass explores the religious and social origins and meaning
of churchwomen's benevolent associations in the early nineteenth
century and links these to the emergence after 1830 of religious
reform movements in which women asserted their own rights, particularly female moral reform and abolitionism. This interpretation of women's expanding sphere of activity argues that "the
ferment of militant Christianity provided the intellectual and
psychological resources which made religious reform a crucial
setting for women's adaptation to and initiative within a changing
society" (p. 297).

115   Bendroth, Margaret L. "The Search for 'Women's Role' in Ameri-
       can Evangelicalism, 1930-1980." In Evangelicalism and Modern
       America, edited by George M. Marsden. Grand Rapids, Mich.:
       Eerdmans Publishing Co., 1984, pp. 122-34.
       Like the "mainline" denominations, evangelicals encountered
confusion with regard to the role of women after the weakening of
the independent women's mission organizations in the 1920s and
1930s; their distinctive response was to adopt more rigid conservative views about gender during the ensuing decades. Bendroth
documents these views, explains their origins, and contrasts them
to the new "evangelical feminism" that emerged in the mid-1970s,
noting that the issue is still far from resolved in evangelical
circles.

116   Berg, Barbara J. The Remembered Gate: Origins of American
       Feminism, The Woman and the City, 1800-1860. New York: Oxford
       University Press, 1978. 334 pp.
       Part 1, "The Woman-Belle Ideal," treats the history, con-
cerns, and images of urban middle- and upper-class women; part 2,
"Towards Feminism," treats the associations these women formed to
help members of their own sex, especially the poor and "fallen."
Berg argues that women's quest for self-realization in an urban

environment, exemplified in organized benevolence, produced a more encompassing feminism than did the movement for legal rights.

117   Blauvelt, Martha Tomhave. "Women and Revivalism." In Women and Religion in America, vol. 1 (entry 78), pp. 1-45.
       Blauvelt's historical essay discusses the social, psychological, and religious meaning of women's activities as revival members and revival promoters, with attention to regional and racial diversity. Eleven documents follow, including ministers' interpretations of female piety; women's private writings, letters, and conversion accounts; and narratives of nineteenth-century revivalists.

118   Boylan, Anne M. "Evangelical Womanhood in the Nineteenth Century: The Role of Women in Sunday Schools." Feminist Studies 4 (1978):62-80.
       This article shows how women Sunday School workers developed an ideal and life-style of "evangelical womanhood" that enabled them to be useful and significant individuals. The role was flexible and could lead to, or be expanded to include, work in organized benevolence, missions, temperance, and other reforms.

119   Bunkle, Phillida. "Sentimental Womanhood and Domestic Education, 1830-1870." History of Education Quarterly 14 (Spring 1974):13-30.
       Bunkle uses a variety of religious concepts to explain the development and significance of the "middle class ideal of sentimental womanhood," including evangelicalism's emphasis on the heart, the role of mothers as religious educators, and the idea of women's superior spirituality.

120   Caskey, Marie. Chariot of Fire: Religion and the Beecher Family. New Haven: Yale University Press, 1978. 442 pp.
       The stories of Lyman Beecher and his eleven offspring touch most of the central themes of nineteenth-century Protestantism. Caskey's discussions of the evangelical household and theology of Lyman, a great leader of the Second Great Awakening, provide the background for individual treatments of seven of his children, all of whom were "ministers or, in the case of the women, virtually ministers" (p. 382). Of particular interest are the chapters on the religious development of the educator and domestic theorist Catharine Beecher, the suffragist and mystic Isabella Beecher Hooker, and the author Harriet Beecher Stowe. The book concludes with chapters on the family's collective interest in spiritualism and a religion conceived in domestic terms. Further information on this family, including essays on the three women named above, may be found in Earl A. French and Diana Royce, eds., Portraits of a Nineteenth-Century Family: A Symposium on the Beecher Family (Hartford, Conn.: Stowe-Day Foundation, 1976); in Notable American Women (entry 35), 1:121-24, 2:212-14, 3:393-402; and in entries 137 and 238.

121   Cott, Nancy F. The Bonds of Womanhood: "Woman's Sphere" in
       New England, 1780–1835. New Haven: Yale University Press,
       1977. 225 pp.
              "Woman's sphere" was a central concept in nineteenth-century
       discussions of the woman question, and Cott's book analyzes its
       origin and meaning. Drawing chiefly on the private writing of
       middle-class women and on sermons, Cott explores the relation of
       the emerging cult of domesticity to the actual circumstances, ex-
       periences, and consciousness of women. Chapters treat work, do-
       mesticity, education, religion, and sisterhood. A concluding
       "sketch" of the longer evolution of women's "group-consciousness"
       suggests the relevance of "woman's sphere" to the emergence of
       feminism. An excerpt from the book appears in Our American Sis-
       ters: Women in American Life and Thought (entry 19), pp. 196–212.

122   Cott, Nancy F. "Passionlessness: An Interpretation of Vic-
       torian Sexual Ideology, 1790–1850." Signs: Journal of Women
       in Culture and Society 4 (1978):219–36. Also in A Heritage of
       Her Own: Toward a New Social History of American Women (entry
       18), pp. 162–81.
              This study of the belief that women's sex drives were less
       than men's is based on women's public and private writings and on
       didactic and popular works, especially religious ones, which in-
       fluenced women. Cott attributes the ideology of passionlessness
       largely to the rise of evangelical religion.

123   Cott, Nancy F. "Young Women in the Second Great Awakening."
       Feminist Studies 3 (1975):15–29.
              Cott draws on modernization theory and developmental psy-
       chology to explain why young unmarried women comprised the largest
       group of converts during the Second Great Awakening. Social and
       economic change bore especially hard on this group, Cott argues,
       and evangelical religion offered a viable resolution of the psy-
       chological conflicts this created.

124   Cross, Whitney R. The Burned-Over District: The Social and
       Intellectual History of Enthusiastic Religion in Western New
       York, 1800–1850. Ithaca, N.Y.: Cornell University Press,
       1950. Reprints. New York: Harper & Row, 1965; New York:
       Octagon Books, 1981. 383 pp.
              Women "should dominate a history of enthusiastic movements,"
       Cross asserts (p. 84), and even though his book does not fulfill
       this purpose in a systematic way, it does contain much information
       on women. Topics include revivalism, benevolence, and "ultraist"
       reform; antimasonry, antislavery, and temperance; Mormonism,
       millenialism, utopianism, and spiritualism. Leading characters
       like Charles Finney, John Humphrey Noyes, and Joseph Smith emerge
       against a rich social background, as do lesser-known male and fe-
       male enthusiasts such as the Fox sisters.

125   Epstein, Barbara Leslie. The Politics of Domesticity: Women,
       Evangelism, and Temperance in Nineteenth-Century America.
       Middletown, Conn.: Wesleyan University Press, 1981. 188 pp.

Epstein traces the development of religious experience and gender group consciousness among middle-class evangelical women from the Great Awakening through the Woman's Christian Temperance Union. In the 1740s, she argues, the conversion experiences of men and women were relatively similar, but after 1800 these experiences diverged, while the culture of domesticity set new norms of female subordination; the Woman's Christian Temperance Crusade and the WCTU provided a transition to feminism, though a socially conservative one. Epstein's interpretation of female piety in terms of women's changing--and usually antagonistic--relations to men makes useful connections between social and religious history and between different historical periods.

126   Fletcher, Robert S. A History of Oberlin College from its Foundation through the Civil War. 2 vols. Oberlin, Ohio: Oberlin College, 1943. 976 pp.
    Fletcher appropriately treats the history of America's first coeducational college in the context of evangelical religion and reform that surrounded its founding (1834). Of particular interest are the chapters in vol. 2 on "Female Reformers" and "Joint Education of the Sexes." For information about some of Oberlin's first women students, see entries 195, 331, and 440.

127   Hardesty, Nancy; Dayton, Lucille Sider; and Dayton, Donald. "Women in the Holiness Movement: Feminism in the Evangelical Tradition." In Women of Spirit: Female Leadership in the Jewish and Christian Traditions (entry 80), pp. 225-54.
    These authors identify the exceptional opportunities for female leadership in an evangelical tradition stretching from John Wesley through the revivals of Charles Finney, the sanctificationism of Phoebe Palmer and Wesleyan Methodists, the Salvation Army, the temperance and religious activities of Frances Willard and Hannah Whitall Smith, the preaching of former slave Amanda Smith, and the late nineteenth-century holiness sects that encouraged women ministers. They suggest the theological, experiential, and social reasons for this tradition's relative openness to women's leadership, as well as noting the decline of this openness in the twentieth century. Much of this information is also presented, in somewhat different form, in chapter 8 of Donald W. Dayton, Discovering an Evangelical Heritage (New York: Harper & Row, 1976), and in Lucille Sider Dayton and Donald W. Dayton, "'Your Daughters Shall Prophesy': Feminism in the Holiness Movement," Methodist History 14 (January 1976):67-92. See also section VII.H of this bibliography.

128   Hogeland, Ronald W. "Charles Hodge, The Association of Gentlemen and Ornamental Womanhood: 1825-1855." Journal of Presbyterian History 53 (Fall 1975):239-55.
    Hogeland discusses the restrictive prescriptions for womanhood published by leaders of Old School Presbyterianism in their journal Biblical Repository and Princeton Review. He argues that they rejected the romantic view of womanhood and the cult of domesticity that were gaining adherents elsewhere in Protestantism and links their views of womanhood to their conservative social and theological positions.

129   Hovet, Theodore. "Phoebe Palmer's 'Altar Phraseology' and the
      Spiritual Dimension of Woman's Sphere." Journal of Religion 63
      (July 1983):264-80.
         Hovet analyzes the theology of the leading nineteenth-century
      teacher of Holiness, arguing that her ideas about the inner spir-
      itual freedom of women within the domestic sphere were both liber-
      ating and constraining. Theological considerations of nineteenth-
      century women's religion are rare, and this one takes Palmer's
      ideas seriously within the longer context of liberalizing tenden-
      cies in Protestantism in the modern world. His treatment may be
      compared to the more sympathetic account offered by Nancy Hardesty,
      Women Called to Witness (entry 288), and the biographical article
      by Anne C. Loveland, "Domesticity and Religion in the Antebellum
      Period: The Career of Phoebe Palmer," Historian 39 (May 1977):
      455-71.

130   Kaufman, Polly Welts. Women Teachers on the Frontier. New
      Haven: Yale University Press, 1984. xxiii, 270 pp.
         Kaufman has added to the chronicle of the wives of overland
      pioneers and of prostitutes the stories of about 250 single women
      who went west in the decade between 1846 and 1856 to teach on the
      frontier. They were recruited and trained by the National Board
      of Popular Education, which required membership in an evangelical
      church and evidence of a conversion experience before it accepted
      applicants. The women saw themselves to be serving God in their
      frontier teaching and were empowered by this to become independent
      and self-reliant. The complete journal of a pioneer teacher in
      Iowa from 1848 to 1851 and letters from other pioneer women
      teachers located throughout the west--all replete with reflections
      on their religious experiences--are included.

131   Kuhn, Anne L. The Mother's Role in Childhood Education: New
      England Concepts, 1830-1860. New Haven: Yale University
      Press, 1947. 224 pp.
         Kuhn's study of popular advice books about mothering pays
      special attention to the religious features of their authors'
      ideals of maternal influence. A bibliographical essay identifies
      the most important primary sources, and an extensive bibliography
      lists other sources from the period.

132   Melder, Keith. "Ladies Bountiful: Organized Female Benevolence
      in Early Nineteenth-Century America." New York History 48
      (1967):231-54.
         This treatment of women's voluntary associations--including
      mission, Bible, tract, and charity societies--analyzes their
      English and religious backgrounds, their development, and their
      consequences in opening the issue of women's rights and leading to
      the more radical efforts of female moral reformers and abolition-
      ists. See also entry 225.

133   Rossi, Alice S. "Social Roots of the Woman's Movement in
      America." In The Feminist Papers (entry 226), pp. 241-81.
         This essay introduces the section on the nineteenth-century
      American women's rights movement in Rossi's rich anthology of

feminist writings. (Those included in this section are Sarah and Angelina Grimkē, Elizabeth and Emily Blackwell, Antoinette Brown Blackwell, Elizabeth Cady Stanton, and Susan B. Anthony, pp. 282-470). Rossi calls these women "moral crusader feminists" and argues that their activities were shaped by revivalism and evangelical movements in benevolence and reform. She also treats the role of domesticity and social change, as well as the lives of the individual authors and the relations among them.

134   Ryan, Mary P. Cradle of the Middle Class: The Family in Oneida County, New York, 1790-1865. New York: Cambridge University Press, 1981. 321 pp.
      Focusing on Utica, a burgeoning commercial center on the Erie Canal and a headquarters of evangelical activism during the Second Great Awakening, Ryan's analysis of one stage in the making of the modern family blends intricate demographic and economic research with insight into the beliefs and values of Utica's residents. The central concern is the emergence of the cult of domesticity and the privatistic middle-class family, a "pivotal turn in family ideology" which Ryan places "at a busy intersection of American history, where structural changes in the household, economics, and class were entangled with the idiosyncratic episodes of evangelism and reform" (p. 15). The changing activities of women in religion and reform--in revivals, missionary societies, maternal associations, abolitionism, female moral reform, temperance, public welfare, and feminism--provide crucial evidence for Ryan's interpretation; this book contains many treasures of new information about women in religion and analyzes that topic within a persuasive social scientific framework.

135   Ryan, Mary P. "A Women's Awakening: Evangelical Religion and the Families of Utica, N.Y.: 1800-1840." In Women in American Religion (entry 75), pp. 89-110.
      After an analysis of the records of four local churches, the Female Missionary Society, and the Maternal Association, Ryan concludes that "Utica women conducted a systematic evangelical campaign" (p. 110). This treatment of women's conversions and their initiatives in securing the conversions of others is based on Ryan's larger study of the family in Utica, Cradle of the Middle Class.

136   Sizer, Sandra S. Gospel Hymns and Social Religion: The Rhetoric of Nineteenth-Century Revivalism. Philadelphia: Temple University Press, 1978. xi, 222 pp.
      Sizer interprets the words of gospel hymns collected by Ira Sankey (partner to revivalist Dwight L. Moody) as a way of understanding the world of meaning to which they belonged. This is not a history of women's religious belief and activity (although Sizer notes that many hymns were written by women and reflects upon the alliance between women and evangelical clergymen), but rather an account of how gender-related imagery concerning home, mother, and family came to dominate revivalists' religious language as they and their followers sought unity of feeling amid the tensions of a rapidly changing society.

137   Sklar, Kathryn Kish. Catharine Beecher: A Study in American
      Domesticity. New Haven: Yale University Press, 1973. 356 pp.
         Sklar portrays Beecher as the architect of a definition of
      domesticity with implications for both personal and national
      values and behavior, and in doing so she presents an "era through
      the life of one woman" (p. xv). The career of Beecher (1800-1878),
      a member of nineteenth-century Protestantism's most notable family
      (see entry 120), included conducting theological and ecclesiasti-
      cal controversies, founding educational institutions for women,
      promoting teaching as a profession for women and educational ven-
      tures in the West, advocating health, housing, and dietary reform,
      and developing a theory of womanly self-sacrifice. This book thus
      sheds light on many aspects of women's culture and women's rela-
      tions to men, to each other, and to American society.

138   Sklar, Kathryn Kish. "The Founding of Mount Holyoke College."
      In Women of America: A History (entry 16), pp. 177-201.
         Sklar's account of Mary Lyon's work for women's education
      emphasizes the contributions of evangelical religion, organized
      female benevolence, and missionary spirit. Two short documents,
      written just before the institution opened in 1837, are included.

139   Smith, Timothy L. Revivalism and Social Reform in Mid-
      Nineteenth-Century America. New York: Abingdon Press, 1957.
      253 pp. Appeared also as Revivalism and Social Reform: Ameri-
      can Protestantism on the Eve of the Civil War. New York:
      Harper Torchbooks, 1965; Baltimore: Johns Hopkins University
      Press, 1980, with new afterword by the author.
         Smith's study of evangelical religion emphasizes the revival
      of 1858 and the emerging doctrine of holiness, sanctification, or
      Christian perfection. Evangelical activities in public welfare
      and social reform became a major source of the Social Gospel of
      later decades, Smith argues. The book includes information on
      many women who were involved in such activities, chief among them
      Phoebe Palmer, and a critical essay on relevant primary and sec-
      ondary sources.

140   Smith-Rosenberg, Carroll. "The Female World of Love and Ritual:
      Relations Between Women in Nineteenth-Century America." Signs:
      Journal of Women in Culture and Society 1 (1975):1-29. Also in
      A Heritage of Her Own: Toward a New Social History of American
      Women (entry 18), pp. 311-42; and in Disorderly Conduct:
      Visions of Gender in Victorian America. New York: Alfred A.
      Knopf, 1985, pp. 53-76.
         In thousands of letters and diaries, Smith-Rosenberg dis-
      covers evidence of deep and lasting intimacy between women; atten-
      tion is given to how this intimacy affected life transitions and
      marriages and to the "homogenous and sexually-segregated groups"
      within which it flourished and received approval. Although the
      article does not treat religion, its depiction of the "homosocial"
      world of middle-class women could be useful to those seeking a
      full understanding of many of the women mentioned elsewhere in
      this chapter.

141   Smith-Rosenberg, Carroll. Religion and the Rise of the Ameri-
      can City: The New York City Mission Movement, 1812-1870.
      Ithaca, N.Y.: Cornell University Press, 1971. 300 pp.
         This study of temporal and religious philanthropy to the
      poor of New York pays substantial attention to the contributions
      of pious women, particularly in early benevolent associations and
      in the American Female Guardian Society (1837-70), which developed
      from a crusade for sexual purity to a shelter, employment agency,
      and educator for slum women and children.

142   Smith-Rosenberg, Carroll. "Women and Religious Revivals:
      Anti-Ritualism, Liminality, and the Emergence of the American
      Bourgeoisie." In The Evangelical Tradition in America, edited
      by Leonard I. Sweet. Macon, Ga.: Mercer University Press,
      1984, pp. 199-232. Also in revised, but basically similar,
      form in Disorderly Conduct: Visions of Gender in Victorian
      America (see entry 140), pp. 129-64, as "The Cross and the
      Pedestal: Women, Anti-Ritualism, and the Emergence of the
      American Bourgeoisie."
         This article explains the remarkable outburst of women's
      activities in the upstate New York revivals of the 1830s, drawing
      heavily upon the theories of anthropologists Mary Douglas and
      Victor Turner.

143   Sweet, Leonard I. "The Female Seminary Movement and Women's
      Mission in Antebellum America." Church History 54 (March 1985):
      41-55.
         Seeking to explain the rapid growth of educational oppor-
      tunities for women from 1820 to the Civil War, Sweet finds a
      rationale in the public speeches of leaders of the female seminary
      movement, most of them evangelicals.

144   Sweet, Leonard I. The Minister's Wife: Her Role in Nineteenth-
      Century Evangelicalism. Philadelphia: Temple University Press,
      1983. viii, 237 pp.
         Sweet identifies a variety of the images and experiences
      attending the role of minister's wife from the time of Frau Luther
      into the early twentieth century, with the emphasis stated in the
      title. In his view, four models predominated (Companion, Sacri-
      ficer, Assistant, and Partner), which he explicates with reference
      to the careers of particular women. Patterns changed over time,
      but on the whole Sweet makes a case for seeing the role as "an
      occupation, a profession, a ministerial vocation" at some moments
      in evangelical history. By setting the careers of these women
      within a rich framework of nineteenth-century women's religious
      history, Sweet also provides insight into other issues in the
      relationship between evangelical religion, domesticity, education,
      benevolence, and reform.

145   Tyler, Alice Felt. Freedom's Ferment: Phases of American
      Social History from the Colonial Period to the Outbreak of the
      Civil War. New York: Harper & Row, 1944, 1962. 608 pp.
         "The religious movements and the adventures in reform of the
      early years of the republic were the truly significant activities

of the men and women of the age, and they contributed much to the
way of life of twentieth-century America," Tyler says in the introduction to this work (p. v), still in print more than 40 years
after its original publication. Tyler provides more than the
usual amount of description of the contributions of women to these
"religious movements and adventures in reform" with coverage of
Margaret Fuller, the Fox sisters, Jemima Wilkinson, Mother Ann
Lee, Frances Wright, women's education, Dorothea Dix, and women in
various reform movements.

146   Welter, Barbara. "The Cult of True Womanhood, 1820–1860."
       American Quarterly 18 (1966):151–74. Also in Dimity Convic-
       tions: American Women in the Nineteenth Century. Columbus:
       Ohio State University Press, 1976, pp. 21–41.
          This study of women's magazines, gift annuals, and religious
       literature identifies the four cardinal virtues of the "true
       woman" they presented: piety, purity, submissiveness, and domes-
       ticity. Welter's emphasis is on norms, not actual behavior.

147   Welter, Barbara. "The Feminization of American Religion, 1800–
       1860." In Clio's Consciousness Raised: New Perspectives in
       the History of Women, edited by Mary S. Hartman and Lois W.
       Banner. New York: Harper & Row, 1974, pp. 137–57. Also in
       Insights and Parallels: Problems and Issues of American Social
       History, edited by William O'Neill. Minneapolis: Burgess Pub.
       Co., 1973, pp. 305–32.
          Welter's definition of feminization encompasses a vast and
       diverse range of ways in which "women in the first half of the
       nineteenth century took Christianity and molded it to their image
       and likeness" (p. 330, ed. O'Neill), including their increased
       numerical prominence in religious institutions, "feminine" adapta-
       tions in religious doctrine and experience by both women and men,
       and the development of new religious forms with "feminine" con-
       tent. On this basis, she detects feminization all over the Ameri-
       can religious landscape--in changing theologies, in literature and
       hymns, among women religious leaders and missionaries, Transcen-
       dentalists and utopians, Mormons and Roman Catholics--and the
       brief article thus becomes a suggestive map of phenomena that
       merit further attention from students of women in American reli-
       gion. In O'Neill's edition, the article is followed by excerpts
       from relevant primary sources (pp. 332–55).

       For Further Information

No aspect of the religious history of American women has been as
thoroughly studied as the evangelical religion of the nineteenth-
century white Northern population, which has attracted the attention
of many social historians in addition to those whose primary interest
is in the history of religion. Research in this field portrays a
vital cultural movement whose ethos was shaped by a mingling of the
images and experiences of domesticity with the themes of evangelical
religion. Religion often shaded imperceptibly into ventures in education, benevolence, and reform; the culture of domesticity influ-
enced church leaders, literary figures, and activists in many causes;

and assertions of women's autonomy, whether or not explicitly linked
to organized feminism, emerged within this cultural framework. The
works listed above depict, in various ways, the connections among
religion, domesticity, education, benevolence, and women's changing
place in American society.

148   Those seeking more understanding of evangelical religion itself
should turn to the general histories and bibliographies of American religion listed in chapter 1. In addition, the following
works by William G. McLoughlin are especially helpful: Modern
Revivalism, Charles Grandison Finney to Billy Graham (New York:
Ronald Press, 1959); The American Evangelicals, 1800-1900 (New
York: Harper & Row, 1968), an edition of primary documents with
a useful introduction that suggests the implications of changing
theology for women; and his introduction to the John Harvard
Library edition of Finney's Lectures on Revivals of Religion
(Cambridge, Mass.: Harvard University Press, 1960), which is the
most important document of American revivalism. A recent work on
evangelical history is by Leonard I. Sweet, ed., The Evangelical
Tradition in America (Macon, Ga.: Mercer University Press, 1984).
In the first chapter, Sweet provides an excellent review of recent
scholarship on American evangelical history, including much on
women.

149   Robert W. Lynn and Elliott Wright, The Big Little School: Two
Hundred Years of the Sunday School, 2d ed. (Nashville: Abingdon
Press, 1980), includes material on women and attributes the suc-
cess of the institution partly to their support. Lois Banner,
"Religious Benevolence as Social Control: A Critique of an Interpretation," Journal of American History 60 (1973):23-41, provides entry into a long-standing debate among historians about the
character and aims of religious benevolence. For general background on benevolence, consult the books and bibliographies on
American religious history listed in chapter 1.

150   The careers of female revivalists provide further insight into
this topic. Information about a number of them may be found by
consulting the category "Ministers and Evangelists" in the index
to Notable American Women (entry 35) and examining the biographical sketches of the women listed there. Each entry includes a
bibliography containing biographies and autobiographies of the
women. See especially Phoebe Worrall Palmer (3:12-14), Amanda
Berry Smith (3:304-5), Hannah Whitall Smith (3:313-16), and
Margaret Anne Newton Van Cott (3:506-7). Individual women who
were important in religious benevolence and education who are
treated in Notable American Women (entry 35) are Catharine
Beecher (1:121-24), Joanna Graham Bethune (1:138-40), Isabella
Graham (2:71-72), Mary Lyon (2:443-47), and Emma Hart Willard
(3:610-13).

151   One group of American Protestant women who deserve further
historical attention (in addition to Leonard Sweet's The Minister's Wife: Her Role in Nineteenth-Century Evangelicalism
[entry 144]), are the wives of clergymen. A sensitive but out-

dated study is William Douglas, <u>Ministers' Wives</u> (New York: Harper & Row, 1965), which includes a brief historical account and an annotated bibliography of historical, contemporary, and fictional resources. On the basis of about 5,000 questionnaire responses from ministers' wives in the range of Protestant tradi- tions, minister and psychologist Douglas analyzes the expecta- tions, conflicts, and tasks that have attended this role. A more recent study that draws on later sources is Roy M. Oswald, Carolyn Taylor Gutierrez, and Liz Spellman Dean, <u>Married to the Minister:</u> <u>Dilemmas, Conflicts, and Joys in the Role of the Clergy Wife</u> (Washington, D.C.: Alban Institute, 1980). For historical ac- counts, see Lois A. Boyd, "Presbyterian Ministers' Wives: A Nineteenth-Century Portrait," in <u>Presbyterian Women in America:</u> <u>Two Centuries of a Quest for Status</u> (entry 306), pp. 189-204; Julie Roy Jeffrey, "Ministry Through Marriage: Methodist Clergy Wives on the Trans-Mississippi Frontier"; and Clotilde Falcon Nanez "Hispanic Clergy Wives: Their Contributions to United Methodism in the Southwest, Later Nineteenth Century to the Pres- ent," in <u>Women in New Worlds</u>, vol. 1 (entry 81), pp. 143-77. Several essays in <u>Women in New Worlds</u>, vol. 2 (entry 76), pp. 97- 161, are relevant: Anne Llewellyn Barstow, "An Ambiguous Legacy: Anglican Clergy Wives after the Reformation"; Frank Baker, "Susanna Wesley: Puritan, Parent, Pastor, Protagonist, Pattern"; Emora T. Brannan, "A Partnership of Equality: The Marriage and Ministry of John and Mary Goucher"; and Rosa Peffly Motes, "The Pacific Northwest: Changing Role of the Pastor's Wife Since 1840."

II.B.2. REFORM MOVEMENTS

152   Bass, Dorothy C. "'In Christian Firmness and Christian Meek- ness': Feminism and Pacifism in Antebellum America." In <u>Immaculate and Powerful: The Female in Sacred Image and Social</u> <u>Reality</u> (entry 57), pp. 201-25.
      This study of a circle of radical abolitionists (including Angelina and Sarah Grimké, Maria Weston Chapman, and William Lloyd Garrison) considers the religious foundations and implications of their views, with emphasis on their espousal of nonresistance as a critique of gender relations.

153   Bordin, Ruth. <u>Woman and Temperance: The Quest for Power and</u> <u>Liberty, 1873-1900</u>. Philadelphia: Temple University Press, 1981. xviii, 221 pp.
      Bordin sets the history of the origins, growth, and ideas of the Woman's Christian Temperance Union in a broad context of re- form and women's history in this study of the WCTU during the pe- riod when it was the largest and most politically powerful reform organization of women ever assembled. Empirical research provides insight into the nature of the organization's constituency, while cultural interpretation explicates its feminist emphases during this period.

154   Fishburn, Janet Forsythe. <u>The Fatherhood of God and the Vic-</u> <u>torian Family: The Social Gospel in America</u>. Philadelphia: Fortress Press, 1981. xi, 208 pp.

This is not a history of women in religious reform but rather a study of six male theologians of religious reform from a feminist perspective that emphasizes the significance of domestic ideals and gender relations in their thought. To explain the apparent paradox that liberal Protestant advocates of social justice and equality (chief among them Walter Rauschenbusch) opposed the feminist movement of their time, Fishburn interprets their attachment to the patriarchal bourgeois family with reference to the social and intellectual changes of the period.

155   Gifford, Carolyn De Swarte. "Women in Social Reform Movements." In Women and Religion in America, vol. 1 (entry 78), pp. 294-340.
      Gifford's introduction (pp. 294-303) summarizes some major themes of women reformers, including their justifications for their activities, and portrays major figures, including those for whom "reform became their religion, a position of faith as much as a cause espoused" (p. 296). Ten pictures and 13 documents follow: Catharine Beecher on the proper limits of women's reform activities; Angelina Grimké's defense of women's equal rights as reformers; Mary Lyon's and Isabella Graham's pleas for women in education; Mary Livermore on Civil War relief efforts; Laura Smith Haviland on postwar aid to freedmen; Margaret Prior on moral reform; "Mother" Stewart on the Temperance Crusade of 1873-74; Frances Willard on the WCTU's woman suffrage strategy; Anna Howard Shaw on woman's mission; Josephine Shaw Lowell on organized charity; Ida B. Wells-Barnett in opposition to lynching; Mary Woodridge on world peace. Gifford's own further explication of the temperance movement is "For God and Home and Native Land: The WCTU's Image of Woman in the Late Nineteenth Century," in Women in New Worlds, vol. 1 (entry 81), pp. 310-27.

156   Hardesty, Nancy A. Women Called to Witness: Evangelical Femininism in the Nineteenth Century. Nashville: Abingdon Press, 1984. 176 pp.
      "Nineteenth-century American feminism was deeply rooted in evangelical revivalism," argues Hardesty (p. 9) in this survey of the wide-ranging reform activities of women who were, or who were influenced by, evangelicals. Her account of evangelicalism emphasizes the contributions of Charles Grandison Finney's theology of free moral agency and Phoebe Palmer's gospel of Holiness as inspirers of women's efforts for the advancement of themselves and others through benevolence, education, and such reforms as abolitionism, temperance, moral reform, and suffrage.

157   Hersh, Blanche Glassman. "To Make the World Better: Protestant Women in the Abolitionist Movement." In Triumph Over Silence: Women in Protestant History (entry 74), pp. 173-202.
      Hersh traces the movement of radical abolitionist women away from orthodox denominations and the institutional churches, the development of the first feminist ideology as a response to clergy challenges to women's participation in abolitionism, and the crusade against racial prejudice as well as against slavery in the radical wing of the abolitionist movement. Her earlier book, The

Slavery of Sex: Feminist-Abolitionists in America (Urbana:
University of Illinois Press, 1978), while paying little attention
to religion as such, closely studies 51 antebellum reformers, the
central patterns of their lives, and the origin and ideology of
their movement.

158   Hewitt, Nancy A. Women's Activism and Social Change: The Case
       of Rochester, New York, 1822-1872. Ithaca, N.Y.: Cornell Uni-
       versity Press, 1984. 192 pp.
          On the basis of thorough research in local records, Hewitt
offers a detailed analysis of women's public activity in a city
long known to have been a hotbed of evangelical religion and reform. She finds that three networks of women devised different
approaches to reform in keeping with their own location within the
city's social structure: the well-to-do "benevolent" women, the
middle-class "perfectionist" women, and the marginal "ultraist"
women. This study's complex analysis of the relationships between
class, religion, and public activism will interest students of
benevolence, abolitionism, moral reform, temperance, and woman
suffrage. An article based upon the same material is her "The
Perimeters of Women's Power in American Religion," in The Evangelical Tradition in America, edited by Leonard I. Sweet (Macon,
Ga.: Mercer University Press, 1984), pp. 233-56.

159   Jones, Jacqueline. Soldiers of Light and Love: Northern
       Teachers and Georgia Blacks, 1865-1873. Chapel Hill: Univer-
       sity of North Carolina Press, 1980. xiii, 273 pp.
          Northern women and men who went south to Georgia after the
Civil War to teach the freed people were "moved by a vision of a
truly unified American society in which competing interests would
be cemented together in national purpose by the tenets of Protestantism and capitalism," says Jones (p. 5). Using the case study
method, she thoroughly examines the motivations and experiences of
368 Northern teachers who served in Georgia between 1865 and 1873,
revealing both "the strength of the neo-abolitionist impulse [and]
the limits of liberal reform" (p. 3).

160   Kraditor, Aileen S. Means and Ends in American Abolitionism:
       Garrison and His Critics on Strategy and Tactics, 1834-1850.
       New York: Pantheon Books, 1969. xvi, 296 pp.
          This controversial and influential study of abolitionist
factionalism includes chapters on two of the issues that separated
the "radical" Garrisonians from their critics: "The Woman Question" and "Religion and the Good Society." This book can lead
researchers into the sources and disagreements on women abolitionists.

161   Lee, Susan Dye. "Evangelical Domesticity: The Woman's
       Temperance Crusade of 1873-74." In Women in New Worlds,
       vol. 1 (entry 81), pp. 293-309.
          Lee describes the nondenominational revival during which
"praying bands" of women closed down saloons, thus moving women
into the front ranks of the temperance movement and preparing the
way for their support of woman suffrage through the WCTU. Her

analysis of the women's ideology of "evangelical domesticity" suggests that it imparted to women reformers weaknesses as well as strengths, however.

162   Lindley, Susan H. "Women and the Social Gospel Novel." Church History 54 (March 1985):56-73.
        Lindley's interpretation of novels by Vida Scudder, Florence Converse, Charles Sheldon, and Elizabeth Stuart Phelps discloses suggestive information about the popularization of the Social Gospel and the place of women therein.

163   McAlister, Pam, ed. Reweaving the Web of Life: Feminism and Nonviolence. Philadelphia: New Society Publishers, 1982. viii, 440 pp.
        This anthology includes a rich variety of personal statements, philosophy, poetry, strategy, reportage, and some history. It suggests resources and themes that would be useful in research on feminism and pacifism in American religious history, though it does not aim to offer adequate coverage of this topic.

164   Ryan, Mary P. "The Power of Women's Networks: A Case Study of Female Moral Reform in Antebellum America." Feminist Studies 5 (Spring 1979):66-88.
        Ryan studies women's involvement in a Utica, New York, moral reform organization in the 1830s and 1840s. Her attention to local detail enables her to arrive at a careful and provocative interpretation of how women exerted social and cultural power through this reform.

165   Smith-Rosenberg, Carroll. "Beauty, the Beast and the Militant Woman: A Case Study in Sex Roles and Social Stress in Jacksonian America." American Quarterly 23 (October 1971):562-84. Also in A Heritage of Her Own: Toward a New Social History of American Women (entry 18), pp. 197-221; and in Disorderly Conduct: Visions of Gender in Victorian America. New York: Alfred A. Knopf, 1985, pp. 109-29.
        This influential article, published early in the new wave of research on women's history, examines the New York Female Moral Reform Society in the 1830s, arguing that middle-class evangelical women's activities on behalf of their "fallen" sisters disclosed their own discontent with prevailing sex roles and their resolve to change them.

166   Tucker, Cynthia Grant. A Woman's Ministry: Mary Collson's Search for Reform as a Unitarian Minister, a Hull House Social Worker, and a Christian Science Practitioner. Philadelphia: Temple University Press, 1984. xviii, 216 pp.
        This biography of the hitherto little-known Collson (1870-1953) relates the story of her attempt to discover a satisfying career in social reform. Her idealism was tested as she sought to help the poor and oppressed in rural Iowa through the church, in Chicago as a juvenile social worker, and finally as a religious healer. The tensions of women's changing status, Tucker believes, were partially responsible for Collson's feelings of failure and chronic depression.

Individual Women

167   Sarah Moore Grimké (1792-1873) and Angelina Emily Grimké Weld
       (1805-79)
       Daughters of a South Carolina slaveholder, these sisters
migrated to the North, where they became prominent abolitionists.
Their religious journey included Episcopalianism, Presbyterianism,
Quakerism, millenarianism, and free thought; Sarah's Letters on
the Equality of the Sexes and the Condition of Woman, written in
1837 at the peak of their controversial career as orators, is a
classic statement of Christian feminism. The Letters receive significant theological explication in Rosemary Radford Ruether, "The
Subordination and Liberation of Women in Christian Theology:
Saint Paul and Sarah Grimké," Soundings 61 (1978):168-81, and in
James L. Cooper and Sheila McIsaac Cooper, "Sarah Grimké: Radical
Sectarian," in Roots of American Feminist Thought (entry 218),
pp. 51-89. Biographies include Gerda Lerner, The Grimké Sisters
from South Carolina: Rebels Against Slavery (Boston: Houghton
Mifflin, 1967); Katharine Du Pre Lumpkin, The Emancipation of
Angelina Grimké (Chapel Hill: University of North Carolina Press,
1974); listing in Notable American Women (entry 35), 2:97-99, and
in American Reformers (entry 171), pp. 379-82. Frank G. Kirk-
patrick, "From Shackles to Liberation: Religion, the Grimké
Sisters and Dissent," in Women, Religion, and Social Change
(entry 64), pp. 433-55, examines the connections between their
evangelical faith and radical social position. A fascinating
record of their reform career and personal lives is by Gilbert H.
Barnes and Dwight L. Dumond, eds., Letters of Theodore Dwight
Weld, Angelina Grimké Weld, and Sarah Grimké, 1822-1844, 2 vols.
(New York: D. Appleton-Century Co., 1934). A thoughtful biographical essay and a good selection from their writings is found
in The Feminist Papers: From Adams to de Beauvoir (entry 226),
pp. 282-322.

168   Lucretia Mott (1793-1880)
       This minister in the Society of Friends was a leader in the
abolitionist, woman suffrage, moral reform, temperance, and peace
movements during her long and fruitful career, grounding her work
in her own theology of "practical righteousness." Both her elo-
quence and the range of her reform commitments are evident in Dana
Greene, ed., Lucretia Mott: Her Complete Speeches and Sermons
(New York: Edwin Mellen Press, 1980). Admiring biographies are
by Margaret Hope Bacon, Valiant Friend: The Life of Lucretia Mott
(New York: Walker & Co., 1980), and Otelia Cromwell, Lucretia
Mott (Cambridge, Mass.: Harvard University Press, 1958). See
also listing in Notable American Women (entry 35), 2:592-95, and
in American Reformers (entry 171), pp. 595-97.

169   Vida Dutton Scudder (1861-1954)
       An Episcopal laywoman and professor of English literature at
Wellesley College, Scudder was active in settlement house work,
labor relations, and Christian Socialism. Her career illuminates
the relationship between the religious reform of the Social Gospel
and the women's movement in the Progressive era. The basic source

is her autobiography, On Journey (New York: E.P. Dutton, 1937);
it is excerpted and published with an interpretive essay in
Journeys: Autobiographical Writings by Women (entry 77),
pp. 147-63. The development of her Christian thought as seen in
her major published works is traced in Theresa Corcoran, Vida
Dutton Scudder (Boston: Twayne Publishers, 1982). Biographical
articles are by Peter J. Frederick, "Vida Dutton Scudder: The
Professor as Social Activist," New England Quarterly 43 (1970):
407-33; listing in Notable American Women: The Modern Period
(entry 36), pp. 636-38; and listing in American Reformers (entry
171), pp. 731-33.

170   Frances E. Willard (1839-98)
       One of the most effective reformers in American history,
Willard headed the Woman's Christian Temperance Union for the last
two decades of her life, leading its large constituency into support for woman suffrage and a host of other reforms. An excellent
biography is by Mary Earhart, Frances Willard: From Prayers to
Politics (Chicago: University of Chicago Press, 1944); Willard is
also prominently featured in all of the works on women and temperance or evangelical reform listed earlier in this section. Among
her own most important works are Woman and Temperance (1883);
Woman in the Pulpit (1888); Occupations for Women (1895); and
Glimpses of Fifty Years (1889), her autobiography. See also listing in Notable American Women (entry 35), 3:613-19, and in American Reformers (entry 171), pp. 885-88.

171   For biographical information about other women engaged in reform movements, see the classified lists of biographies in Notable
American Women (entry 35) and Notable American Women: The Modern
Period (entry 36) under the following categories: abolitionists,
peace advocates, prison reformers, settlement house leaders,
social and civil reformers, social reform, temperance advocates,
and temperance and prohibition. Alden Whitman's American Reformers (Bronx, N.Y.: H.W. Wilson Co., 1985) contains brief
biographies of more than 500 principal reformers, about half of
whom are women. Dozens of women are listed in Mark Edward
Lender's Dictionary of American Temperance Biography (Westport,
Conn.: Greenwood Press, 1984) and hundreds of reformers are found
in Frances E. Willard and Mary A. Livermore, eds., A Woman of the
Century (entry 37).

       For Further Information

Religion has often been evident in women's organized activities for
social reform. The best examples in American history are abolitionism, temperance, and moral reform (a movement that sought to redeem
"fallen" women and transform male behavior, in opposition to the
sexual double standard); these reformers are emphasized in the sources
above. Less research has been published on the place of religious
women in the more secular reform movements of the early twentieth
century, though some is included here. The civil rights movement is
covered in the section on the South (II.B.5) and in the chapter on
Afro-American religion (V); the movement for women's legal rights is

treated in a later section of this chapter (II.B.6). Readers are
also advised to consult works in the preceding section (II.B.1),
since many reforms of the nineteenth century grew from these roots;
see especially the works by Altschuler and Saltzgaber (entry 112),
Bass (entries 113-14), Berg (entry 116), Epstein (entry 125), Melder
(entry 132), Rossi (entry 133), and Tyler (entry 145).

II.B.3. MISSIONARIES

172   Beaver, R. Pierce. All Loves Excelling: American Protestant
       Women in World Mission. 1968. 227 pp. 2d ed. as American
       Protestant Women in World Mission: A History of the First
       Feminist Movement in North America. Grand Rapids: Eerdmans,
       1980. 237 pp.
       This standard institutional history of women's missionary
efforts treats activities both in the mission field and in state-
side missionary societies in the nineteenth and twentieth centuries. The second edition includes an eight-page chapter about
the 1970s. The bibliography cites most key primary sources.

173   Brumberg, Joan Jacobs. "The Ethnological Mirror: American
       Evangelical Women and Their Heathen Sisters, 1870-1910." In
       Women and the Structure of Society, edited by Barbara J. Harris
       and JoAnn K. McNamara. Durham: Duke University Press, 1984,
       pp. 108-28.
       Following a description of the activities, size, and cul-
tural origins of Baptist, Congregational, Methodist, and Presbyterian women's missionary societies, Brumberg shows how their
publications developed "women's overall conception of the emanci-
patory nature of Christianity versus the oppressions of the ethnic
religions" (p. 115). Her well-researched and thought-provoking
analysis of these accounts of foreign women's oppression and
American women's complex responses to them suggests that American
women's self-perceptions in relation to the other women of the
world had significant implications for their participation in
religion, reform, and American society generally.

174   Brumberg, Joan Jacobs. Mission for Life. New York: Free
       Press, 1980. 302 pp.
       This book is written for both academic and general readers,
and it largely fulfills the promise of its subtitle: "The story
of the family of Adoniram Judson, the dramatic events of the first
American foreign mission, and the course of evangelical religion
in the nineteenth century." Of particular interest are Brumberg's
treatment of the Burma missionary's first wife, Ann Hasseltine
(who would be a saint if Baptists had saints), his third wife, the
author Emily Chubbuck, and his daughter Abby Ann Judson, who became a well-known spiritualist. In "The Case of Ann Hasseltine
Judson: Missionary Hagiography and Female Popular Culture, 1815-
1850," in Women in New Worlds, vol. 2 (entry 76), pp. 234-48,
Brumberg explores the extraordinary hold of the first Mrs. Judson,
the earliest heroine of the foreign mission field, on the religious imagination of evangelical women.

175   Drucker, Alison R. "The Influence of Western Women on the
       Anti-Footbinding Movement, 1840-1911." In Women in China:
       Current Directions in Historical Scholarship, edited by Richard
       W. Guisso and Stanley Johannesen. Youngstown, N.Y.: Philo
       Press, 1981, pp. 179-99.
          Following discussion of some Chinese efforts to stop foot-
       binding, Drucker demonstrates the extent to which Western Protes-
       tant missionaries influenced not only Chinese Christians but non-
       Christians against this practice, which they told the Chinese and
       the Western world was "barbaric." She asserts that this pressure,
       with women missionaries prominently involved, "set the stage for,
       and later reinforced, the spread of secular egalitarian ideologies
       among non-Christian Chinese" (p. 184).

176   Drury, Clifford Merrill. First White Women over the Rockies:
       Diaries, Letters, and Biographical Sketches of the Six Women of
       the Oregon Mission who made the Overland Journey in 1836 and
       1838. 2 vols. Glendale, Calif.: Arthur H. Clark Co., 1963.
       280 pp; 382 pp.
          This is a large collection of documents by and about the
       wives of six missionaries sent by the American Board of Commis-
       sioners for Foreign Missions to work among the Native Americans
       of the Pacific Northwest. Drury adds extensive introductions and
       biographical and historical notes on their journeys, their lives
       in Oregon, and their piety. The women are Narcissa Whitman, Eliza
       Spalding, Mary Walker, Myra Eels, Mary Gray, and Sarah Smith.

177   Garrett, Shirley S. "Sisters All: Feminism and the American
       Women's Missionary Movement." In Missionary Ideologies in the
       Imperialist Era, 1820-1920, edited by Torben Christensen and
       William R. Hutchison. Arhus, Denmark: Aros, 1982,
       pp. 221-30.
          Garrett asserts that in the missionary field "women's work
       for defenseless girls set a personal and compassionate tone for
       the missionary movement as a whole" and, because it threatened
       deeply rooted cultural beliefs, "presented a challenge to women's
       status that was dangerous business" (p. 228). She argues that
       although "missionary feminist ideology hardly looked like radical
       feminism in the United States," abroad it was indeed "missionary
       feminism" and, beyond that, even "feminist imperialism" (p. 229).

178   Grimshaw, Patricia. "Christian Woman, Pious Wife, Faithful
       Mother, Devoted Missionary: Conflicts in Roles of American
       Missionary Women in Nineteenth-Century Hawaii." Feminist
       Studies 9 (Fall 1983):489-521.
          Believing foreign missionary work could widen their sphere
       of activity while they remained faithful to the ideology of the
       supreme moral and spiritual worth of home and family, women mar-
       ried virtual strangers who were departing for the mission fields
       and traveled to places where they hoped to "enlighten the dark
       minds of . . . ignorant heathen" (p. 498). Homemaking duties in
       less-than-congenial settings and their insistence on raising their
       children isolated from Hawaiian influence served to make indepen-
       dent missionary work virtually impossible. Grimshaw concludes

that true women's emancipation would have necessitated both an assault on powerful domestic ideologies and on the racism and classism that was endemic to nineteenth-century women's struggle for sexual equality.

179   Hageman, Alice L. "Women and Missions: The Cost of Libera-
       tion." In Sexist Religion and Women in the Church: No More
       Silence! (entry 65), pp. 167-93.
       Hageman surveys the history of women's missionary activities
and assesses their meaning in two areas: the dynamics of women's
oppression and liberation in the church and the problem of American cultural imperialism in missionary work.

180   Hill, Patricia R. "The World Their Household": The American
       Woman's Foreign Mission Movement and Cultural Transformation,
       1870-1920. Ann Arbor: University of Michigan Press, 1985.
       231 pp.
       Hill treats her subject as a mass movement (with 3 million
adherents in 1915) that transcended denominational boundaries.
The changing appeal and style of women's missionary activism were
integrally related to the general cultural history of American
women, she argues, showing how works of popular fiction portrayed
the "romance of missions" and analyzing the inception, growth, and
decline of the movement in correlation with other cultural changes.
A major theme is how the professionalization and secularization of
missions after the turn of the century ultimately eroded their
base of support in the local auxiliaries of nonprofessional
churchwomen who had earlier seen missions as a grand and special
female calling.

181   Hunter, Jane. The Gospel of Gentility: American Women Mis-
       sionaries in Turn-of-the-Century China. New Haven: Yale
       University Press, 1984. xxi, 318 pp.
       Hunter's study, based on the private papers of about forty
women and the archives of the Congregational and Methodist missions boards, provides a rich portrait of American women missionaries and their meaning in two cultures. Analyzing who they had
been in the U.S., why they went to China, and their reactions to
their unexpected authority as Westerners in a colonial land,
Hunter follows their changing views and experiences as Christian
women through the challenges and rewards of their situation.
Hunter is particularly sensitive to differences between the experiences of single and married missionaries and to Chinese responses
to missionary activity; on this basis, her work becomes a rare
example of comparative women's history. In addition, the encounter of the two cultures is vividly and poignantly displayed in
dozens of excellent photographs taken in turn-of-the-century
China.

182   Hyatt, Irwin T. Our Ordered Lives Confess: Three Nineteenth-
       Century American Missionaries in East Shantung. Cambridge,
       Mass.: Harvard University Press, 1976. xiv, 323 pp.
       In the course of his treatment of Baptist missionary
Charlotte Diggs Moon (pp. 65-136), Hyatt surveys women's work in

East Shantung, China, covering such subjects as missionary service
as opportunity to escape restricted roles; the women's understanding of, attitudes toward, and relationships with Chinese women;
their development of a Christian literature in Chinese; education
of Chinese women and girls; and the efficacy of their evangelistic
work. In addition to Charlotte Diggs Moon, attention is given to
Baptist missionaries Martha Foster Crawford, Helen Coan Nevius,
and Sally Little Holmes, as well as Presbyterians Julia Brown
Mateer and Annette Thompson Mills. Extensive footnotes and bibliography (pp. 297-313) lead the reader to further resources. See
also annotation to entry 244.

183   Jeffrey, Julie Roy. Frontier Women: The Trans-Mississippi
      West, 1840-1880. New York: Hill & Wang, 1979. xvi, 240 pp.
      For eastern seaboard Christians, the American West was a
vast area in need of missions. Jeffrey's book pays little attention to religion overall, but her treatment of the wives of missionaries and women's participation in churches, schools, and
Sunday Schools does provide a place to begin study of the role of
women in frontier missions.

184   Keller, Rosemary Skinner. "Lay Women in the Protestant Tradi-
      tion." In Women and Religion in America, vol. 1 (entry 78),
      pp. 242-93.
      Keller's historical essay discusses organizations
of women founded after the Civil War--deaconess orders and home
and foreign mission societies--with attention to the women who
founded them, the female lay workers they employed, and the re-
cipients of their work, which was conceived as "woman's work for
woman." Sixteen documents follow, most of them excerpts from
periodicals published by these societies.

185   Montgomery, Helen Barrett. Western Women in Eastern Lands: An
      Outline Study of Fifty Years of Woman's Work in Foreign Mis-
      sions. New York: Macmillan, 1910. 286 pp.
      Montgomery, a leading organizer of support for women's mis-
sions, produced this book for an ecumenical consultation of women's societies, which distributed it widely for use in local
churches. It sets women's missions in the context of women's
social and religious status in the U.S. and the Orient; gives
histories of women's societies, missionaries, and Eastern women;
includes bibliographical references to important nineteenth- and
early twentieth-century books on missions; and concludes with a
feminist analysis of problems and policies facing women in missionary work. It is excerpted in Keller's article (entry 184);
Keller justly calls it "perhaps the most important single piece
produced from this era of 'woman's work for woman'" (p. 289).

186   Taylor, Sandra C. "Sisterhood of Salvation and the Sunrise
      Kingdom: Congregational Women Missionaries in Meiji Japan."
      Pacific Theological Review 48 (1979):27-45.
      Taylor emphasizes the feminist perspective of three mis-
sionaries. Another article by Taylor that focuses on one of the

women treated here, who served in Japan from 1879 to 1917, is "Abby M. Colby: The Christian Response to a Sexist Society," New England Quarterly 52 (1979):68-79.

187   Welter, Barbara. "She Hath Done What She Could: Protestant Women's Missionary Careers in Nineteenth-Century America." In Women in American Religion (entry 75), pp. 111-25.
        This article--based on biographies, autobiographies, and missionary society publications--treats many aspects of the nineteenth-century mission effort: the missionary wives of early decades and unmarried women missionaries of later ones; recruitment at home and trials in the field; views of churchmen and the empowering self-images of women missionaries.

        For Futher Information

188   Many biographies of missionaries by Christian admirers have been published in the last two centuries. As a genre, these biographies are a type of Protestant hagiography; they shed light not only on the activities of the missionaries but also on the piety of their authors. Many also include substantial excerpts from the letters and diaries of the missionaries. Among the earliest and most popular examples of this genre are by James D. Knowles, Memoir of Mrs. Ann H. Judson (Boston: Lincoln & Edmands, 1829), and Leonard Woods, Memoirs of Mrs. Harriet Newell (Boston: Samuel T. Armstrong, 1814); an interesting later one is by James M. Thoburn, Life of Isabella Thoburn (Cincinnati: Jennings and Pye, 1903). Collections of biographical sketches that adopt a similar style are by Daniel Clark Eddy, Heroines of the Missionary Enterprise (Boston: Ticknor, Reed & Fields, 1850); Emma Raymond Pitman, Heroines of the Mission Field (New York: Anson D.R. Randolph & Co., 1880); and Annie Ryder Gracey, Eminent Missionary Women (New York: Eaton & Mains, 1898). References to many more such works may be found in the bibliographies in Notable American Women (entry 35).

189   The categorized list of subjects at the end of vol. 3 of Notable American Women (entry 35) includes the names of 38 missionaries and 12 missionary society leaders; short biographies and guides to sources on these women may be found under their names in the appropriate volumes. Notable American Women: The Modern Period (entry 36), which treats women who died between 1950 and 1975, includes articles on these Protestant missionaries: Donaldina Mackenzie Cameron, Rosetta Sherwood Hall, Vida Scudder, and Matilda Calder Thurston.

190   The missionary movement has produced countless documents that historians have only begun to explore. Of particular interest are the periodicals produced by the denominational women's missionary boards, a number of which are listed at the end of All Loves Excelling: American Protestant Women in World Mission (entry 172, both editions). Further sources on these organizations may be found in the final sections of this chapter under listings for individual denominations (entries 239-339). A particularly fine

example of research of this kind is John Patrick McDowell's The
Social Gospel in the South: The Woman's Home Mission Movement in
the Methodist Episcopal Church, South, 1886-1939 (entry 291).
Note also eight articles on national and foreign missions in Women
in New Worlds, vol. 2 (entry 76), pp. 162-289.

191   Serious researchers should be aware of the special collections
       at the Missionary Research Library, Union Theological Seminary,
       New York City (for which there is a 17-volume published catalog:
       Dictionary Catalog of the Missionary Research Library, New York
       [Boston: G.K. Hall, 1968]); at the Divinity School of Yale Uni-
       versity, New Haven, Connecticut; and at Houghton Library, Harvard
       University, Cambridge, Massachusetts. For resources about mis-
       sionaries in China see Scholars' Guide to China Mission Resources
       in the Libraries and Archives of the United States, compiled by
       Archie R. Crouch (Princeton: Princeton Theological Seminary,
       1983-). Denominational historical societies and libraries are
       also likely to contain important records. For archival resources
       on missionary activities by more conservative evangelical Protes-
       tants, consult the collections at the Billy Graham Center for the
       Study of American Evangelicalism, Wheaton, Illinois.

192   For further bibliography on women and missions, see Arthur L.
       Allen, "Women and Missions: A Bibliography," Duke Divinity Review
       39 (1979):103-4; Kwang-Ching Liu, Americans and Chinese: A His-
       torical Essay and a Bibliography (Cambridge, Mass.: Harvard Uni-
       versity Press, 1963), works by and about women, pp. 112-32 and
       passim; and G.O.M. Tasie et al., "History of Mission: Urgent
       Research Fields: Role of Women in Mission (Workshop 6),"
       Missiology 7 (1979):92-96. Recent general bibliography on mis-
       sions may be found in the chapter "Missionary Impulse," in Reli-
       gion and Society in North America (entry 6), and in Missions and
       Evangelism: A Bibliography Selected from the ATLA Religion Data-
       base, 3d rev. ed. (Chicago: American Theological Library Associa-
       tion, 1985).

II.B.4. ORDAINED MINISTRY

193   Brereton, Virginia Lieson, and Klein, Christa Ressmeyer.
       "American Women in Ministry: A History of Protestant Beginning
       Points." In Women of Spirit: Female Leadership in the Jewish
       and Christian Traditions (entry 80), pp. 301-32. Also, in re-
       vised form, in Women in American Religion (entry 75),
       pp. 171-90.
           The authors place the historical background for women's
       ordination in lay movements of the nineteenth and early twentieth
       centuries and the access to theological education they created:
       the missionary societies, deaconesses, and religious training
       schools of 1861-1925, and the increasing power of laywomen in
       church governance and as professional religious educators between
       1920 and 1945. They then treat the institutional, theological,
       and historical factors explaining the increase in the number of

women attending seminary and being ordained from 1945 to the present in these denominations: Disciples, Baptist, Congregational
and Reformed, Methodist, Presbyterian, and Lutheran.

194   Carroll, Jackson W.; Hargrove, Barbara; and Lummis, Adair T.
        Women of the Cloth: A New Opportunity for the Churches. San
        Francisco: Harper & Row, 1983. xi, 276 pp.
            This sociological study focuses on women in parish ministry
        in nine Protestant denominations: American Baptist, American
        Lutheran, Christian (Disciples of Christ), Episcopal, Lutheran
        Church in America, Presbyterian U.S., United Church of Christ,
        United Methodist, and United Presbyterian U.S.A. Chapter 2,
        "American Churches and 'Women's Place,'" is a useful historical
        survey; other chapters report on the recent experiences of women
        in seminaries, the job market, and the parish. Questionnaire and
        interview responses from more than 600 female and 700 male clergy
        provide one data base; numerous lay leaders, denominational offi-
        cials, and seminary professors were also surveyed. The result is
        a combination of quantitative evidence with personal experience
        that substantially clarifies the major issues and attitudes facing
        women in ordained ministry.

195   Cazden, Elizabeth. Antoinette Brown Blackwell: A Biography.
        Old Westbury, N.Y.: Feminist Press, 1983. xii, 315 pp.
            This narrative of the life of the first woman to become a
        regularly ordained minister (by the Congregationalists in 1853) is
        set amid the ethos of religion, reform, and feminism that also
        nurtured other early feminists, some of them ministers. The cor-
        respondence between Blackwell and Oberlin College schoolmate Lucy
        Stone appears in Soul Mates: The Oberlin Correspondence of Lucy
        Stone and Antoinette Brown, 1846-1850, edited by Carol Lasser and
        Marlene Merrill (Oberlin, Ohio: Oberlin College, 1983). See also
        entry 331.

196   Fraser, Dorothy Bass. "Women With a Past: A New Look at the
        History of Theological Education." Theological Education 8
        (1972):213-24.
            This article treats both the fortunes of women who attended
        theological seminaries (beginning in 1847 with Antoinette Brown)
        and the formal or informal educations for lay leadership acquired
        by women's society leaders, deaconesses, missionaries, and reli-
        gious educators in nineteenth- and twentieth-century Protestantism.

197   Gibson, Elsie. When the Minister is a Woman. New York: Holt,
        Rinehart & Winston, 1970. 174 pp.
            Drawing on questionnaire responses from 270 ordained women,
        Gibson (herself ordained in the United Church of Christ) considers
        the career patterns of women ministers, particularly in relation
        to their marriage and family lives. The book also includes gen-
        eral historical and theological reflections on women in ministry.

198   Hardesty, Nancy A. "Minister as Prophet? or As Mother?: Two
       Nineteenth-Century Models." In Women in New Worlds, vol. 1
       (entry 81), pp. 88-101.
              Hardesty analyzes two important nineteenth-century arguments
       in favor of women's right to preach: Phoebe Palmer's Promise of
       the Father: or, A Neglected Specialty of the Last Days and
       Frances Willard's Woman in the Pulpit. Although both authors
       appeal to biblical support, male endorsements, and female prece-
       dents, they advocate different models of ministry. The notes to
       this article will lead researchers to other important nineteenth-
       century statements on women's preaching.

199   Harkness, Georgia. Women in Church and Society: A Historical
       and Theological Inquiry. Nashville: Abingdon Press, 1972.
       240 pp.
              This short but wide-ranging book includes some information
       on women ministers of the past and advocacy for women's ministries
       in the modern world. It is primarily of interest, however, be-
       cause its author was the leading liberal Protestant clergywoman of
       mid-twentieth-century America. For information on Harkness, see
       listing in Notable American Women: The Modern Period (entry 36),
       pp. 112-14; Martha L. Scott, "Georgia Harkness: Social Activist
       and/or Mystic," in Women in New Worlds, vol. 1 (entry 81),
       pp. 117-40; and Joan Chambers Engelsman, "The Legacy of Georgia
       Harkness," in Women in New Worlds, vol. 2 (entry 76), pp. 338-58.

200   Palmer, Phoebe. Promise of the Father: or, A Neglected Spe-
       cialty of the Last Days. New York: W.C. Palmer, 1859. 421 pp.
       See also reprints.
              Here Palmer, a lay leader who was a prominent preacher and
       promoter of the Holiness revival, develops biblical, theological,
       and practical arguments for women's right to preach. For informa-
       tion on Palmer, see entry in Notable American Women (entry 35),
       3:12-14; Anne C. Loveland, "Domesticity and Religion in the Ante-
       bellum Period: The Career of Phoebe Palmer," Historian 39 (1977):
       455-71; and entries 129 and 288. Other manifestations of the
       Holiness movement are treated in section VII.H of this bibliog-
       raphy.

201   Willard, Frances E. Woman in the Pulpit. Chicago: Woman's
       Temperance Publishing Association, 1889. Reprint. Washington,
       D.C.: Zenger Publishing Co., 1978. 173 pp.
              Willard, a Methodist laywoman who as head of the Woman's
       Christian Temperance Union was the most prominent Christian fem-
       inist of her time, argues here for women's right to preach and
       minister. She criticizes church policies toward women, finds
       biblical support for her views, shows the compatability of minis-
       try and motherhood, presents the supportive testimony of male and
       female preachers, and prints articles by clergymen on both sides
       of the issue. The "ecclesiastical emancipation of women" was one
       of Willard's lifelong causes; the story of her own rejection as a
       lay delegate to the Methodist General Conference in 1888 is told
       in her autobiography, Glimpses of Fifty Years (Chicago: H.J.
       Smith, 1889). For more information see entry 170.

202   Zikmund, Barbara Brown. "The Struggle for the Right to
       Preach." In Women and Religion in America, vol. 1 (entry 78),
       pp. 193-241.
           Zikmund's historical essay treats nineteenth-century debates
       over women's right to preach, explaining the biblical, practical,
       social, and intellectual arguments of those on both sides of the
       issue. Eight documents follow, including excerpts from Frances
       Willard and Phoebe Palmer, the black preacher Jarena Lee, the
       sermon Luther Lee preached at the ordination of Antoinette Brown,
       and three male and female opponents of women's preaching.

       For Further Information

203   Throughout religious history, women have ministered in many
       ways without benefit of the title "minister." Therefore readers
       interested in the ministries of American Protestant women should
       consult other sections of this bibliography, for example, mis-
       sionaries, benevolence and education, and reform. Moreover, in
       some traditions even the right to preach is conferred not insti-
       tutionally but charismatically; an interesting source on an early
       figure is by Almond H. Davis, ed., The Female Preacher, or Memoir
       of Salome Lincoln (Providence: Elder J.S. Mowry, 1843; reprint,
       New York: Arno Press, 1972; excerpts in The Female Experience in
       Eighteenth- and Nineteenth-Century America [entry 17]). A strong
       tradition of female preaching has also existed in the black
       churches (see chapter V of this bibliography).

204   The categorized list of subjects at the end of vol. 3 of
       Notable American Women (entry 35) includes the names of 28 minis-
       ters and evangelists; short biographies and guides to sources on
       these women may be found under their names in the appropriate
       volumes.

205   Woman's Pulpit (1921-) is the quarterly newspaper of the Inter-
       national Association of Women Ministers, c/o the Reverend Carol
       Brown, 579 Main St., Stroudsburg, PA 18360.

206   In many Protestant denominations, deaconesses have been profes-
       sionally trained and ecclesiastically set apart as church workers.
       For information about them, see the denominational histories in
       section II.C.

II.B.5. THE SOUTH

207   Evans, Sara. "Southern White Women in a Southern Black Move-
       ment." In Personal Politics: The Roots of Women's Liberation
       in the Civil Rights Movement and the New Left. New York:
       Knopf, 1979, pp. 24-59.
           Evans argues that "virtually without exception white southern
       women who joined the civil rights movement came to it first through
       the church" (p. 35). She tells the stories of several such women
       and emphasizes the religious ethos of the Southern student move-
       ment, including the Methodist campus organization, the YWCA, and
       SNCC. Although religion figures little in the book's other

chapters, which treat Northern radicals and the events leading to
the new feminism of the late 1960s, they provide an interesting
account based on primary documents and interviews with partici-
pants.

208   Friedman, Jean E. The Enclosed Garden: Women and Community in
        the Evangelical South, 1830-1900. Chapel Hill: University of
        North Carolina Press, 1985. xvi, 180 pp.
        Friedman argues that the Southern women's reform movement
lagged behind the Northern feminist movement because the evangelical, kin-dominated church in the predominately rural south pre-
vented women from forming same-sex organizations out of which
reform activities could grow. She uses traditional historical
sources and quantitative methods as well as private diaries, correspondence, slave narratives, and literary analysis to support
her thesis. Her thesis is more succinctly advanced in "Piety
and Kin: The Limits of Antebellum Southern Women's Reform," in
Women and the Structure of Society, edited by Barbara J. Harris
and JoAnn K. McNamara (Durham: Duke University Press, 1984),
pp. 12-19.

209   Hall, Jacquelyn Dowd. Revolt Against Chivalry: Jessie Daniel
        Ames and the Women's Campaign Against Lynching. New York:
        Columbia University Press, 1979. 373 pp.
        Here the biography of Ames, a Texas suffragist and anti-
lynching organizer, is interwoven with an account of the origins,
ideas, and strategies of the campaign itself. Hall emphasizes the
religious backgrounds of the white middle-class women of the campaign, argues that it was based in local women's missionary societies (especially Methodist ones), and shows how it linked the
concerns of faminism with the cause of racial justice in the 1920s
and 1930s. The bibliography contains numerous primary sources on
Southern women. A shorter treatment of the same material is
Hall's "'A Truly Subversive Affair': Women Against Lynching in
the Twentieth-Century South," in Women of America: A History
(entry 16), pp. 360-88.

210   LeLoudis, James L. "Subversion of the Feminine Ideal: The
        Southern Lady's Companion and White Male Morality in the Ante-
        bellum South, 1847-1854." In Women in New Worlds, vol. 2
        (entry 76), pp. 60-75.
        According to LeLoudis, this publication of the Methodist
Episcopal Church, South (edited by clergymen and filled largely
with correspondence from white Southern women), offered substantial
criticism of the moral behavior of white men, thereby belying the
ideology of women's submissiveness and laying the foundations for
women's postwar activism in religion and reform. The part played
by ideas about gender in the perpetuation of slavery is also
considered.

211   Mathews, Donald G. Religion in the Old South. Chicago:
       University of Chicago Press, 1977. 288 pp.
       Mathews considers white evangelical views of woman's sphere
on pp. 101–24, with attention to domesticity, role in the church,
individual and organized benevolence toward slaves, and the psychological and cultural significance of Southern ideals of womanhood.

212   Mitchell, Norma Taylor. "Women in Religion." In Encyclopedia
       of Religion in the South, edited by Samuel S. Hill. Macon,
       Ga.: Mercer University Press, 1984, pp. 845–51.
       Mitchell summarizes the general trends of white and black
women's participation in Southern religion from the colonial period to the present, with emphasis on popular movements such as
the First and Second Great Awakenings, the feminization of American religion, women's missionary organizations, and civil rights.
She assesses the state of current research, notes needs for
further studies, and provides a brief bibliography. Researchers
on women in Southern religion may also benefit from other articles
in this encyclopedia, which include information on individual
women and women's organizations among some two hundred entries on
a wide range of theological, denominational, and social topics.

213   Myers, Robert Manson, ed. Children of Pride: A True Story of
       Georgia and the Civil War. New Haven: Yale University Press,
       1972. 1,845 pp.
       This is a voluminous collection of letters from the family
of Charles Colcock Jones, a prominent Presbyterian minister and
plantation owner. Written between 1854 and 1868, the letters re-
veal the private lives of a group of deeply religious men and
women during peace, war, and reconstruction, as well as offering
glimpses into the workings of slavery and emancipation.

214   Scott, Anne Firor. The Southern Lady: From Pedestal to Poli-
       tics, 1830–1930. Chicago: University of Chicago Press, 1970.
       xv, 247 pp.
       Scott traces the story of Southern "ladies" from the re-
strictive setting of the plantation through the victory of woman
suffrage, with attention to both cultural ideals of womanhood and
women's actual experiences. Of particular interest are chapter 1,
which includes discussion of the role of religion in confirming
women's inferior status in the antebellum South, and chapter 6,
which treats women's empowerment in late nineteenth-century voluntary societies, especially missions, and the Woman's Christian
Temperance Union. Scott's treatment of religion is expanded in
her article, "Women, Religion, and Social Change in the South,
1830–1930," in Religion and the Solid South, edited by Samuel S.
Hill (Nashville: Abingdon Press, 1972), pp. 92–121.

215   Shankman, Arnold M. "Civil Rights, 1920–1970: Three Southern
       Methodist Women." In Women in New Worlds, vol. 2 (entry 76),
       pp. 211–33.
       This article summarizes the careers, accomplishments, and
difficulties of three key advocates of interracial harmony

among the white women of the South: Carrie Parks Johnson, Jessie
Daniel Ames, and Dorothy Rogers Tilly.

216   Smith, Lillian. <u>Killers of the Dream</u>. 1949, 256 pp. Rev. and
      enl. ed. 1961, 1978. 253 pp. New York: W.W. Norton.
         In this very personal book, Smith mixes autobiography, fic-
      tion, history, allegory, and theology as she explores the pain and
      passions of life in a segregated culture. She writes as a white
      Southerner, a Christian, and a woman, weaving connections between
      sexuality, race, religion, and power in her effort to explain the
      tragic roots and consequences of Southern race relations.

         For Further Information

Other material about Protestant women in the South appears in sections II.A.2 (especially entry 104), II.B.2 (especially entry 159),
II.C.2, and II.C.6 (especially entry 291), and in chapter V.

II.B.6. ORGANIZED FEMINISM

217   Brown, Olympia. <u>Suffrage and Religious Principle: Speeches</u>
      <u>and Writings of Olympia Brown</u>. Edited by Dana Greene.
      Metuchen, N.J.: Scarecrow Press, 1983. 192 pp.
         Brown was the first woman to be ordained as a Universalist
      minister, and her wide-ranging activities in religion and reform
      contributed to the suffrage movement of the late nineteenth cen-
      tury.

218   Cooper, James L., and Cooper, Sheila M., eds. <u>The Roots of</u>
      <u>American Feminist Thought</u>. Boston: Allyn & Bacon, 1973.
      298 pp.
         A general introduction and historical/biographical introduc-
      tions to each section are provided for this collection of excerpts
      from seven major feminist thinkers: Mary Wollstonecraft, Sarah
      Grimké, Margaret Fuller, Charlotte Perkins Gilman, John Stuart
      Mill, Margaret Sanger, and Suzanne LaFollette.

219   Gage, Matilda Joslyn. <u>Woman, Church, and State</u>. 1893.
      Reprint. Watertown, Mass.: Persephone Press, 1980. xxxix,
      294 pp.
         Gage, a prominent suffragist, surveys the history of women's
      oppression from women's initial favorable position under "the
      matriarchate" through the persecutions associated with canon law,
      sexual exploitation, witchcraft, domestic tyranny, polygamy,
      labor, and the nineteenth-century American churches. This is an
      impressive and important early work of feminist scholarship which
      is dominated by Gage's angry conviction that the church has always
      been "the bulwark of woman's slavery." In a rousing preface to
      the 1980 edition, feminist theologian Mary Daly claims Gage as
      "one of the great foresisters of contemporary feminists" (p. vii).
      Sally Roesch Wagner's extensive, well-researched introduction to
      the same edition describes Gage's involvement in the nineteenth-
      century women's movement and the controversies which her radical
      opposition to Christianity aroused.

220   Gilman, Charlotte Perkins. <u>His Religion and Hers: A Study of</u>
       <u>the Faith of Our Fathers and the Work of Our Mothers</u>. New
       York: Century Co., 1923. xi, 300 pp. Reprint. Westport,
       Conn.: Hyperion Press, 1976.
           An important feminist theorist and leading suffragist here
       upholds what she sees as women's natural "birth-based" religion
       against the "death-based" religion of men, which she holds ac-
       countable for many of the world's misfortunes. Gilman's novel
       <u>Herland</u> (1915-16; reprint, edited by Ann J. Lane [New York:
       Pantheon Books, 1979]) depicts an all-female society where such a
       religion is practiced. Gilman, whose major works drew on evolu-
       tionary theory to analyze and improve the economic and social con-
       dition of women, was not primarily a religious thinker, but <u>His</u>
       <u>Religion and Hers</u> and <u>Herland</u> do foreshadow some issues in con-
       temporary feminist spirituality. A fine biography is Mary A.
       Hill's <u>Charlotte Perkins Gilman</u> (Philadelphia: Temple University
       Press, 1980).

221   Grimes, Alan P. <u>The Puritan Ethic and Woman Suffrage</u>. New
       York: Oxford University Press, 1967. xiii, 159 pp.
           Seeking to explain why woman suffrage was enacted remark-
       ably early in some western frontier states and territories (e.g.,
       1869 in Wyoming, 1870 in Utah), Grimes argues that the (male)
       electorate hoped that women's votes would support the "puritan"
       values of the majority against disorderly frontier elements.

222   Harrison, Beverly W. "Early Feminists and the Clergy: A Case
       Study in the Dynamics of Secularization." <u>Review and Expositor</u>
       72 (1975):41-52. Also in <u>Making the Connections: Essays in</u>
       <u>Feminist Social Ethics</u>, edited by Carol S. Robb. Boston:
       Beacon Press, 1985, pp. 193-205.
           Harrison traces an issue of contemporary concern--enmity be-
       tween many feminists and organized religion--to its roots in the
       nineteenth century. In spite of the religious earnestness of
       early feminists, she argues, clerical opposition to their activi-
       ties ultimately propelled them out of the churches.

223   Harrison, Beverly W. "Sexism and the Contemporary Church:
       When Evasion Becomes Complicity." In <u>Sexist Religion and</u>
       <u>Women in the Church</u> (entry 65), pp. 195-216.
           As historical background for her own proposals for women's
       full equality in the contemporary church, Harrison sketches two
       strategies by which nineteenth-century American women sought to
       increase their role in religious and public life. Her distinction
       between "hard" and "soft" feminism has been influential.

224   Kraditor, Aileen S. <u>The Ideas of the Woman Suffrage Movement,</u>
       <u>1890-1920</u>. 1965. Reprint. Garden City, N.Y.: Doubleday,
       1971; New York: W.W. Norton, 1981. xii, 313 pp.
           This analysis of the suffragists' major arguments includes a
       chapter on religion, which tells the story of the controversy sur-
       rounding Elizabeth Cady Stanton's <u>The Woman's Bible</u> (entry 227)
       and analyzes the leadership of Anna Howard Shaw, a Methodist

minister who was president of the National American Woman Suffrage Association from 1904 to 1915.

225   Melder, Keith E. The Beginnings of Sisterhood: The American
       Woman's Rights Movement, 1800-1850. New York: Shocken Books,
       1977. 199 pp.
           Melder surveys the growing involvement of women in extra-
       familial reform activities, from the social changes of the early
       nineteenth century, through the benevolent and abolitionist so-
       cieties of the 1830s, to the emergence of an organized movement
       for women's rights in the decade before the Civil War. Religion
       and reform figure prominently in this work; it is placed in this
       section because the overall narrative drives steadily toward the
       origins of organized feminism.

226   Rossi, Alice, ed. The Feminist Papers from Adams to
       de Beauvoir. New York: Columbia University Press, 1973.
       Reprint. New York: Bantam Books, 1974. xix, 716 pp.
           This anthology displays rare excellence by presenting ex-
       cerpts that are sufficiently long, and Rossi's editorial essays
       are also substantial and insightful. Among the authors whose
       excerpts possess special interest for students of women's reli-
       gious history are Judith Sargent Murray, who wrote a feminist
       exposition of the Adam and Eve story in 1790; Frances Wright and
       Harriet Martineau, Englishwomen who observed (and deplored) the
       religious behavior of American women in the early nineteenth cen-
       tury; Margaret Fuller (entry 237); Sarah and Angelina Grimke
       (entry 167); Antoinette Brown Blackwell (entry 195); and Elizabeth
       Cady Stanton (entry 227). Other major American and European
       feminists are also represented.

227   Stanton, Elizabeth Cady. The Woman's Bible. 2 vols. New
       York: European Publishing Co., 1895-98. 152, 217 pp.
       Reprint in 1 vol. Seattle: Coalition Task Force on Women and
       Religion, 1974; New York: Arno Press, 1974.
           Stanton, the leading theorist of the nineteenth-century
       feminist movement, believed that the plain sense of the English
       Bible served to enforce the oppression of women. At the end of
       her career, she gathered a "Revising Committee" of about two
       dozen women, including several noted suffragists and a number of
       Universalist ministers, to write a biblical commentary from
       women's perspective. They divided the passages that dealt with
       women among themselves and wrote their responses, which display a
       considerable diversity of feminist and religious views. The
       Woman's Bible, though not uniformly hostile to the Bible and
       Christianity, was repudiated by most Christian suffragists. All
       editions conclude with two fascinating sets of documents: the
       minutes of the National American Woman Suffrage Association meet-
       ing at which this book was explicitly repudiated by the organiza-
       tion, and the letters of response to The Woman's Bible from nota-
       ble feminists of the day, including Antoinette Brown Blackwell,
       Frances Willard, and Matilda Joslyn Gage. Useful articles about
       The Woman's Bible include Dorothy C. Bass, "Women's Studies and
       Biblical Studies: An Historical Perspective," Journal for the

Study of the Old Testament 22 (1982):6-12; Suzan E. Hill, "The
Woman's Bible: Reformulating Tradition," Radical Religion 3
(1977):23-30; Elaine C. Huber, "They Weren't Prepared to Hear: A
Closer Look at The Woman's Bible," Andover Newton Quarterly 16
(March 1976):271-76; James H. Smylie, "The Woman's Bible and the
Spiritual Crisis," Soundings 59 (1976):305-28; and Barbara Welter's
introduction to the Arno Press edition. Barbara Brown Zikmund,
"Biblical Arguments and Woman's Place in the Church," in The Bible
and Social Reform, edited by Ernest R. Sandeen (Philadelphia:
Fortress Press, 1982), pp. 85-104, permits comparison by treating
The Woman's Bible alongside other contemporary interpretations of
the Bible; shorter discussion of similar issues by the same author
is "Feminist Consciousness in Historical Perspective," in Feminist
Interpretation of the Bible, edited by Letty M. Russell (New York:
Westminster Press, 1985), pp. 21-29. The Woman's Bible leads some
contemporary feminist hermeneutes to claim Stanton as a pioneer;
see Elisabeth Schüssler Fiorenza, In Memory of Her (entry 51).
Important sources on Stanton herself include her autobiography,
Eighty Years or More (New York: European Publishing Co., 1898);
Elisabeth Griffith, In Her Own Right: The Life of Elizabeth Cady
Stanton (New York: Oxford University Press, 1984); Ellen Carol
DuBois, ed., Elizabeth Cady Stanton and Susan B. Anthony: Cor-
respondence, Writings, Speeches (New York: Shocken Books, 1981);
and listing in Notable American Women (entry 35), 3:342-47.

228   Stanton, Elizabeth Cady; Anthony, Susan B.; and Gage, Matilda
       Joslyn. History of Woman Suffrage. 6 vols. Rochester, 1881-
       1902; New York, 1922. Vol. 4 edited by Susan B. Anthony and
       Ida Husted Harper; vols. 5-6 edited by Ida Husted Harper.
           Each of these volumes is a thick compendium of documents,
    personal statements, institutional narratives, and feminist inter-
    pretation. Together they comprise the basic source for the study
    of the woman suffrage movement, compiled by leaders who were fully
    convinced of the great historical importance of their cause and
    thus sought to leave a good record of it. Religion appears
    sporadically throughout; it is a particularly strong presence in
    vol. 1, which treats the women's rights movement before the Civil
    War, when it was closely linked to other movements of religious
    reform and embroiled in controversy with ecclesiastical opponents.
    A useful abridgment, which includes an extensive introduction on
    woman suffrage and American reform, is by Mary Jo Buhle and Paul
    Buhle, eds., The Concise History of Woman Suffrage (Urbana:
    University of Illinois Press, 1978).

       For Further Information

The works assembled in this section make explicit connections between
religion and the movement for women's legal and political rights. We
do not seek to isolate feminism here; for instance, readers should be
aware that the Woman's Christian Temperance Union (see section II.B.2
above) was the largest organization working in support of woman suffrage in the late nineteenth century, and most authors of the works
listed in all of the preceding sections of this chapter consider how
and whether women's religious activism incorporated feminist

assertions, at least implicitly. Readers interested in feminism and religion in general are therefore advised to look far beyond the bounds of this section. More thorough treatment of the general social and cultural history of American feminism may be found in and through the sources listed in section I.B.

II.B.7. LITERATURE

229 Christ, Carol P. Diving Deep and Surfacing: Women Writers on
      Spiritual Quest. Boston: Beacon Press, 1980. xvi, 159 pp.
          Seeking resources for feminist theology, the author turned
      to works of imaginative literature in which women "spoke in their
      own language, not forced into structures of male theology"
      (p. xii). Christ analyzes works by Kate Chopin, Margaret Atwood,
      Doris Lessing, Adrienne Rich, and Ntozake Shange; her methods and
      insights will also be suggestive to those interested in reading
      other authors from a feminist spiritual perspective.

230 Douglas, Ann. The Feminization of American Culture. New York:
      Knopf, 1977. 403 pp.
          A long subtitle on this book's cover identifies the inter-
      pretive emphasis of Douglas's study of thirty women writers and
      thirty liberal (mostly Congregational and Unitarian) ministers
      between 1820 and 1875: "how the Victorian alliance between women
      and clergy, and the popular literature to which that alliance gave
      birth, fostered a sentimental society and the beginnings of modern
      mass culture." Deploring the Victorians' loss of the rigor of
      mind that had characterized their Calvinist forebears, Douglas
      detects in the writings of women and ministers a sentimentalism
      that contained the seeds of many of modern America's cultural
      flaws; her explanation of this development treats the changing
      status of women and ministers in a commercial society and the re-
      grettable cultural strategies by which these groups sought an emo-
      tionally manipulative "influence" in that society. This interpre-
      tation has provoked some controversy, attaining considerable
      influence but limited support among historians and critics. Essay
      reviews that take issue with Douglas include William R. Leach,
      "Dictatorship of the Powerless," Marxist Perspectives 1 (1978):
      158-71; David Schuyler, "Inventing a Feminine Past," New England
      Quarterly 51 (1978):291-308; and David S. Reynolds, "The Feminiza-
      tion Controversy: Sexual Stereotypes and the Paradoxes of Piety
      in Nineteenth-Century America," New England Quarterly 53 (1980):
      96-106.

231 Duke, Maurice; Bryer, Jackson R.; and Inge, M. Thomas, eds.
      American Women Writers: Bibliographical Essays. Westport,
      Conn.: Greenwood Press, 1983. xvi, 434 pp.
          Competent scholarly essays will lead readers to criticism on
      24 authors, of whom several would be of interest as sources of
      religious history: Anne Bradstreet, Mary Rowlandson, Sara Kemble
      Knight, Sarah Orne Jewett, Mary E. Wilkins Freeman, Mary N.
      Murfree, Kate Chopin, Edith Wharton, Gertrude Stein, Djuna Barnes,
      Anaïs Nin, Ellen Glasgow, Katherine Anne Porter, Eudora Welty,
      Flannery O'Connor, Carson McCullers, Zora Neale Hurston, Constance

Rourke, Pearl Buck, Marjorie Kinnan Rawlings, Margaret Mitchell, Marianne Moore, Anne Sexton, and Sylvia Plath.

232   Martin, Wendy. An American Triptych: Anne Bradstreet, Emily Dickinson, Adrienne Rich. Chapel Hill: University of North Carolina Press, 1984. x, 272 pp.
    Martin interprets the life and work of each of these major poets to reveal both the continuities among them and how their differences reflect changes in the lives and imaginations of women at disparate moments in the history of American culture. Although only Bradstreet was conventionally religious, Martin sees strong religious emphases in the poetry of all three as a central element in the "female aesthetic-ethic" they created.

233   Parker, Gail, ed. The Oven Birds: American Women on Womanhood, 1820-1920. Garden City, N.Y.: Doubleday, 1972. xii, 387 pp.
    Parker's lengthy introduction traces the rise and fall of a "Romantic-sentimental ideology" in literature by and about women, with attention to its relation to religious history. This is a provocative early interpretation, to be read in conjunction with other works in this section. Selections from the works of the following authors are found here: Lydia Huntley Sigourney, Lydia Maria Child, Angelina Grimké Weld, Catharine Beecher, Harriet Beecher Stowe, Sarah Orne Jewett, Elizabeth Cady Stanton, Jane Addams, and Charlotte Perkins Gilman.

234   Porterfield, Amanda. Feminine Spirituality in America: From Sarah Edwards to Martha Graham. Philadelphia: Temple University Press, 1980. 238 pp.
    Porterfield draws heavily on imaginative literature in tracing the domestic, aesthetic, personal, and sexual imagery of "feminine spirituality" in nineteenth- and twentieth-century culture. The novels of Harriet Beecher Stowe and Elizabeth Stuart Phelps represent the "domestication" of theology; Hawthorne's and Melville's fictions reveal the complex relation between sexuality and spirituality; Charlotte Perkins Gilman and Edith Wharton explore women's subjectivity and spiritual power in modern terms. Emily Dickinson, whose "poetics of feminine spirituality" are central to Porterfield's interpretation, receives extensive treatment.

235   Welter, Barbara. "Defenders of the Faith: Women Novelists of Religious Controversy in the Nineteenth Century." In Dimity Convictions: The American Woman in the Nineteenth Century. Athens: Ohio University Press, 1976, pp. 103-29.
    Welter treats novelists Augusta Evans Wilson, Elizabeth Stuart Phelps Ward, and Margaret Deland as lay theologians who popularized theological change and advocated an important religious role for women.

Individual Women

Works by authors treated in the books listed above will repay the
attention of students of women in American religion. Notable American Women (entry 35) provides brief biographies and identifies important titles by each author. In addition, see the following sources
on three nineteenth-century authors who have attracted an exceptional
amount of critical attention.

236 Emily Dickinson (1830-86)
        The basic source is The Complete Poems of Emily Dickinson,
    edited by Thomas H. Johnson (Boston: Little, Brown, 1960); see
    also Johnson's shorter collection, Final Harvest: Emily Dickin-
    son's Poems (Boston: Little, Brown, 1951), and his Emily Dickin-
    son: An Interpretive Biography (Cambridge, Mass.: Harvard
    University Press, 1955). There are several major biographies of
    Dickinson: among these, Richard B. Sewall, The Life of Emily
    Dickinson, 2 vols. (New York: Farrar, Straus & Giroux, 1974;
    reprint in 1 vol., 1980), is especially thorough, and John Cody,
    After Great Pain: The Inner Life of Emily Dickinson (Cambridge,
    Mass.: Harvard University Press, 1971), employs psychoanalysis to
    study the poet's religious life. Treatments of Dickinson's reli-
    gious views include chapter 7 in Feminine Spirituality in America
    (entry 234); section 2 of An American Triptych (entry 232); Joan
    Burbick, "'One Unbroken Company': Religion and Emily Dickinson,"
    New England Quarterly 53 (1980):62-75; and Barton L. St. Armand,
    Emily Dickinson and Her Culture: The Soul's Society (New York:
    Cambridge University Press, 1984), which also treats the important
    religious novelist Elizabeth Stuart Phelps. See also Suzanne
    Juhasz, ed., Feminist Critics Read Emily Dickinson (Bloomington:
    Indiana University Press, 1983).

237 Margaret Fuller (1810-50)
        A woman of letters rather than a religious figure, Fuller is
    included here because the intellectual movement to which she be-
    longed, Transcendentalism, has interested many historians of
    American religion and because of her advocacy of intellectual,
    social, and spiritual freedom for women. A good place to begin a
    study of Fuller is Bell Gale Chevigny, The Woman and the Myth:
    Margaret Fuller's Life and Writings (Old Westbury, N.Y.: Feminist
    Press, 1976), which includes excerpts from Fuller's autobiographi-
    cal and literary writing as well as excerpts from contemporary
    and critical works about her. Fuller's feminist position is set
    forth in Woman in the Nineteenth Century (1845; reprint, New York:
    W.W. Norton, 1971); this is excerpted, with a helpful introduc-
    tion, in The Roots of American Feminist Thought (entry 218). Joel
    Myerson has edited three important reference works: Margaret
    Fuller: An Annotated Bibliography (New York: Burt Franklin &
    Co., 1977); Margaret Fuller: A Descriptive Bibliography (Pitts-
    burgh: University of Pittsburgh Press, 1978); and Critical Essays
    on Margaret Fuller (Boston, G.K. Hall, 1980). The Letters of
    Margaret Fuller, edited by Robert N. Hudspeth (Ithaca, N.Y.:
    Cornell University Press, 1983-), are being published in multiple
    volumes.

238   Harriet Beecher Stowe (1811-96)
         To set the novelist in the context of her prominent reli-
gious family, see relevant chapters in Portraits of a Nineteenth-
Century Family and Chariot of Fire: Religion and the Beecher
Family (entry 120). Charles H. Foster, The Rungless Ladder:
Harriet Beecher Stowe and New England Puritanism (Durham: University of North Carolina Press, 1954), treats religious themes in
Stowe's life and fiction. Agreeing to the centrality of these
themes but interpreting them with more attention to Stowe's understanding of womanhood are Gayle Kimball's "Harriet Beecher Stowe's
Revision of New England Theology," Journal of Presbyterian History
58 (1980):64-81, and The Religious Ideas of Harriet Beecher Stowe:
Her Gospel of Womanhood (New York: Edwin Mellen Press, 1982);
and Jane P. Tompkins, "Sentimental Power: Uncle Tom's Cabin and
the Politics of Literary History," Glyph 9 (1980):79-102. Eliza-
beth Ammons, ed., Critical Essays on Harriet Beecher Stowe (Boston:
G.K. Hall, 1980), includes important nineteenth- and twentieth-
century views; on women and religion, see especially Dorothy
Berkson, "Millenial Politics and the Feminine Fiction of Harriet
Beecher Stowe," and Lawrence Buell, "Calvinism Romanticized:
Harriet Beecher Stowe, Samuel Hopkins, and The Minister's Wooing."
For other sources, see Jean Willoughby Ashton, Harriet Beecher
Stowe: A Reference Guide (Boston: G.K. Hall, 1977), and Margaret
Holbrook Hildreth, Harriet Beecher Stowe: A Bibliography (Hamden,
Conn.: Archon Books, 1976).

         For Further Information

Fiction and poetry often contain fascinating evidence of women's
religious beliefs and experiences, and some scholars have thus based
interpretations of aspects of women's religious history on literary
sources. Scholarship on black women and religion, for example, often
employs literary sources; see chapter V of this bibliography. We
have listed here only a selection of influential works on imaginative
literature and the religious history of women, as an introduction to
the possibilities of this topic. The reader is urged to follow the
bibliographical suggestions for further information.

II.C. DENOMINATIONAL HISTORIES

II.C.1. BAPTIST

239   Allen, Catherine B. The New Lottie Moon Story. Nashville:
         Broadman Press, 1980. 320 pp.
         The author tells in full the story of Charlotte Diggs Moon
(1840-1912), born of aristocratic lineage in Virginia, who became
one of the best-educated women in the South and served nearly
forty years as a beloved and well-known Baptist missionary in
China until her death. For more on Lottie Moon, see entry 244.

240   Baptist History and Heritage 12 (1977):1-64.
         This special issue of the Southern Baptist historical jour-
nal focuses on the role of women in Baptist history and includes
the following articles: "The Role of Women in Southern Baptist

History," by Harry Leon McBeth (entry 247); "Baptist Women in
Missions Support in the Nineteenth Century," by Helen Emery Falls;
"The Status of Women in the Southern Baptist Convention in His-
torical Perspective," by Norman H. Letsinger (entry 245); "South-
ern Baptists and Women's Right to Vote, 1910-1920," by Bill
Sumners; and "Deaconesses in Baptist History: A Preliminary
Study," by Charles W. Deweese.

241   Brumberg, Joan Jacobs. "The Case of Ann Hasseltine Judson."
      In Women in New Worlds, vol. 2 (entry 76), pp. 234-48.
          In her Mission for Life (entry 174), Brumberg chronicles the
      life of the family of the early nineteenth-century Baptist mis-
      sionary to Burma, Adoniram Judson, and his three wives. Ann
      Hasseltine Judson (1789-1826) was the most famous of them and re-
      ceives the most attention in the literature. Biographical treat-
      ment of Judson's second wife, Sarah Hall Boardman Judson (1803-45),
      and third wife, Emily Chubbuck Judson (1817-54), as well as Ann
      Hasseltine Judson, may be found in Notable American Women (entry
      35), 2:295-300, in addition to Brumberg's Mission for Life.

242   Hoyt, Frederick B. "'When a Field was Found too Difficult for
      a Man, a Woman Should be Sent': Adele M. Fielde in Asia, 1865-
      1890." Historian 44 (1982):314-34.
          Reaching Siam in 1865 to marry a Baptist missionary only to
      discover that he had died while she was en route, Adele Fielde
      became the first unmarried Baptist woman missionary in Bankok.
      Hoyt chronicles her great difficulty finding satisfying work and
      building healthy relationships with her co-workers. After five
      years, she was posted to the South China (American) Baptist Mis-
      sion in Swatow where she worked among Chinese women and children.
      A growing interest in Chinese scholarship and science gradually
      distanced her from this work, and in 1889 her superiors' unhappi-
      ness with her and deteriorating health forced her resignation.
      Back in the United States she lived for 25 more years engaged in
      scholarly and reform work.

243   Hull, Eleanor. Women Who Carried the Good News: The History
      of the Woman's American Baptist Home Missions Society. Valley
      Forge, Pa.: Judson Press, 1975. 96 pp.
          Hull provides both an institutional history of the Society
      and a description of the kinds of ministry performed by members
      of the Society in focusing on specific women who exemplified par-
      ticular kinds of work.

244   Hyatt, Irwin T., Jr. "Charlotte Diggs Moon." In Our Ordered
      Lives Confess: Three Nineteenth-Century American Missionaries
      in East Shantung (entry 182), pp. 65-136.
          Introducing his discussion of the well-known Southern Bap-
      tist missionary to China with a survey of woman's work in East
      Shantung (see entry 182), Hyatt provides valuable contextual mate-
      rial for understanding Moon and other East Shantung Baptist women
      missionaries Martha Foster Crawford, Helen Coan Nevius, and Sally
      Little Holmes. Biographical material on Charlotte Diggs Moon may

also be found in The New Lottie Moon Story (entry 239) and Notable American Women (entry 35), 2:570-71.

245   Letsinger, Norman H. "The Status of Women in the Southern Bap-
       tist Convention in Historical Perspective." Baptist History
       and Heritage 12 (1977):37-44.
            The period from 1860 to 1975 has included improvement in the
       ecclesiastical position of women in the S.B.C., Letsinger argues,
       though he acknowledges that restrictions still exist.

246   Lumpkin, William L. "The Role of Women in Eighteenth-Century
       Virginia Baptist Life." Baptist History and Heritage 8 (1973):
       158-67.
            Lumpkin focuses on the last 35 years of the century, a pe-
       riod of Baptist revivalism and patriotism in reaction to the op-
       pressive and arid Anglicanism of Virginia. He surveys women's
       roles and provides biographical sketches of three outstanding
       Baptist women: Martha Marshall, Margaret Meuse Clay, and Hannah
       Lee.

247   McBeth, Leon. Women in Baptist Life. Nashville: Broadman
       Press, 1979. 190 pp.
            McBeth provides a general descriptive treatment touching on
       all areas of Southern Baptist women's participation in the life of
       the denomination and is cautiously supportive of women in church
       leadership roles. A shorter version of this material is his "The
       Role of Women in Southern Baptist History," Baptist History and
       Heritage 12 (1977):3-25.

248   Mondello, Salvatore. "Isabel Crawford: The Making of a Mis-
       sionary"; "Isabel Crawford and the Kiowa Indians"; and "Isabel
       Crawford: Champion of the American Indians." Foundations: A
       Baptist Journal of History and Theology 21 (1978):322-39; 22
       (1979):28-42; 22 (1979):99-115.
            Mondello portrays the life of Baptist Isabel Crawford (1865-
       1961) from her childhood through her training and work among the
       poor in Chicago to her missionary and advocacy work for Indians in
       Oklahoma, Arizona, Western New York, and Florida.

       For Further Information

249   A number of women--Nannie Burroughs, for example (entry 456)--
       about whom material appears in chapter V, were Baptist. For cur-
       rent scholarship on Baptist women see Women and Religion: A
       Bibliography Selected from the ATLA Religion Database (entry 15)
       and the periodical indexes from which it was compiled; America:
       History and Life (entry 1); and issues of Baptist History and
       Heritage and Foundations: A Baptist Journal of History and
       Theology.

           II.C.2. CHRISTIAN CHURCH (DISCIPLES OF CHRIST)

250   Bailey, Fred A. "Woman's Superiority in Disciple Thought,
       1865-1900." Restoration Quarterly 23 (1980):151-60.

Bailey provides an historical-theological survey of late nineteenth-century opinions by Disciples about women. He concludes that liberal and conservative Disciples were in essential agreement that woman was man's moral superior but were divided on the religious and social role that women could play.

251   Lollis, Lorraine. The Shape of Adam's Rib: A Lively History of Women's Work in the Christian Church. St. Louis: Bethany Press, 1970. 219 pp.

Narrating the organizational history of women's work in the Christian Church (Disciples of Christ) from 1874 to 1969, the author examines three major chronological periods. The women worked from 1874 to 1919 out of their own organization, the Christian Woman's Board of Missions. In 1919, this organization was merged into the denomination's United Christian Missionary Society, but after 1949 women's work was again carried out through the women's own organization. Within the narrative, the author examines three overall themes: the worldwide missionary enterprise; the movement toward unification and consolidation of the work; and the search for woman's place in church and community. Footnotes and bibliography aid in locating further resources on the women's story in this denomination.

For Further Information

252   The history of Disciples of Christ women in one area of the country has been written by Phyllis G. Brown: A Century with Christian Women in Virginia (Richmond, Va.: Christian Women's Fellowship in Virginia, 1975). A special issue of the periodical Disciple celebrated 100 years of organized women's work (1 [23 June 1974]).

253   For current scholarship on Disciples of Christ women, see Women and Religion: A Bibliography Selected from the ATLA Religion Database (entry 15) and the periodical indexes from which it was compiled; and America: History and Life (entry 1).

II.C.3.   EPISCOPAL

254   Bellamy, V. Nelle. "Participation of Women in the Public Life of the Church from Lambeth Conferences, 1867-1978." Historical Magazine of the Protestant Episcopal Church 51 (1982):81-98. "Participation of Women in the Public Life of the Anglican Communion." In Triumph Over Silence: Women in Protestant History (entry 74), pp. 229-60.

Bellamy's first essay provides a concise but thorough chronology of the statements and commentary on the status of women from the international consultations of Anglican bishops held roughly every ten years. Her second essay profiles the activities of women in leadership roles in two of the national constituent bodies of the Anglican communion, the Church of England and the Episcopal Church, U.S.A.

255   Boyd, Sandra Hughes, ed. <u>Cultivating Our Roots: A Guide to</u>
      <u>Gathering Church Women's History</u>. Cincinnati, Ohio: Forward
      Movement Publications for the Episcopal Women's History Project.
      1984. 111 pp.
           Aimed at encouraging church women to engage in the process
      of collecting their history, the essays include personal accounts
      by women who have discovered women's church history and "how-to's"
      for researching, doing oral histories, and organizing conferences.
      A bibliography of resources on these topics is also included.

256   Boyd, Sandra Hughes. "The History of Women in the Episcopal
      Church: A Select Annotated Bibliography." <u>Historical Magazine</u>
      <u>of the Protestant Episcopal Church</u> 50 (1981):423-33.
           Intended to serve as a beginning bibliography, this covers
      the subject areas of general history and resources, sisterhoods,
      deaconesses and the diaconate, and the ordination of women to the
      priesthood.

257   Donovan, Mary Sudman. "Women and Mission: Towards a More
      Inclusive Historiography." <u>Historical Magazine of the Protes-</u>
      <u>tant Episcopal Church</u> 53 (1984):297-305.
           Illustrating her chronicles with Episcopal women mission-
      aries who served from Greece to China, Donovan examines husband
      and wife missionary teams, women as publicists for the missionary
      enterprise, and women as innovators in the missionary programs.

258   Hiatt, Suzanne R. "How We Brought the Good News from Graymoor
      to Minneapolis: An Episcopal Paradigm." <u>Journal of Ecumenical</u>
      <u>Studies</u> 20 (1983):576-84.
           A participant and prime mover in the "irregular" but his-
      toric first ordination of women to the Episcopal priesthood in
      1974 tells the story of the movement from its organizational in-
      ception at a women's meeting in 1970 to the 1976 national church
      convention where the canons were changed to allow the ordination
      of women to the priesthood. An earlier version of this story is
      "Entering the Sanctuary: The Struggle for Priesthood in the Con-
      temporary Episcopalian and Roman Catholic Experience" (the Episco-
      pal story by Norene Carter), in <u>Women of Spirit: Female Leader-</u>
      <u>ship in the Jewish and Christian Traditions</u> (entry 80), pp. 356-72.
      Heather Huyck's article on the same subject, "Indelible Change:
      Women Priests in the Episcopal Church" (<u>Historical Magazine of</u>
      <u>the Protestant Episcopal Church</u> 51 [1982]:385-98), is based on
      her Ph.D. dissertation. For further bibliography on this topic,
      see entry 256.

259   <u>Historical Magazine of the Protestant Episcopal Church</u> 51
      (December 1982).
           This special issue contains a selection of papers from a
      1982 conference entitled "Notable Episcopal Women: The Feminine
      Dimension of Church History." In addition to articles mentioned
      within other annotations of this bibliography, the following
      appear: "The Non-Institutional Church: The Religious Role of
      Women in Eighteenth-Century Virginia," by Joan R. Gunderson, and
      "Carrie, or The Child in the Rectory: 19th-Century Episcopal

Sunday School Prototype," by Joanna B. Gillespie. The conference
keynote speech appeared in revised form as "Women and Religion,
Women as Episcopalians: Some Methodological Observations," by
Catherine M. Prelinger, in Historical Magazine of the Protestant
Episcopal Church 52 (1983):141-52.

260   Sherman, Margaret Marston. True to Their Heritage: A Brief
       History of the Woman's Auxiliary, 1871-1958. New York:
       Episcopal Church, National Council, [ca. 1958]. 43 pp.
         Written by an administrator who served the woman's auxiliary
for 30 years, this work traces its history from the formal beginnings to the mid-twentieth century. Another of the organization's
pillars, Avis E. Harvey, wrote a history of its national meetings
and the decisions made there: Every Three Years: The Triennial
Meetings, 1874-1967 (New York: Episcopal Church, Executive Council, [ca. 1969]. Mary Sudman Donovan provides a more contemporary
perspective on this story in "Zealous Evangelists: The Woman's
Auxiliary to the Board of Missions" (Historical Magazine of the
Protestant Episcopal Church 51 [1982]:371-83). A biography of the
woman who guided the auxiliary for 30 years from 1876 to 1916 is
Margaret A. Tomes, Julia Chester Emery (New York: Protestant
Episcopal Church, National Council, Woman's Auxiliary, 1924).
Julia Chester Emery's history of Episcopal missions is A Century
of Endeavor, 1821-1921 (New York: Department of Missions, 1921).

261   Young, Frances M. Thankfulness Unites: The History of the
       United Thank Offering, 1889-1979. Cincinnati, Ohio: Forward
       Movement Publications for the United Thank Offering, 1979.
       85 pp.
         The author sets not only the story of the women's missionary
funding organization, the United Thank Offering, but the history
of Episcopal women's organizations into their historical context,
telling the story decade-by-decade. Illustrations and a brief
bibliography are included. Young, a participant in many of the
events about which she writes, continues her historical chroni-
cling in issues of the newsletter published by the Episcopal
Women's History Project (entry 262).

       For Further Information

262   Several local jurisdictions of Episcopal women's organizations
       have recently published histories: A Goodly Heritage: A History
       of Episcopal Churchwomen in the Diocese of South Carolina, by
       Harriet Linen Goodbody (Charleston: Episcopal Churchwomen,
       Diocese of South Carolina, 1984); Morning Glories and Evensong:
       A Century of the Episcopal Churchwomen in Connecticut, by Ann
       Harding Robinson (Hartford, Conn.: Church Missions Publishing
       Co., 1981); and Women Who Made a Difference, by the Episcopal
       Women's History Project, the Diocese of California (San Francisco:
       Episcopal Women's History Project, Diocese of California, 1985).

The Episcopal Women's History Project, which in addition to its
guidebook Cultivating Our Roots (entry 255) publishes a quarterly
newsletter reprinting primary source material and providing news
items about ongoing historical projects, has its office at
175 Ninth Avenue, New York, NY 10011.

263   Among the Episcopal women whose biographies appear in Notable
American Women (entry 35) and Notable American Women: The Modern
Period (entry 36) are Anne Ayres, Kate Harwood Waller Barrett,
Evadel Vakia Bowles, Harriet Starr Cannon, Adelaide Teague Case,
Helena Stuart Dudley, Emily Bradley Neal Haven, and Vida Scudder.
See also, in other chapters of this bibliography, the entries for
"The Religious Experience of Southern Women" (entry 103), Vida
Scudder (entry 169), Anna Julia Cooper (entry 457), and Pauli
Murray (entry 460).

264   Some examples of recent scholarship on the English foremothers
of Episcopal women are Anne Llewellyn Barstow, "An Ambiguous
Legacy: Anglican Clergy Wives after the Reformation," in Women
in New Worlds, vol. 2 (entry 76), pp. 97-111; Nancy Boyd, Three
Victorian Women Who Changed Their World: Josephine Butler,
Octavia Hill, Florence Nightingale (New York: Oxford University
Press, 1982); Brian Heeney, "The Beginnings of Church Feminism:
Women and the Councils of the Church of England, 1897-1919,"
Journal of Ecclesiastical History 33 (1982):89-109; and Frederica
Harris Thompsett, "Women Inclined to Holiness: Our Reformation
Ancestry," Historical Magazine of the Protestant Episcopal Church
51 (1982):337-45.

265   For other periodical publications on Episcopal women, see Women
and Religion: A Bibliography Selected from the ATLA Religion
Database (entry 12) and the indexes from which it was compiled;
America: History and Life (entry 1); and articles appearing in
the Historical Magazine of the Protestant Episcopal Church.

II.C.4.   LUTHERAN

266   Albers, James W. "Perspectives on the History of Women in the
Lutheran Church-Missouri Synod During the Nineteenth Century."
Lutheran Historical Conference: Essays and Reports, 1980 9
(1982):137-83.
      This paper, the first on women's history to be presented at
the Lutheran Historical Conference, is based largely on research
in the official publications of the Missouri Synod, though helpful notes point toward sources from other synods as well. Albers
considers ideas of domesticity, pastors' wives, teachers, women's
organizations, woman suffrage (opposed by this body), and early
manifestations of deaconess work (not officially recognized until
after World War I). The views of these Lutherans, Albers reports,
were similar to those of Lutherans in Germany and of other Americans, except that there was in this synod no discoverable feminist minority.

267   Diehl, Nona M.; Hass, Dorothy E.L.; and Nold, Lieselotte.
       "Woman's Place in the Church." In The Encyclopedia of the
       Lutheran Church, vol. 3. Minneapolis: Augsburg Publishing
       House, 1965, pp. 2490-97.
            This article provides historical survey from prebiblical
       times through Luther to "present problems" and covers "practical
       aspects" ranging from women in mission work to the ordination of
       women.

268   Ermarth, Margaret Sittler. Adam's Fractured Rib. Philadelphia:
       Fortress Press, 1970. xvi, 159 pp.
            Highly illustrative of the debate about women in the late
       1960s, this book is the result of four years of effort by a sub-
       committee of the Lutheran Church in America's Commission on the
       Comprehensive Study of the Doctrine of Ministry. Ermarth surveys
       at some length the status of women in other denominations and
       church bodies in this country and abroad with 25 pages devoted to
       Lutheran Churches in North America. She concludes with biblical
       and theological discussion about ordination, the diaconate, and
       the future of the debate.

269   Fjellman, Burnice. "Women in the Church." In Centennial
       Essays: Augustana Lutheran Church, 1860-1960, edited by Emmer
       Engberg. Rock Island, Ill.: Augustana Press, 1960,
       pp. 200-226.
            Writing in the context of Lutheran mergers and discussion of
       combining women's work into the larger structure of the denomina-
       tion, Fjellman provides historical background by chronicling the
       participation of parish women's groups, women missionaries,
       deaconesses, and denominational women's groups in the church's
       life.

270   Graebner, Alan. "Birth Control and the Lutherans: The
       Missouri Synod as a Case Study." In Women in American Religion
       (entry 75), pp. 229-52.
            Graebner, in this thorough study, traces the movement from
       opposition to silence to acceptance of birth control in the con-
       servative Missouri Synod and posits several causes for the shift:
       changes in behavior of the laity, erosion of clerical authority,
       decline in Lutheran pastors' own family birth rates, new biblical
       exegesis of critical passages, and turnover of "Old Guard" church
       leadership.

271   Meyer, Ruth Fritz. Women on a Mission: The Role of Women in
       the Church from Bible Times up to and Including a History of
       the Lutheran Women's Missionary League During the First Twenty-
       Five Years. St. Louis: Concordia Publishing House, 1967.
       300 pp.
            After brief accounts of biblical precedents, the work of
       women in other denominations, and the work of Lutheran women in
       other synods (the predecessor groups of the American Lutheran
       Church and the Lutheran Church in America), Meyer provides a
       detailed narrative of women's organizational efforts in support
       of the missions of the Missouri Synod.

272   Telleen, Jane. "'Yours in the Master's Service': Emmy Evald
      and the Woman's Missionary Society of the Augustana Lutheran
      Church, 1892-1942." Swedish Pioneer History Quarterly 30
      (1979):183-95.
          Telleen asserts that the desire of Swedish Lutheran women to
      combine the traditional goals of motherhood and marriage with that
      of executive autonomy in the church led them in 1892 to found
      their own organization where "their leadership roles . . . vali-
      dated them in the same way that being a minister brought automatic
      prestige to men" (p. 184). She traces the history of the W.M.S.
      through its prosperous years to 1921, when it challenged the Synod
      over the site of a women's dormitory--for which the W.M.S. had
      raised the money--and lost. By 1942, decision-making was out of
      the hands of the W.M.S. and under the control of the Synod.

273   Weiser, Frederick A. Love's Response: A Story of the Lutheran
      Deaconesses in America. Philadelphia: United Lutheran Church
      in America, 1962. xi, 164 pp.
          Weiser's account begins with the origins of the modern
      deaconess movement in mid-nineteenth-century Germany and follows
      its development in all of the American Lutheran synods, with
      emphasis upon its most successful period from 1884 to 1916. He
      pays special attention to the question of why the diaconate did
      not prove to be more successful in the United States.

      For Further Information

274   A description of material in Lutheran archives is Helen M.
      Knubel's An Introductory Guide to Lutheran Archives and Collec-
      tions (New York: Lutheran Council in the U.S.A., Archives of
      Cooperative Lutheranism, 1981).

275   For ongoing periodical resources on Lutheran women, see Women
      and Religion: A Bibliography Selected from the ATLA Religion
      Database (entry 12) and the periodical indexes from which it was
      compiled, and America: History and Life (entry 1).

                        II.C.5. MENNONITE

276   Cummings, Mary Lou, ed. Full Circle: Stories of Mennonite
      Women. Newton, Kans.: Faith and Life Press, 1978. viii,
      204 pp.
          Here are found 19 biographical sketches of Mennonite women
      of Dutch, Prussian, and Russian background who immigrated to the
      Western prairies in 1874 and later. Portraits of all the women
      preface their stories and bibliographical notes accompany a number
      of the stories.

277   Goering, Gladys V. Women in Search of Missions: A History of
      the General Conference Mennonite Women's Organization. Newton,
      Kans.: Faith and Life Press, 1980. vii, 128 pp.
          Goering presents here the organizational history from 1917
      to the present of the women's society of the General Conference

Mennonite Church, a branch whose members of Dutch, Prussian, and Russian heritage had migrated to the Western prairies in the late nineteenth century.

278   Klingelsmith, Sharon. "Women in the Mennonite Church, 1900-1930." Mennonite Quarterly Review 54 (1980):163-207.
        The author documents the role of women in the development of the Mennonite Woman's Missionary Society from the early twentieth century to its subsequent appropriation in 1928 by the denominational Mennonite Board of Missions and Charities.

279   Nyce, Dorothy Yoder. Which Way Women? Akron, Pa.: Mennonite Central Committee, Peace Section, Task Force on Women, 1980. 156 pp.
        This collection of articles and poetry from contemporary Mennonite women ranging from biblical commentary to modern issues facing women will serve as a resource for learning about late twentieth-century Mennonite women. Correspondingly useful is her collection of contemporary Mennonite women's sermons, Weaving Wisdom: Sermons by Mennonite Women (Notre Dame, Ind.: Womansage, Fatima Research Center, 1983).

280   Rich, Elaine Sommers. Mennonite Women: A Story of God's Faithfulness, 1683-1983. Scottdale, Pa.: Herald Press, 1983. 257 pp.
        Women in the Mennonite branches of Swiss, South German, and Alsatian background who immigrated to the eastern United States and Canada from 1683 to the 1850s are treated in this book. Rich's thorough survey ranges from Old World forebears to twentieth-century peace activists and includes women in the home, education, overseas and home missions, health-care ministries, and church organizations. Many photographs enliven the text, and notes, bibliography, and index are included.

281   Weibe, Katie Funk, ed. Women Among the Brethren: Stories of Fifteen Mennonite Brethren and Krimmer Mennonite Brethren Women. Hillsboro, Kans.: General Conference of Mennonite Brethren Churches, Board of Christian Literature, 1979. x, 197 pp.
        Women in two branches of the Mennonite tradition (now merged as the Mennonite Brethren Church in North America) of Dutch, Prussian, and Russian background are included here. There are biographies of five who spent the major part of their lives in the United States—Justine Friesen Wiebe, Sarah Block Eitzen, Magdalena Hergert Becker, Elizabeth Pauls Wiebe, and Mary J. Hiebert—along with biographical sources.

        For Further Information

282   The Mennonite Encyclopedia, jointly published by the Mennonite Publishing House, the Mennonite Publication Office, and the Mennonite Brethren Publishing House (Scottdale, Pa.; Newton, Kans.; and Hillsboro, Kans., 1959), provides in its fourth volume articles on the status of women in the Mennonite tradition and institutional histories of two Mennonite women's organizations (pp. 972-76).

283   For current scholarship on Mennonite women, see Women and
      Religion: A Bibliography Selected from the ATLA Religion Database
      (entry 12) and the periodical indexes from which it was compiled,
      and America: History and Life (entry 1).

                         II.C.6. METHODIST

284   Blauvelt, Martha Tomhave, and Keller, Rosemary Skinner. "Women
      and Revivalism: The Puritan and Wesleyan Traditions." In
      Women and Religion in America, vol. 2 (entry 79), pp. 316-67.
           Asserting that "colonial revivalism witnessed an awakening
      of women's power as well as of religion and prepared the way for
      women's much wider participation in evangelicalism in the nine-
      teenth century" (pp. 316-17), the authors describe and compare
      revivalism for women in the two traditions and support their
      argument with excerpts from a dozen documents of the period.

285   Hale, Harry, Jr., et al. New Witnesses: United Methodist
      Clergywomen. Nashville: Board of Higher Education and Min-
      istry, Division of Ordained Ministry, 1980. 127 pp.
           Based on responses to a survey of nearly 1,000 Methodist
      clergywomen, this report examines the personal and social charac-
      teristics of the women, their career histories, and the satisfac-
      tions and problems they experienced. Statistical tables derived
      from the responses are included in the appendix.

286   Hill, Patricia R. "Heathen Women's Friends: Role of the
      Methodist Episcopal Women in the Foreign Mission Movement,
      1869-1915." Methodist History 19 (1981):146-54.
           This organizational chronicle is especially interesting
      because of the unusual degree of autonomy this denominational
      society maintained over its own work for women. For further work
      by Hill, see "The World Their Household": The American Woman's
      Foreign Mission Movement and Cultural Transformation, 1870-1920
      (entry 180).

287   Hoover, Theressa. With Unveiled Face: Centennial Reflections
      on Women and Men in the Community of the Church. New York:
      United Methodist Church, General Board of Global Ministries,
      Women's Division, 1983. 126 pp.
           Hoover explores the recent history of the Women's Division
      and its national grassroots organization, United Methodist Women,
      noting that together these organizations form "one continuing
      women's organization . . . having denominational authority to
      function as a reasonably autonomous body with significant rights
      and responsibilities" (p. 7). Thorough bibliographical footnotes
      lead the reader to further resources.

288   Hovet, Theodore. "Phoebe Palmer's 'Altar Phraseology' and the
      Spiritual Dimension of Woman's Sphere." Journal of Religion 63
      (July 1983):264-80.
           Arising from a contemporary approach to the study of women's
      role and incorporating a theological perspective, Hovet's work is
      an example of the steady stream of scholarly publication about

perhaps the most well-known of American Methodist women. Phoebe
Palmer (1807-74), evangelist and leader of the nineteenth-century
Holiness movement, is also featured in Nancy Hardesty, Women
Called to Witness (entry 156), "Minister as Prophet? or As
Mother?" (entry 198), and "Women in the Holiness Movement: Fem-
inism in the Evangelical Tradition" (entry 127). See also Timothy
L. Smith, Revivalism and Social Reform (entry 139), and "The
Struggle for the Right to Preach" in Women and Religion in America,
vol. 1 (entry 78), pp. 193-241. For biographical and bibliograph-
ical coverage, see Notable American Women (entry 35), 3:12-14, and
Methodist Women: A Guide to the Literature (entry 293).

289   Keller, Rosemary S. "Women and the Nature of Ministry in the
       United Methodist Tradition." Methodist History 22 (January
       1984):99-114.
       Keller provides an overview of women in three periods:
eighteenth-century England; the American Revolution and the first
Methodist societies in the colonies; and the founding of missionary societies and deaconess orders as well as the struggle for
laity rights and ordination for women.

290   Keller, Rosemary Skinner; Queen, Louise L.; and Thomas,
       Hilah F., eds. Women in New Worlds: Historical Perspectives
       on the Wesleyan Tradition, vol. 2 (entry 76).
       This second volume of papers presented at a 1980 United
Methodist conference (see entry 299 for the first volume) contains
essays about "the attitudes toward the place of women in Wesleyan
and related traditions [and] the ways women and men actually have
related as laity and clergy in the ministries of the church"
(p. 11). Of particular interest to United Methodist women's history in this country are the following: "John Wesley and Sophy
Hopkey: A Case Study in Wesley's Attitude Toward Women," by Alan
L. Hayes; "'The Sun in Their Domestic System': The Mother in
Early Nineteenth-Century Methodist Sunday School Lore," by Joanna
Bowen Gillespie; "Subversion of the Feminine Ideal: The Southern
Lady's Companion and White Male Morality in the Antebellum South,
1847-1854," by James L. LeLoudis, II (entry 210); "Distress from
the Press: Antifeminism in the Editorials of James Monroe
Buckley, 1880-1912," by Saranne Price O'Donnell; "A Partnership of
Equality: The Marriage and Ministry of John and Mary Goucher," by
Emora T. Brannan; "The Pacific Northwest: Changing Role of the
Pastor's Wife Since 1840," by Rosa Peffly Motes; "Sisterhoods of
Service: Women's Clubs and Methodist Women's Missionary Societies
in North Carolina, 1890-1930," by Anastatia Sims; "Civil Rights,
1920-1970: Three Southern Methodist Women," by Arnold M. Shankman
(entry 215); "Ordination of Women: The Issue in the Church of the
United Brethren in Christ," by James E. Will; "Maggie Newton Van
Cott: The Methodist Episcopal Church Considers the Question of
Women Clergy," by Janet S. Everhart; "The Function of Female Bond-
ing: The Restored Diaconessate of the Nineteenth Century," by
Catherine M. Prelinger and Rosemary S. Keller; and "The Legacy of
Georgia Harkness," by Joan Chamberlain Engelsman.

291   McDowell, John Patrick. The Social Gospel in the South: The
      Woman's Home Mission Movement in the Methodist Episcopal
      Church, South, 1886-1939. Baton Rouge: Louisiana State
      University Press, 1982. 167 pp.
         Challenging the widely held belief that Southern church
      people were concerned with individual salvation to the exclusion
      of social reform issues, McDowell buttresses his argument by means
      of this study of women's missionary work in one of the constituent
      bodies that formed the Methodist Church in the 1940 merger. A
      bibliography includes articles and books "by or about Southern
      Methodist women." See also entry 190.

292   Norwood, Frederick A. "Expanding Horizons: Women in the
      Methodist Movement." In Triumph Over Silence: Women in
      Protestant History (entry 74), pp. 151-72.
         Norwood's essay is a broad survey covering the origins of
      Methodism, a few early American notable women, the institutional-
      ization of women's work and its absorption into denominational
      structures, the training of women for church work, black women's
      participation in the church, lay delegates, the ordination of
      women, holiness women, and women in social gospel activities.

293   Rowe, Kenneth E. Methodist Women: A Guide to the Literature.
      Lake Junaluska, N.C.: United Methodist Church, General Com-
      mission on Archives and History, 1980. 50 pp.
         The nearly 400 entries in this bibliography of secondary
      sources make it a basic resource for the study of Methodist women.
      Covered are historical studies; biographical studies, womanhood,
      and the church; marriage, motherhood, and the family; the struggle
      for laity rights; women organized for mission; the deaconess move-
      ment; the struggle for clergy rights; ethnic women; and images of
      Methodist women. Brief annotations and an author index are in-
      cluded. Of the works listed in Rowe's bibliography, the following
      highlight some particularly important themes for a contemporary
      consideration of the role of Methodist women in the church's
      history:

294   Gorrell, Donald K., ed. "Women's Rightful Place." Dayton,
         Ohio: United Theological Seminary, 1980. 62 pp.
            This small work is helpful for the light it throws on the
         struggle for laity and clergy rights among the Evangelicals
         and the United Brethren, among the oldest of the constituent
         bodies of the United Methodist Church.

295   Magalis, Elaine. Conduct Becoming to a Woman: Bolted Doors
         and Burgeoning Missions. New York: United Methodist Church,
         Board of Global Ministries, Women's Division, 1973. 140 pp.
            Surveying women in the constituent bodies of the present-
         day United Methodist Church, Magalis focuses on missionary
         work and the ordination of women.

296   Mitchell, Norma Taylor. "From Social to Radical Feminism."
        Methodist History 13 (1975):21-44.
             Mitchell surveys the history of Methodist women's organi-
        ations from the establishment of women's missionary societies
        after the Civil War through the advocacy groups of the 1970s,
        ending with the Women's Caucus and the Commission on the
        Status and Role of Women in the United Methodist Church,
        with analysis of their changing approaches to feminism.

297   Tatum, Noreen Dean. Crown of Service: A Story of Women's
        Work in the Methodist Episcopal Church, South, from 1878-
        1940. Nashville: Parthenon Press, 1960. 418 pp.
             Tracing the history of organized women's work in one
        branch of Methodism from the mid-nineteenth century to the
        1940 merger of three branches, Tatum tells of the gradual
        loss of women's autonomy in their work and the fight for
        women's laity and clergy rights.

298   To a Higher Glory: The Growth and Development of Black
        Women Organized for Mission in the Methodist Church, 1940-
        1968. Cincinnati, Ohio: United Methodist Church, Board of
        Global Ministries, Task Group on the History of the Central
        Jurisdiction Women's Organization, Women's Division, 1978.
        153 pp.
             This work tells of the all-black Central Jurisdiction
        through which black women related to the missions and women's
        organizations of the Methodist Church prior to the merger
        which created the United Methodist Church.

299   Thomas, Hilah F., and Keller, Rosemary Skinner, eds. Women in
      New Worlds: Historical Perspectives on the Wesleyan Tradition,
      vol. 1 (entry 81).
           This first of two volumes of papers presented at the 1980
      United Methodist Conference on women's history (for the second
      volume, see entry 290), contains articles about the experience of
      Methodist women in the United States: "Minister as Prophet? or
      As Mother?," by Nancy Hardesty (entry 198); "Mary McLeod Bethune
      as Religionist," by Clarence G. Newsome (entry 455); "Georgia
      Harkness: Social Activist and/or Mystic," by Martha L. Scott
      (entry 199); "Ministry Through Marriage: Methodist Clergy Wives
      on the Trans-Mississippi Frontier," by Julie Roy Jeffrey; "His-
      panic Clergy Wives: Their Contribution to United Methodism in the
      Southwest, Later Nineteenth Century to the Present," by Clotilda
      Falcon Nanez; "Preparing Women for the Lord's Work: The Story of
      Three Methodist Training Schools, 1880-1940," by Virginia Lieson
      Brereton; "The Social Gospel According to Phoebe: Methodist
      Deaconesses in the Metropolis, 1885-1918," by Mary Agnes
      Dougherty; "Laity Rights and Leadership: Winning Them for Women
      in the Methodist Protestant Church, 1860-1900," by William T.
      Noll; "'A New Impulse': Progress in Lay Leadership and Service by
      Women of the United Brethren in Christ and the Evangelical Asso-
      ciation, 1870-1910," by Donald K. Gorrell; "Creating a Sphere for
      Women: The Methodist Episcopal Church, 1869-1906," by Rosemary
      Skinner Keller; "The Laity Rights Movement, 1906-1918: Woman's
      Suffrage in the Methodist Episcopal Church, South," by Virginia

Shadron; "Nineteenth-Century A.M.E. Preaching Women: Cutting Edge
of Women's Inclusion in Church Polity," by Jualynne Dodson (entry
431); "Evangelical Domesticity: Korean Women in Hawaii, 1903-
1945: The Role of Methodism in Their Liberation and in Their
Participation in the Korean Independence Movement," by Alice Chai;
"Shaping a New Society: Methodist Women and Industrial Reform in
the South, 1880-1940," by Mary E. Frederickson; and "Everybody on
the Left Knew Her," by Miriam J. Crist.

300   Van Scoyoc, Nancy J. <u>Women, Change, and the Church</u>. Nash-
       ville: Abingdon Press, 1980. 96 pp.
           One of a series of volumes published in preparation for the
       1984 celebration of the 200th anniversary of Methodism in the
       United States, this work addresses the changing roles of women in
       American society and the impact of those changes on the ministry
       of the church.

       For Further Information

301   Under the aegis of the United Methodist Church's General Com-
       mission on Archives and History, The Women's and Ethnic History
       Project (P.O. Box 127, Madison, NJ 07940) sponsors ongoing work in
       oral history and workshops on the recovery of Methodist women's
       history.

302   For information on individual Methodist women, see <u>Methodist</u>
       <u>Women: A Guide to the Literature</u> (entry 293). The chapters on
       biographical studies there include citations for sketches appear-
       ing in <u>Notable American Women</u> (entry 35) as well as book-length
       biographies. <u>Notable American Women: The Modern Period</u> (entry
       36), not referred to in Rowe's bibliography, has biographical
       sketches of Mary McLeod Bethune and Georgia Harkness.

303   For current scholarship on Methodist women, consult <u>The United</u>
       <u>Methodist Periodical Index</u> (Nashville: United Methodist Publish-
       ing House, 1961-); <u>Women and Religion: A Bibliography Selected</u>
       <u>from the ATLA Religion Database</u> (entry 12) and the periodical
       indexes from which it was compiled; <u>America: History and Life</u>
       (entry 1); and articles appearing regularly in <u>Methodist History</u>.

304   A multivolume union catalog of Methodist materials in 200 re-
       search collections is being edited by Kenneth E. Rowe: <u>Methodist</u>
       <u>Union Catalog: Pre-1976 Imprints</u> (Metuchen, N.J.: Scarecrow
       Press, 1975-).

305   For resources about English foremothers of American Methodist
       women, see the several chapters about British women in <u>Methodist</u>
       <u>Women: A Guide to the Literature</u> (entry 293). Recent examples of
       scholarship are Frank Baker, "Susanna Wesley: Puritan, Parent,
       Pastor, Protagonist, Pattern," in <u>Women in New Worlds</u>, vol. 2
       (entry 76), pp. 112-31; Earl Kent Brown, <u>Women of Mr. Wesley's</u>
       <u>Methodism</u> (New York: Edwin Mellen Press, 1983); Mollie C. Davis,
       "The Countess of Huntingdon: A Leader in Missions for Social and

Religious Reform," in Women in New Worlds, vol. 2 (entry 76),
pp. 162-75; and Charles Wallace, "Susanna Wesley's Spirituality,"
Methodist History 22 (April 1984):158-73.

II.C.7. PRESBYTERIAN

306   Boyd, Lois A., and Brackenridge, R. Douglas. Presbyterian
       Women: Two Centuries of a Quest for Status. Westport, Conn.:
       Greenwood Press, 1983. xiv, 308 pp.
           This work traces the history of women in the United Presby-
       terian Church in the U.S.A., incorporating material from the other
       branches of Presbyterianism into the narrative. A chronological
       arrangement covers the following periods: the first century of
       the denomination's existence when women were unable to exercise
       any power; the late nineteenth century when they exerted influence
       through their own successful church-related organizations; the
       early twentieth-century loss of this power base in the co-optation
       of their work into denominational structures; and the subsequent
       twentieth-century constitutional changes that allowed women's
       ordination as elders and ministers. A 12-page bibliography of
       archival material, official church records, primary and secondary
       sources, articles, and a list of periodicals is included. A
       concise treatment of the official actions of the Presbyterian
       church is found in Boyd and Brackenridge's "United Presbyterian
       Policy on Women and the Church: An Historical Overview," Journal
       of Presbyterian History 59 (1981):383-407. A short survey of
       women in the Presbyterian Church in the U.S.A. appeared in their
       "Questions of Power and Status: American Presbyterian Women,
       1870-1980," in Triumph Over Silence: Women in Protestant History
       (entry 74), pp. 203-228. Their book is the place to begin re-
       search into the history of Presbyterian women. Several works
       noted in its survey and bibliography recommend themselves for
       particular attention:

307   Penfield, Janet Harbison. "Women in the Presbyterian
       Church: An Historical Overview." Journal of Presbyterian
       History 55 (1977):107-23.
           Penfield traces the activities of Presbyterian women,
       emphasizing the missions movement of the nineteenth century
       and the twentieth-century struggle for equal ecclesiastical
       rights.

308   Smylie, James H. "Notable Presbyterian Women." Journal of
       Presbyterian History 52 (1974):99-121.
           Biographical sketches of 25 black and white Presbyterian
       women from the late eighteenth century to the 1970s are in-
       cluded.

309   Verdesi, Elizabeth Howell. In But Still Out: Women in the
       Church. Philadelphia: Westminster Press, 1973. 218 pp.
           As an advocate of women's full participation in all
       aspects of the life and ministry of the United Presbyterian
       Church (the former northern branch of the denomination)
       Verdesi analyzes the ways in which women have lost power at

important moments in the church's history, with emphasis
upon the co-optation of the women's missions boards in the
1920s and the declining status of religious educators after
World War II. This book offers provocative insights into
issues of institutional organization and power as they
affect women.

310   Campbell, Penelope. "Presbyterian West African Missions:
       Women as Converts and Agents of Social Change." Journal of
       Presbyterian History 56 (1978):121-32.
           African women, because of social pressures more easily con-
       verted to Christianity than men, became the foundation of indige-
       nous mission churches during the latter half of the nineteenth
       century. Campbell also discusses education work in the West
       African missions field for the same period.

311   Lehman, Edward C. Women Clergy: Breaking Through Gender
       Barriers. New Brunswick, N.J.: Transaction Books, 1985.
           Lehman reports the findings of a sociological survey of
       clergywomen and parishes in the United Presbyterian Church in the
       U.S.A. on the problems and prospects of women in ministry.

312   Miller, Page Putnam. A Claim to New Roles. Metuchen, N.J.:
       Scarecrow Press, 1985. ix, 241 pp.
           Focusing on the antebellum period of the nineteenth century,
       Miller seeks to locate the reasons for Presbyterian women's
       emergence into new prominence in the church. She examines Presby-
       terian policy on female behavior, mother as spiritual guardian,
       organized benevolence, foreign missions, the Sunday School move-
       ment, and female education. A number of prominent Presbyterian
       women are also featured. A 19-page bibliography, photographs,
       and an index enhance this work.

313   Smylie, James H. "Of Secret and Family Worship: Historical
       Meditations." Journal of Presbyterian History 58 (1980):
       95-115.
           Though Presbyterians have long been enjoined to pray in
       private and as families as well as in public worship, this aspect
       of Presbyterian piety has confronted various social historical
       challenges, including secularization and changes in family life.
       Much of Smylie's analysis would be applicable to other similar
       denominations.

       For Further Information

314   Presbyterian women were heavily involved in many of the activi-
       ties of nineteenth-century evangelical women described earlier in
       this bibliography, including evangelical religion, reform, mis-
       sions, and the ordained ministry. Examples are the description of
       the careers of Julia Brown Mateer and Annette Thompson Mills in

Our Ordered Lives Confess (entry 182); the story of Presbyterian
Rhoda Bement as told in Revivalism, Social Conscience, and Community in the Burned-Over District (entry 112); Sylvia M. Jacob's
recounting of the careers of five women who served the Southern
Presbyterian Congo Mission in "Their Special Mission: Afro-
American Women as Missionaries to the Congo, 1894-1937" (entry
437); and the discussion of restrictive prescriptions for womanhood in Old School Presbyterianism described by Ronald W. Hogeland
(entry 128).

315   The bibliography in Presbyterian Women (entry 306) may be sup-
       plemented by use of the bibliography in Verdesi's In But Still
       Out: Women in the Church (entry 309) and Miller's A Claim to New
       Roles (entry 312). For current scholarship see entries about
       Presbyterian women in Women and Religion: A Bibliography Selected
       from the ATLA Religion Database (entry 15) and the periodical in-
       dexes from which it was compiled; America: History and Life
       (entry 1); and issues of Journal of Presbyterian History.

                  II.C.8. THE SOCIETY OF FRIENDS

316   Bacon, Margaret. As The Way Opens: The Story of Quaker Women
       in America. Richmond, Ind.: Friends United Press, 1981. xiv,
       132 pp.
            This popularly written survey by the much-published Quaker
       author treats Colonial Quaker women, educators, ministers, re-
       formers, abolitionists, suffragists, and peace activists. A list
       of biographies of Quaker women completes the book.

317   Calvo, Janis. "Quaker Women Ministers in Nineteenth-Century
       America." Quaker History 63 (1974):75-93.
            Calvo's account of women who traveled as preachers empha-
       sizes these women's acceptance of many conventional female roles.

318   Dunn, Mary Maples. "Women of Light." In Women of America:
       A History (entry 16), pp. 114-36.
            Dunn contrasts Quaker theology and views of women in the
       beginnings and growth of seventeenth- and eighteenth-century
       Quakerism. Individual women discussed here include Margaret Fell,
       Jane Hoskins, Mary Dyer, Susannah Morris, and Abigail Pike. Six
       documents are included. See also Dunn's "Saints and Sisters:
       Congregational and Quaker Women in the Early Colonial Period"
       (entry 96).

319   Speizman, Milton D., and Kronick, Jane C., eds. "A Seventeenth-
       Century Quaker Women's Declaration." Signs: Journal of Women
       in Culture and Society 1 (1975):231-45.
            The editors introduce a long letter from English Quakers to
       Quakers in Philadelphia, setting forth Quaker views on the equal-
       ity of the sexes, the organization of women's meetings, and
       women's charitable duties. For further information on the lib-
       erating legacy of English Quakers to the Quakers of the American
       colonies, see the selection by Margaret Fell in Womanhood in
       Radical Protestantism, 1525-1675 (entry 98) and the article by

Elaine C. Huber, "'A Woman Must Not Speak': Quaker Women in the
English Left Wing," in Women of Spirit: Female Leadership in the
Jewish and Christian Traditions (entry 80), pp. 153-81.

320   Tolles, Frederick B., ed. Slavery and the Woman Question:
      Lucretia Mott's Diary of Her Visit to Great Britain to Attend
      the World's Anti-Slavery Convention of 1840. Haverford, Pa.:
      Friends' Historical Association, 1952.
         Tolles's introduction and Mott's journal entries shed light
      on the way in which Quaker beliefs about the spiritual equality
      of all--male and female, slave and free--shaped one important
      leader and the members of her community. Further resources on
      Mott, a Quaker minister, may be found in entry 168.

321   West, Jessamyn, ed. The Quaker Reader. New York: Viking
      Press, 1962. xviii, 523 pp.
         West's essays on the history and spirit of the Society of
      Friends and a useful historical chronology introduce this collec-
      tion of documents from three centuries of British and American
      Quakerism. Among important women represented here are Margaret
      Fell, Mary Penington, Elizabeth Fry, Caroline Fox, Elizabeth
      Buffum Chace, Hannah Whitall Smith, Helen Thomas Flexner, and
      Caroline Stephen. A bibliography is included.

      For Further Information

322   A list of biographies of Quaker women may be found in As The
      Way Opens (entry 316), pp. 129-32. Amanda Way, ·born of Quaker
      pioneers, served as an itinerant Methodist preacher until the
      Methodist Episcopal Church discontinued licensing women as local
      preachers, effecting her return to the Society of Friends where
      she served as a pastor the rest of her life. See Notable American
      Women (entry 35), 3:552-53, for biographical information about her.
      Two women with roots in the Quaker tradition who founded indepen-
      dent religious movements were Ann Lee (entry 547) and Jemima
      Wilkinson (entry 563). One resource on a British forebear of
      American Quakers is Isabel Ross, Margaret Fell: Mother of
      Quakerism (London: Longmans, Green, 1949).

323   The Quaker periodical Quaker History frequently publishes
      articles about women in the Society of Friends. For current
      scholarship on Quaker women, see Women and Religion: A Bibliog-
      raphy Selected from the ATLA Religion Database (entry 15) and the
      periodical indexes from which it was compiled; and America:
      History and Life (entry 1).

324   The Quaker publishing house, Pendle Hill Publications (Walling-
      ford, PA 19086), has produced a number of pamphlets about women,
      for example, Women and Quakerism, by Hope Elizabeth Luder, Women
      Ministers: Quaker Contribution, by Robert J. Leach, and Lucretia
      Mott Speaking, compiled by Margaret Hope Bacon. Useful background
      for a study of Quaker women may be found in J. William Frost, The
      Quaker Family in Colonial America: A Portrait of the Society of

Friends (New York: St. Martin's Press, 1973). The Catalog of the
Book and Serials Collections of the Friends Historical Library [of
Swarthmore College] (Boston: G.K. Hall, 1982-) is a multivolume
resource on Quaker history.

II.C.9. UNITARIAN UNIVERSALIST

325   Cazden, Elizabeth. Antoinette Brown Blackwell: A Biography.
      Old Westbury, N.Y.: Feminist Press, 1983. xii, 315 pp.
         This biography of Blackwell recounts her quest for higher
      education (at Oberlin College and Seminary in the 1840s) and her
      ordination to the ministry of the Congregational Church. Ordained
      in 1853, she served a parish for a year before returning to her
      activities as a reformer (chiefly for abolitionism and women's
      rights), which continued until her death a few months after she
      cast her first ballot in 1920 at age ninety-six. In 1878, she
      entered into fellowship with the Unitarians among whom she minis-
      tered in her latter years. For fuller annotation of this biog-
      raphy, see entry 331.

326   Hitchings, Catherine F. "Universalist and Unitarian Women
      Ministers." Journal of the Universalist Historical Society 10
      (1975):3-165.
         A brief introduction to women in the ordained ministry of
      the Universalist and Unitarian denominations and the merged (1961)
      Unitarian Universalist Association is followed by a biographical
      directory (with footnotes and resources) of the some 200 women who
      served in the United States. A lengthier biography of Antoinette
      Brown Blackwell, the first woman ordained in the United States--to
      the Congregational ministry in 1853, but who later was in fellow-
      ship with the Unitarians--is included. A name index provides
      access to women by their maiden names and to other women mentioned
      in the biographical sketches.

327   Miller, Russell E. "God Bless and Make Us Grateful for Our
      Women!" In The Larger Hope: The First Century of the Uni-
      versalist Church in America, 1770-1870. Boston: Unitarian
      Universalist Association, 1979, pp. 534-73.
         Surveying the position of women in the Universalist Church,
      Miller discusses women and higher learning, women and the minis-
      try, and women and literature, and also profiles some Universalist
      "movers and shapers" in the struggle for women's rights. Exten-
      sive footnotes lead the reader to further resources.

328   "Olympia Brown: A Centennial Volume Celebrating Her Ordination
      and Graduation in 1863." Annual Journal of the Universalist
      Historical Society 4 (1963). xii, 110 pp.
         Olympia Brown, ordained to the Universalist ministry in
      1863, is here claimed to be the first woman ordained in a denom-
      ination, based on the fact that Antoinette Brown Blackwell did not
      have the full ecclesiastical support of her denomination at the
      time of her ordination. The autobiography of Olympia Brown which

is reprinted here was written by her daughter, Gwendolen B. Willis, in consultation with her mother and from notes written by her mother when in her late eighties. Also included are two chapters from a book written by Brown in 1911 supporting the women's suffrage campaign and a reconstruction of two of Brown's sermons. Selections from Brown's works have been edited by Dana Greene in Suffrage and Religious Principle: Speeches and Writings of Olympia Brown, (entry 217). For more recent biographical data on Brown, see Notable American Women (entry 35), 1:256-58.

For Further Information

329   A very early Universalist laywoman, Judith Sargent Murray, in 1790 wrote a feminist exposition of the Adam and Eve story. For biographical information, see Notable American Women (entry 35), 2:603-5, and for the exposition itself, see The Feminist Papers (entry 226), pp. 18-24. The story of Mary Collson's service as a Unitarian minister in late nineteenth-century rural Iowa is told in A Woman's Ministry (entry 166). In Notable American Women (entry 36), see entries for Unitarian and Universalist ministers and activists Alice and Phoebe Cary (1:295-97), Caroline Julia Bartlett Crane (1:401-2), Augusta Jane Chapin (1:320-21), Phoebe Ann Coffin Hanaford (2:126-27), Mary A. Livermore (2:410-13), Caroline August White Soule (3:325-27), and Anna Carpenter Garlin Spencer (3:331-33).

330   For current scholarship on Unitarian Universalist women, see Women and Religion: A Bibliography Selected from the ATLA Religion Database (entry 15) and the periodical indexes from which it was compiled; America: History and Life (entry 1); and the denominational historical journals.

II.C.10.   UNITED CHURCH OF CHRIST

331   Cazden, Elizabeth. Antoinette Brown Blackwell: A Biography. Old Westbury, N.Y.: Feminist Press, 1983. xii, 315 pp.
      This biography of Blackwell recounts her struggle to obtain an education and answer a call to ordained ministry in the Congregational Church. Serving less than a year in the parish where she was ordained in 1853, Blackwell maintained no religious affiliation for the next twenty-five years until in 1878 she entered into fellowship with the Unitarians. Ministering there in her later years, Blackwell was also a leader of the woman's suffrage movement. She voted in 1920, a few months before her death at the age of ninety-six. Correspondence between Antoinette Brown and her Oberlin schoolmate Lucy Stone (1818-93) has been edited by Carol Lasser and Marlene Merrill in Soul Mates: The Oberlin Correspondence of Lucy Stone and Antoinette Brown, 1846-1850 (Oberlin, Ohio: Oberlin College, 1983). See also entry 133.

332   Rasche, Ruth W. "The Deaconess Sisters: Pioneer Professional
       Women." In Hidden Histories in the United Church of Christ,
       edited by Barbara Brown Zikmund. New York: United Church
       Press, 1984, pp. 95-109.
          Beginning with a description of the revival of deaconess
       work at Kaiserswerth, Germany, in the middle of the nineteenth
       century, Rasche then traces the development of the deaconess move-
       ment in the Evangelical Synod with an emphasis on the opportuni-
       ties it created for women in health care and social services. In
       his biography of the father of Reinhold and Richard Niebuhr (A
       Father's Mantle: The Legacy of Gustav Niebuhr [New York: Pilgrim
       Press, 1982]), William G. Chrystal devotes nearly a chapter to the
       elder Niebuhr's championing of the deaconess movement in the
       Evangelical Synod.

333   Taylor, Sandra C. "Abby M. Colby: The Christian Response to
       a Sexist Society." New England Quarterly 52 (1979):68-79.
       Also "Sisterhood of Salvation and the Sunrise Kingdom: Congre-
       gational Women Missionaries in Meiji, Japan" (entry 186).
          Congregational women missionaries are here discussed in the
       larger context of women's secular and religious rights issues.
       Congregational women were heavily involved in the nineteenth-
       century missions movement and are prominently featured in the
       historical literature. For example, in section II.B.3 see
       entries 172, 178, 180-81, and 187.

334   Withers, Barbara A. Women of Faith and Our History. Phila-
       delphia: United Church Press, 1976. 17 pp.
          This survey of women's participation in the traditions that
       have formed the United Church of Christ emphasizes the contribu-
       tions of eminent individual women, including Anne Bradstreet, Anne
       Marbury Hutchinson, Mercy Otis Warren, Abigail Smith Adams, Emma
       Hart Willard, Sarah Pierce, Nancy Gove Cram, Abigail Roberts, and
       Cynthia Farrar.

335   Zikmund, Barbara Brown. "Abigail Roberts: 'Female Laborer'
       in Christian Churches." Historical Intelligencer 2 (1982):
       3-10.
          After being converted under the preaching of Nancy Cram in
       upstate New York in 1814, Abigail Roberts conducted a wide-ranging
       (though unordained) preaching ministry in the churches of this
       frontier denomination until her death in 1841. This is a bio-
       graphical account.

336   Zikmund, Barbara Brown, and Dries, Sally A. "Women's Work and
       Woman's Boards." In Hidden Histories in the United Church of
       Christ, edited by Barbara Brown Zikmund. New York: United
       Church Press, 1984, pp. 140-53.
          This article surveys the organization and attitudes that
       supported women's missionary activities from the early nineteenth
       century into the twentieth, through the women's boards of each of
       the four denominations that have since joined to become the U.C.C.
       Helpful notes will lead researchers to many primary sources. The
       anthology from which this essay comes, edited by Zikmund and with

her historiographical introduction, also includes articles on various ethnic constituences within the denomination, advocating a broader consciousness of the diversity within a denomination's history.

For Further Information

The United Church of Christ is a young denomination, born in a 1957 merger. The four major streams from which it flowed (the Congregational churches, the Christian Connection, the Evangelical Synod, and the [German] Reformed Church) have much longer historical records. Congregationalism, the established church in most of the New England colonies, is probably the most studied branch of American Protestantism on account of its cultural hegemony in a very influential region, though the historical literature emphasizes its character as a denomination less than its cultural, social, and theological aspects. Puritans were Congregationalists (see section II.A.1 of this bibliography), and Congregational women are also strongly represented in the sources on evangelical religion, domesticity, education, and benevolence (section II.B.1), reform movements (II.B.2), missionaries (II.B.3), ordained ministry (II.B.4), and literature (II.B.7).

337   The Historical Intelligencer (1981-), the historical journal of the denomination, often includes articles on the history of women. For other current scholarship, see Women and Religion: A Bibliography Selected from the ATLA Religion Database (entry 15) and the periodical indexes from which it was compiled, and America: History and Life (entry 1).

II.C.11.   INTERDENOMINATIONAL

338   Calkins, Gladys Gilkey.   Follow Those Women: Church Women in the Ecumenical Movement.   New York: National Council of Churches, 1961.   108 pp.
       A second subtitle for this book tells the reader that it is "A History of the Development of United Work Among Women of the Protestant Churches in the United States."   Calkins draws together the threads of cooperative work among Protestant women from the mid-nineteenth century to the founding in 1941 of the United Council of Church Women, which in 1950 became the "General Department of United Church Women" of the National Council of the Churches of Christ in the United States of America.

339   Shannon, Margaret.   Just Because: The Story of the National Movement of Church Women United in the U.S.A., 1941 through 1975.   Corte Madera, Calif.:   Omega Books, 1977.   464 pp.
       This book by the executive director of Church Women United, a large orgnization of Protestant, Roman Catholic, and Orthodox women, draws on C.W.U. records and its publication, the Church Woman.   Topics treated include international peace concerns, human rights, social action, and ecumenism.

III. Roman Catholicism

340   Allen, Christine. "Women in Colonial French America." In
      Women and Religion in America, vol. 2 (entry 79), pp. 79-131.
          Strongly influenced by the Roman Catholic Counter-
      Reformation, some early French settlers in the New World were
      determined to establish a world order free of class, sex, and
      racial barriers. This chapter describes six women who, between
      1600 and 1800, "seemed to exemplify the best kind of Christian
      vocations in New France" (p. 80). They founded hospitals, schools,
      and religious orders, and one of them (Kateri Tekakwitha) was a
      well-known Christian mystic. Along with description of the his-
      torical context and biographical information, the chapter provides
      excerpts from primary sources by and about the women.

341   Billington, Ray Allen. The Protestant Crusade 1800-1860:
      A Study of the Origins of American Nativism. New York:
      Macmillan, 1938. Also several reprints. 514 pp.
          This classic work on the pre-Civil War anti-Catholic move-
      ment contains a full account of the burning of the Charlestown,
      Massachusetts, Ursuline convent and the acquittal of those accused
      in 1834. The exploitation by Protestant leaders of the writings
      of two women who claimed to have escaped from the Hotel Dieu con-
      vent in Montreal is chronicled and an extensive bibliography of
      primary sources is included. A slightly revised version of the
      account of the convent burning appeared in Billington's article
      "The Burning of the Charlestown Convent," New England Quarterly
      10 (1937):4-24.

342   Cuneen, Sally. Sex: Female; Religion: Catholic. New York:
      Holt, Rinehart, & Winston, 1968. xv, 171 pp.
          Cuneen reports the results of a 1965 survey of Roman Catho-
      lic opinion about women. The detailed questionnaire dealt with
      issues such as sex, birth control, marriage, celibacy, women's
      theology, etc. Although the material was quickly dated and the
      questionnaire inadequate--both acknowledged by the author--she
      provided an important opportunity for women to speak for them-
      selves about these issues and the work thus serves as a primary
      source for the period.

343   Foley, Nadine. "Women in Vatican Documents, 1960 to the Pres-
       ent." In Sexism and Church Law: Equal Rights and Affirmative
       Action, edited by James A. Coriden. New York: Paulist Press,
       1977, pp. 82-108.
           Surveying selected texts from official Vatican documents,
       Foley concludes that they reflect a distinctive "ontology of
       women" and upon that rests a specific theology of woman. This
       ontology and theology have served as the foundation upon which the
       church's treatment of women is based and the author calls for a
       new anthropology with a fresh look at authority and ministry in
       the church.

344   Iadarola, Antoinette. "The American Catholic Bishops and
       Women: From the Nineteenth Amendment to ERA." In Women,
       Religion and Social Change (entry 64), pp. 457-67.
           This chronological treatment examines views of women as
       illustrated in the official documents of the Roman Catholic
       hierarchy through the twentieth century.

345   Kenneally, James J. "Catholic and Feminist: A Biographical
       Approach." U.S. Catholic Historian 3 (1984):229-53.
           Kenneally provides lengthy biographical accounts of three
       Roman Catholic lay women who, while remaining dedicated to the
       institutional church, which opposed political, social, and eco-
       nomic equality with men, "publicly espoused female equality and
       pursued non-traditional, self-assertive careers" (p. 229). The
       women are poet Mary Elizabeth Blake (1840-1907), labor reformer
       Mary Kenney O'Sullivan (1864-1943), and suffagist Margaret Foley
       (1875-1957).

346   Kenneally, James J. "Eve, Mary and the Historians: American
       Catholicism and Women." In Women in American Religion (entry
       75), pp. 191-206.
           Reviewing Roman Catholicism's early encounters with the suf-
       fragist movement, female education, and women working outside the
       home, Kenneally goes on to describe later efforts of the church to
       reconcile with these exigencies of American life and urges Ameri-
       can Catholic historians to consider the historical role of women.

347   Kenneally, James J. "Catholicism and Woman Suffrage in Massa-
       chusetts." Catholic Historical Review 53 (1967):43-57.
           The author catalogs various efforts by Roman Catholic
       leaders in politically liberal Massachusetts to prevent the exten-
       sion of voting rights to women. A critical factor in this move-
       ment was late nineteenth-century anti-Catholic nativism and the
       use of women's suffrage as a means of defending Protestantism.

348   Lavrin, Asuncion. "Women and Religion in Spanish America." In
       Women and Religion in America, vol. 2 (entry 79), pp. 42-78.
           The religious life--in cloistered convents or in lay Third
       Orders--was a very popular alternative for increasing numbers of
       marginalized women in colonial New Spain. This chapter treats
       women's religious vocation in that particular historical context
       in Mexico and Central and South America and provides a collection

of documents illustrating various aspects of that experience ranging from the founding of convents to the writings of a mystic.

349 McCarthy, Esther. "Catholic Women and the War: The National
     Council of Catholic Women, 1919-1946." Peace and Change 5
     (1978):23-32.
          The National Council of Catholic Women, established as a
     committee of the National Catholic War Council (later renamed the
     National Catholic Welfare Conference), reflected the conservative
     attitude of its parent organization on the war issue during both
     world wars. McCarthy illustrates from organizational literature
     that men and women were given different justification for the
     necessity of war and participation in war efforts.

350 Patrick, Anne E. "Women and Religion: A Survey of Significant
     Literature, 1965-1974." Theological Studies 36 (December 1975):
     737-65. Also in Woman: New Dimensions, edited by Walter J.
     Burghardt. New York: Paulist Press, 1977, pp. 161-89.
          Four types of literature are presented in this bibliographi-
     cal essay: "general analysis of the 'current' situation"; histori-
     cal studies; works on selected issues; and "constructive efforts
     and radical challenges." She updates this work with a focus on
     the ordination of women as priests in "Studies on Women Priests,"
     in Women Priests: A Catholic Commentary on the Vatican Declara-
     tion (entry 379), pp. 70-74.

351 Rosenberg, Florence R., et al. Women and Ministry: A Survey
     of the Experience of Roman Catholic Women in the United States.
     Washington, D.C.: Center for Applied Research in the Aposto-
     late, 1980. 241 pp.
          An extensive national study undertaken for the Leadership
     Conference of Women Religious focused first on women as ministers
     and second on women as recipients of the church's ministry. Most
     of the women-in-ministry tended to favor some change as opposed to
     retaining tradition and approved some expansion of women's par-
     ticipation in the church. About two thirds of the women who were
     recipients of the church's ministry experienced no problems in
     this regard while about one third expressed difficulties with the
     exclusive maleness of the clergy and lack of decision-making power
     in the church.

352 Swidler, Arlene. "Creative Teaching: Women in American
     Catholic History." Horizons 10 (1983):334-40.
          From her own experience in teaching the history of American
     Catholic women at the university level, Swidler makes recommenda-
     tions and lists a variety of resources for that endeavor.

353 Weaver, Mary Jo. New Catholic Women: A Contemporary Challenge
     to Traditional Religious Authority. San Francisco: Harper &
     Row, 1985. xviii, 270 pp.
          Weaver provides a helpful survey of the historical expe-
     rience of American Catholic women, covering a range of topics in-
     cluding women in the parish, sisters and the women's movement,

Roman Catholic feminist theologians and feminist spirituality, and the women's ordination movement.

For Further Information

354   Two general histories that serve as background in this area are Jay Dolan, <u>American Catholic Experience: A History from Colonial Times to the Present</u> (New York: Doubleday, 1985), and James Hennessey, <u>American Catholics: A History of the Roman Catholic Community in the United States</u> (New York: Oxford University Press, 1981). Very helpful in locating further information is John Tracy Ellis and Robert Trisco, <u>A Guide to American Catholic History</u>, 2d ed. (Santa Barbara, Calif.: ABC-CLIO, 1982), an annotated bibliography of sources that includes many about women among its 1,258 entries.

355   The <u>U.S. Catholic Historian</u>, published quarterly by the U.S. Catholic Historical Society, has provided several articles on women's history in recent years: "Catholic Women: Service to God and the Community" 2 (Winter 1982); "'I Can't Imagine Our Lady on an Outdoor Platform': Women in the Catholic Street Propaganda Movement" 3 (Spring-Summer 1983); "The Self-Image of Three Philadelphia Catholic Intellectuals" (two of them are women) 3 (Spring-Summer 1985); "The Grail Movement to 1962: Laywomen and a New Christendom" 3 (Fall-Winter 1983); and "Catholic and Feminist: A Biographical Approach" (entry 345). Vol. 3, no. 1 (1983) was devoted to an overview of organizations dealing with American Catholic history.

356   The index volume of Andrea Hinding's monumental compendium of primary sources <u>Women's History Sources: A Guide to Archives and Manuscript Collections in the United States</u> (entry 41) contains a large number of entries under the headings "Catholic" and "Sisters" as well as under the names of organizations and individual women.

357   For a subject approach to contemporary and historical material in the Catholic periodical literature, consult the <u>Catholic Periodical and Literature Index</u> (entry 12). <u>Origins</u>, published since 1971 by the independent National Catholic News Service in Washington, D.C., is an excellent guide to current Catholic opinion. It reproduces official documents together with background and bibliographical notes.

358   Documentary material that illuminates official Roman Catholic attitudes toward women may be approached by way of <u>The Papal Encyclicals 1740-1980</u>, edited by Claudia Carlen (Wilmington, N.C.: McGrath Pub. Co., 1981), a five-volume set of the teachings of eighteen popes with lists of commentaries and comprehensive subject index. The <u>Official Catholic Teachings</u> series (Wilmington, N.C.: McGrath Pub. Co., 1978) and the <u>Papal Teachings</u> series (Boston: Daughters of St. Paul, 1959-67) each contain a volume of documents about women and sexuality issues.

359   For a variety of opinions as to the role that women played in
      the Nativist movement see David H. Bennett, "Women in the Nativist
      Movement," in "Remember the Ladies": New Perspectives on Women in
      American History: Essays in Honor of Nelson Manfred Blake, edited
      by Carol V.R. George (Syracuse: Syracuse University Press, 1975),
      pp. 71-89, and Jean Gould Hales, "'Co-Laborers in the Cause':
      Women in the Ante-bellum Nativist Movement," Civil War History 25
      (1979):119-38.

360   For information about the cult of Mary in the United States,
      see Anna Wirtz Domas's Mary: U.S.A. (Huntington, Ind.: Our
      Sunday Visitor, 1978). Although her approach is very traditional
      and contains no analysis, Domas has collected and presented a
      large number of pictures that reflect a widespread devotion to
      Mary throughout the history of the United States.

III.B.   WOMEN RELIGIOUS

III.B.1.   HISTORICAL WORKS

361   Bradshaw, Sue. "Catholic Sisters in China: An Effort to Raise
      the Status of Women." In Women in China: Current Directions
      in Historical Scholarship, edited by Richard W. Guisso and
      Stanley Johannesen. Youngstown, N.Y.: Philo Press, 1981,
      pp. 201-13.
         Bradshaw provides a thoroughgoing but concise survey of the
      missionary service of Catholic sisters in China from the middle of
      the nineteenth century to 1949.

362   Curb, Rosemary, and Manahan, Nancy, eds. Lesbian Nuns: Break-
      ing Silence. Tallahassee, Fla.: Naiad Press, Inc., 1985.
      xliii, 383 pp.
         Because the publication of this book was attended by nega-
      tive publicity, the reader might miss the value of its helpful
      collection of first-person accounts by some fifty women who en-
      tered religious orders in the 1950s and 1960s. Some of the women
      have remained in their orders, some have left; some are open
      lesbians, some write with pseudonyms. All have insightful re-
      flections on their motivations for entering religious life and
      about the significant changes that have come within many of those
      orders during the last several decades.

363   Ewens, Mary. The Role of the Nun in Nineteenth-Century
      America: Variations on the International Theme. New York:
      Arno Press, 1978. 427 pp.
         Ewens provides an interdisciplinary look at role conflicts
      experienced by American nuns who tried to live according to canon
      laws based on medieval European concepts of women. Not able to
      counter the anti-Catholic ideas about them reflected in the popu-
      lar literature of the antebellum period, sisters found that atti-
      tudes changed from hostility to acceptance and respect as a result
      of their continuing interaction with the American people. Canon
      law changes came in 1900 but thorough adaptation of religious life
      to the needs of American culture did not happen until the 1960s.

An extensive bibliography includes histories of religious communities and nursing, as well as lists of novels and popular literature.

364   Ewens, Mary. "Removing the Veil: The Liberated American Nun."
        In Women of Spirit: Female Leadership in the Jewish and
        Christian Traditions (entry 80), pp. 256-78.
             This is a brief overview of some of the points made in her
        complete study (entry 363), aimed at encouraging the study of
        American nuns. A three-page bibliography of sources appears at
        the end of the article.

365   Ewens, Mary. "The Leadership of Nuns in Immigrant Catholi-
        cism." In Women and Religion in America, vol. 1 (entry 78),
        pp. 101-49.
             Introductory material surveys the work of nuns and is fol-
        lowed by photographs and a series of documents ranging from the
        letter granting approval of the constitution of the first indige-
        nous American women's order to an excerpt from the trial transcript
        describing the burning of the Ursuline convent in Charlestown,
        Massachusetts.

366   Kolmer, Elizabeth. "Catholic Women Religious and Women's His-
        tory: A Survey of the Literature." In Women in American Reli-
        gion (entry 75), pp. 127-39.
             This bibliographical essay is the starting point for research
        in this subject. Kolmer evaluates the existing literature,
        identifies bibliographical aids, indicates archival and other
        sources, surveys scholarly works on American religious history,
        the histories of individual congregations and biographies of
        foundresses, and unpublished dissertations on the role of sisters,
        and, finally, comments on the materials available for studying the
        relationship of Catholic sisters to the women's movement of the
        1960s and 1970s.

367   Kolmer, Elizabeth. Religious Women in the United States:
        Survey of the Influential Literature from 1950 to 1983.
        Wilmington, Del.: Michael Glazier, 1984. 111 pp.
             Concisely surveying the renewal of religious orders since
        1950, Kolmer reviews the literature and provides a bibliography of
        primary and secondary sources that document the profound changes
        in the life of sisters in the United States over the three decades.

368   Oates, Mary J. "Organized Voluntarism: The Catholic Sisters
        in Massachustts, 1870-1940." In Women in American Religion
        (entry 75), pp. 141-69.
             Using women's community archival materials in the Arch-
        diocese of Boston, Oates surveys the membership and work of the
        sisters who staffed most of the church's charitable and educa-
        tional institutions. A significant percentage of sisters moved
        into parochial school teaching as early as 1880, and this examina-
        tion of teacher recruitment, demand for parish schools, class
        size, inadequate and sex-segregated compensation, and lack of

parish support and training opportunities illustrates how the women subsidized that parochial school system.

369   Rector, Theresa A.   "Black Nuns as Educators." Journal of
        Negro Education 51 (1982):238-53.
        About three quarters of the black Roman Catholic nuns in the United States belong to three black religious communities. This article presents brief historical sketches and the current status of these orders: the Oblate Sisters of Providence, the Sisters of the Holy Family, and the Franciscan Handmaids of Mary.

370   Thomas, Evangeline. Women Religious History Sources: A Guide
        to Repositories. New York: R.R. Bowker, 1983. xxvii, 329 pp.
        This guide to source materials in archives and manuscript collections of women religious reports the results of a survey of more than 500 repositories of congregational collections of Roman Catholic and non-Catholic sisterhoods and deaconess orders in the United States. The guide represents approximately 98 percent of the medium and large Motherhouse archives and most of the smaller archives maintained in the continental United States. Each collection is fully described and cross-referenced. A table of founding dates, biographical register of foundresses and major superiors, and a name-place index are included.

III.B.2.   SOCIOLOGICAL WORKS

371   Bernstein, Marcelle.   The Nuns. Philadelphia: Lippincott Co.,
        1976. 326 pp.
        Here a British journalist of Jewish heritage provides a readable and thorough survey of women religious. A particular strength of the book is its placing of contemporary developments within historical perspective.

372   Chittister, Joan, et al. Climb Along the Cutting Edge: An
        Analysis of Change in Religious Life. New York: Paulist
        Press, 1977. 304 pp.
        Utilizing the results of a survey of leaders who were involved in religious life changes during the decade 1966-76, five Benedictine sisters focus on five areas: religious life prior to 1966, the dynamics of renewal, the Vatican II context for renewal, the development of Benedictine monasticism, and the personal effects of change.

373   Ebaugh, Helen Rose Fuchs. Out of the Cloister: A Study of
        Organizational Dilemmas. Austin: University of Texas Press,
        1977. 155 pp.
        This book provides an organizational analysis of a movement in American female religious orders away from a "cloistered enclosed way of life toward a more open and socially involved existence" (p. xi). The author, a former nun and trained sociologist, looks at that movement from historical, sociological, and social psychological perspectives and concludes that religious orders must be able to assist members in achieving their own

personal growth and development goals and in providing meaningful corporate goals.

374   Neal, Marie Augusta. Catholic Sisters in Transition: From the
      1960's to the 1980's. Wilmington, Del.: Michael Glazier,
      1984. 173 pp.
           Based on data collected in surveys conducted in 1966 and
      1982, this report examines and compares information ranging from
      the numbers of sisters entering and leaving orders to their opin-
      ions on various aspects of religious life.

375   SanGiovanni, Lucinda F. Ex-Nuns: A Study of Emergent Role
      Passage. Norwood, N.J.: Ablex Pub. Corp., 1978. 184 pp.
           This sociological inquiry is intended to illuminate the
      passage from one social role into a new one by Roman Catholic nuns
      who, in the late 1960s and early 1970s, left their convents to
      begin secular lives. They are representative of persons at the
      social frontier who, because their changes are not institutional-
      ized in the society, must shape their own passage. The focus is
      on their process of adaptation to life on the outside.

III.C. THE ORDINATION OF WOMEN

376   Dwyer, Maureen, ed. New Woman, New Church, New Priestly Min-
      istry: Proceedings of the Second Conference on the Ordination
      of Roman Catholic Women, November 10-12, 1978. Baltimore,
      Maryland. Rochester, N.Y.: Women's Ordination Conference,
      1980. 178 pp.
           This publication includes, in addition to the "formal" pre-
      sentations, a description of and commentary on the design and
      process of the conference, reports from participant discussions,
      and texts of the conference liturgical events.

377   Gardiner, Anne Marie, ed. Women and Catholic Priesthood, An
      Expanded Vision: Proceedings of the Detroit Ordination Con-
      ference. New York: Paulist Press, 1976. 259 pp.
           This work includes papers, liturgical celebrations, process
      reflections, and the list of participants for the first Roman
      Catholic Ordination Conference (1975), and concludes with a
      selected bibliography, 1965-75.

378   Ruether, Rosemary. "Entering the Sanctuary: The Roman Catho-
      lic Story." In Women of Spirit: Female Leadership in the
      Jewish and Christian Traditions (entry 80), pp. 373-83.
           This brief history of the contemporary Roman Catholic
      women's ordination movement begins with the St. Joan's Inter-
      National Alliance in the late 1950s and concludes with commentary
      on the Vatican Declaration against the ordination of women issued
      in early 1977.

379   Swidler, Leonard, and Swidler, Arlene, eds. Women Priests: A
      Catholic Commentary on the Vatican Declaration. New York:
      Paulist Press, 1977. 352 pp.

This paragraph-by-paragraph commentary on the Vatican
declaration against the ordination of women as priests covers the
subjects of historical tradition, the attitude of Christ, the
practice of the Apostles, contemporary application of these attitudes and practices, the ministerial priesthood, the mystery of
Christ and the mystery of the Church, and includes a bibliography
by Anne E. Patrick entitled "Studies on Women Priests" (pp. 70-
74).

380   Weaver, Mary Jo. "Ordination, Collective Power, and Sister-
       hood: Foundations for the Future." In New Catholic Women: A
       Contemporary Challenge to Traditional Religious Authority
       (entry 353), pp. 109-44.
       Weaver's essay from her summary of Roman Catholic women's
historical and contemporary issues traces the women's ordination
movement from its initial demand for "equal rights" for women's
priestly ordination to its concern and demand for fundamental
institutional structural change before such ordinations should
take place. A bibliography is included.

For Further Information

381   Listed above is a very limited selection of works about the
       ordination of women to the priesthood of the Roman Catholic
       church, mostly those which describe the historical development of
       the movement in the United States. Women Priests: A Catholic
       Commentary on the Vatican Declaration (entry 379) gathers
       material on the broad range of issues related to the
       ordination of women to the priesthood: biblical, theological,
       ecumenical, and psychological, as well as historical. See also
       "Canon Law and the Battle of the Sexes," in Religion and Sexism:
       Images of Woman in the Jewish and Christian Traditions (entry 67).
       The literature in the field is extensive and may be further ap-
       proached in several ways. In addition to bibliographies in the
       indicated works annotated above, the reader may consult "Can We
       Not Also Break Bread: A Bibliography on the Ordination of Women,"
       compiled by Myriel Crowley Eykamp (Rochester, N.Y.: Women's
       Ordination Conference, 1979) and the Catholic Periodical and
       Literature Index (entry 12).

III.D. THEOLOGY

382   Daly, Mary. The Church and the Second Sex. 2d ed. New York:
       Harper & Row, 1975. 229 pp.
       The first edition of this work, published in 1968 when Daly
saw herself as a Roman Catholic philosopher-theologian, reflects
a view that the church was guilty of contributing to the subjec-
tion of women but was nevertheless capable of radical transforma-
tion. She repudiates this in her autobiographical "new feminist
postchristian" introduction to the 1975 edition, asserting that
the church is hopelessly sexist and oppressive. For further
development of her thought, see her Beyond God the Father: Toward
a Philosophy of Women's Liberation (Boston: Beacon Press, 1973),
Gyn/Ecology: The Metaethics of Radical Feminism (Boston: Beacon

Press, 1978), and Pure Lust: Elemental Feminist Philosophy
(Boston: Beacon Press, 1984).

383   Fiorenza, Elisabeth Schüssler. In Memory of Her: A Feminist
       Theological Reconstruction of Christian Origins. New York:
       Crossroad Publishing Co., 1983. xxv, 351 pp.
            Although her official field of study is New Testament, the
       depth of the theological reflection in all of Fiorenza's work and
       her self-identification as a Catholic feminist earn her the addi-
       tional title "Catholic theologian." Her major work, exceptionally
       well exemplified in this book, is (as the subtitle suggests) that
       of a critical feminist hermeneutical approach to the scriptures.
       Only in this way, she says, can scriptures be claimed as an
       empowering resource for women. Her methodology is described in
       her Bread Not Stone: The Challenge of Feminist Biblical Inter-
       pretation, (Boston: Beacon Press, 1984). See also entries 51
       and 58.

384   Ruether, Rosemary Radford. Liberation Theology: Human Hope
       Confronts Christian History and American Power. New York:
       Paulist Press, 1972. 194 pp.
            Holding classical Christianity's soul-body dualism responsi-
       ble for Western cultural oppression, Ruether challenges the church
       to integrate the dualism. Building on this in New Woman, New
       Earth: Sexist Ideologies and Human Liberation (New York: Seabury
       Press, 1975), she sees the liberation of women as the key to over-
       coming patterns of dualistic thinking. In To Change the World:
       Christology and Cultural Criticism (New York: Crossroad Press,
       1981), she reflects on domination and empowerment issues inherent
       in traditional Christology and in methodology for feminist theol-
       ogy. For autobiographical thought on her self-identification as
       a Catholic Christian, see "Beginnings: An Intellectual Auto-
       biography," in Journeys: the Impact of Personal Experience on
       Religious Thought, edited by Gregory Baum (New York: Paulist
       Press, 1975), pp. 34-56, and for wide-ranging personal reflection
       on critical issues of the Christian faith, see her Disputed Ques-
       tions: On Being a Christian (Nashville: Abingdon Press, 1982).
       Consult the name index of this volume for other works edited by
       Ruether.

385   Weaver, Mary Jo. "Enlarging the Discipline: Roman Catholic
       Feminist Theologians." In New Catholic Women: A Contemporary
       Challenge to Traditional Religious Authority (entry 353),
       pp. 146-49.
            Weaver's essay surveys Roman Catholic feminist theology be-
       ginning with the theology of Alfred North Whitehead and Karl
       Rahner, on whose work "many of the creative insights of 20th cen-
       tury Roman Catholic theology rest," and concluding with substantive
       descriptions of the work of Anne Carr, Elisabeth Schussler
       Fiorenza, Rosemary Radford Ruether, and Mary Daly.

For Further Information

386   For a summary and commentary on Daly, Ruether and other feminist theologians, see Carter Heyward's "Reuther and Daly: Theologians Speaking and Sparking, Building and Burning." Christianity and Crisis 39 (April 2, 1979):66-72. See also "Methodology"
section of Chapter IC in this bibliography and issues of Catholic
Periodical and Literature Index (entry 12).

III.E. INDIVIDUAL WOMEN

387   Sidney Cornelia Callahan (1933-).
        In Why Catholic?, edited by John J. Delaney ([Garden City,
N.Y.: Doubleday, 1979], pp. 15-33), this educator and writer describes her conversion to Roman Catholicism as an adult after
growing up in the Bible-belt South, noting that her experience of
the church was not anti-intellectual, that it was racially and by
class inclusive, and that it was feminine and motherly. She calls
for improved leadership in the church, opening it to women, including ordination as priests and bishops. Callahan has written
a number of books and articles about women and the family and
values, including The Illusion of Eve: Modern Woman's Quest for
Identity (New York: Sheed & Ward, 1965) and (with her husband
Daniel Callahan, coeditor) Abortion: Understanding Differences
(New York: Plenum Press, 1984).

388   Dorothy Day (1897-1980)
        The life of this radical activist and journalist is told in
William D. Miller's Dorothy Day: A Biography (San Francisco:
Harper & Row, 1982); see also Miller's A Harsh and Dreadful Love:
Dorothy Day and the Catholic Worker Movement (New York: Liveright,
1973). The best account of the movement Day founded and led is
Mel Piehl's Breaking Bread: The Catholic Worker and the Origin of
Catholic Radicalism in America (Philadelphia: Temple University
Press, 1982). An account of her life that emphasizes the news-
paper she founded, edited, and wrote for is Nancy L. Roberts's
Dorothy Day and the Catholic Worker (Albany: State University of
New York Press, 1985). Further information may be found in
Dorothy Day and The Catholic Worker: A Bibliography and Index,
by Anne and Alice Klejment (New York: Garland Press, 1984).
Readers will also wish to consult Day's own works, especially her
autobiography, The Long Loneliness (1952; reprint, with introduc-
tion by Daniel Berrigan [San Francisco: Harper & Row, 1981]).
An excerpt is in Journeys: Autobiographical Writings by Women
(entry 77), pp. 195-211. An extensive selection from her writings
is found in By Little and By Little: The Selected Writings of
Dorothy Day, edited by Robert Ellsberg (New York: Alfred A.
Knopf, 1983).

389   Mary McCarthy (1912-)
        In her popular Memories of a Catholic Girlhood (New York:
Harcourt Brace, 1957), this journalist and well-known personality
describes her early family life in the Midwest and education in a

convent school. McCarthy has continued to produce fiction,
essays, and other literature, amassing a considerable body of
work.

390   Flannery O'Connor (1925-64)
       Her biography in Notable American Women: The Modern Period
(entry 36), 2:512-15, highlights the strong Roman Catholic faith of
this Southern author and the ways it manifested itself in her
writing. A bibliography leads to further sources, but to it must
be added Sally Fitzgerald's Letters of Flannery O'Connor: The
Habit of Being (New York: Vintage Books, 1979) and a discussion
of O'Connor's theology in "Flannery O'Connor's Literary Biography," by Lorine M. Getz, in Flannery O'Connor: Her Life,
Library and Book Reviews (New York: Edwin Mellen Press, 1980),
pp. 3-55. For bibliographic guidance to O'Connor's works, see
essay in American Women Writers: Bibliographical Essays (entry
231) and exhaustive bibliographical coverage in Flannery O'Connor
and Caroline Gordon: A Reference Guide, by Robert E. Golden and
Mary C. Sullivan (Boston: G.K. Hall, 1977).

391   Elizabeth Ann Bayley Seton (1774-1821)
       Biographical treatment of the founder of the first sister-
hood in the United States and recently canonized saint may be seen
in Notable American Women (entry 35), 3:263-65. Full-length biographies of her are listed there and modern discussion of her
spiritual life may be found in Feminine Spirituality in America:
From Sarah Edwards to Martha Graham (entry 234), pp. 110-19,
137-38. A collection of her writings appears in Elizabeth Seton:
Selected Writings, edited by Annabelle Melville and Ellin M. Kelly
(New York: Paulist Press, 1984).

       For Further Information

392   Notable American Women (entry 35) and Notable American Women:
The Modern Period (entry 36) contain biographies of more than
seventy Roman Catholic leaders. Most of them may be located by
consulting the classified lists of biographies under such headings
as "missionaries," "religion," "religious educators," "religious
founders and leaders," and "school founders and administrators."
A biography of each woman is followed by bibliographical references for further study.

IV. Judaism

393   Baum, Charlotte; Hyman, Paula; and Michel, Sonya. The Jewish
Woman in America. New York: American Library, 1975. xiii,
290 pp.
   In this historical survey, the authors draw on memoirs,
biographies, and literature to depict the daily lives of Jewish
women, especially in the late nineteenth and early twentieth centuries. The book is also a general social and cultural history,
with chapters on women in the Jewish tradition, German Jewish
women in America, Eastern European Jewish women in the old country and America, Jewish women in labor unions, and relations among
Jewish women of different classes and origins. The last two chapters discuss women in Jewish-American fiction, analyzing and com-
batting the stereotypes found there. An extensive bibliography
completes the work.

394   Beck, Evelyn Torton, ed. Nice Jewish Girls: A Lesbian
Anthology. Watertown, Mass.: Persephone Press, 1982.
xxxix, 286 pp.
   Beck has collected here 29 first-person accounts by Jewish
lesbians that are particularly helpful in their dual examination
of and reflection on religious-cultural and sexuality-based oppression in twentieth-century Western experience.

395   Braude, Ann. "The Jewish Woman's Encounter with American Culture." In Women and Religion in America, vol. 1 (entry 78),
pp. 150-92.
   Braude's introductory essay describes the different heri-
tages of Sephardic, German, and East European Jews and traces the
expanding role of women as these immigrant groups became Ameri-
canized. She then introduces excerpts from the writings of the
following women: Rebecca Gratz (early nineteenth-century educator), Rose Kohler (an artist prominent in Reform Judaism late in
the century), Anzia Yezierska (feminist novelist), Lucy Robins
Lang (labor union leader), Ray Frank Litman (learned Reform leader
and ad hoc rabbi), and Hannah Greenebaum Solomon (founder of the
National Council of Jewish Women in 1893).

396   Cohen, Steven Martin. "American Jewish Feminism: A Study in
       Conflicts and Compromises." American Behavioral Scientist 23
       (March-April 1980):519-58.
            Cohen depicts feminism and Judaism as "systems" divided by
       "substantive differences" and explores the variety of ways in
       which Jewish feminists reduce "conflict" between them. His scheme
       relies heavily on social and scientific theory, but the article
       contains much useful information on the history and dilemmas of
       Jewish feminism in the 1970s, based primarily on interviews with
       its leaders.

397   Glanz, Rudolf. The Jewish Woman in America: Two Female Immi-
       grant Generations, 1820-1929. Vol. 1, The Eastern European
       Jewish Woman, vii, 209 pp.; vol. 2, The German Jewish Woman,
       xiii, 213 pp. New York: KTAV Publishing House, 1976.
            Glanz emphasizes the social history of Jewish women, with
       treatments of their situation in the Old World, family life, and
       work, including the leadership of Jewish women in labor unions,
       education, and social service. There is some attention to cul-
       tural activities and portrayals of women; several pages of photo-
       graphs. Glanz tends to idealize his subject, and the two volumes
       seem hastily written, but they can lead a researcher to helpful
       resources.

398   Greenberg, Blu. On Women and Judaism: A View from Tradition.
       Philadelphia: Jewish Publication Society of America, 1981.
       xi, 178 pp.
            Greenberg, a committed Orthodox Jew and a prominent advocate
       of Jewish feminism, writes in the conviction that important fem-
       inist goals can be fulfilled within law-observant Judaism. Draw-
       ing on her own experience as daughter, wife, and mother, she
       explores the theoretical basis of women's equality in Judaism and
       such issues as liturgy, divorce, and abortion. Her appreciation
       of the religious benefits of the Orthodox way of life is evident
       throughout, especially in her chapter on niddah and mikveh (sexual
       abstinence during and after menstruation, and the subsequent
       ritual bath).

399   Gross, Rita. "Female God Language in a Jewish Context." In
       Womanspirit Rising: A Feminist Reader in Religion (entry 59),
       pp. 167-73.
            Gross presents a theological proposal for developing "an
       imagery of bisexual androgynous deity by reintroducing the image
       of God as female to complement the image of God as male" (p. 168),
       an option that she sees as consistent with Jewish theism. Follow-
       ing this article in the anthology are three rituals, developed by
       Jewish feminists, that incorporate female God language and other
       feminist themes into traditional Jewish celebrations. Each is
       accompanied by thoughtful comments on how the authors arrived at
       these ritual formulations. See Naomi Janowitz and Maggie Wenig,
       "Sabbath Prayers for Women," pp. 174-78; Judith Plaskow, "Bringing
       a Daughter into the Covenant," pp. 179-84; and Aviva Cantor, "A
       Jewish Woman's Haggadah," pp. 185-92.

400 Heschel, Susannah, ed. On Being a Jewish Feminist: A Reader.
New York: Schocken Books, 1983. xxxvi, 256 pp.
Twenty-six articles, most by notable Jewish feminists, are
divided into three parts: "Old Myths and Images," "Forging New
Identities," and "Creating a Feminist Theology of Judaism." A
glossary of relevant Hebrew and Yiddish terms is included.

401 Koltun, Elizabeth, ed. The Jewish Woman: New Perspectives.
New York: Shocken Books, 1976. xx, 194 pp.
Twenty-five articles comprise this anthology, which is
divided into sections on "Spiritual Quest," "The Life Cycle and
New Rituals," "Women in Jewish Law," "Models from Our Past,"
"Jewish Women in Modern Society," and "Women in Jewish Litera-
ture." The volume represents the positions and resources of the
Jewish feminism that emerged, especially in New York City, in the
early 1970s. Koltun and several contributors belonged to Ezrat
Nashim, a women's group formed in 1971, and to the national Jewish
Feminist Organization (active 1973-75). It is a revision and ex-
pansion of the special issue on women, also edited by Koltun, of
Response: A Contemporary Jewish Review 7 (Summer 1973). There is
also a helpful selective bibliography.

402 Kramer, Sydelle, and Masur, Jenny, eds. Jewish Grandmothers.
Boston: Beacon Press, 1976. xvi, 174 pp.
Kramer and Masur have collected the oral histories of ten
Jewish women who immigrated from Eastern Europe to the United
States early in the twentieth century. Divided into sections on
why they came to America, how they came, and how they fared, the
stories of these women are moving portraits of the experience of
immigration.

403 Lacks, Roslyn. Women and Judaism: Myth, History, and Struggle. Garden City, N.Y.: Doubleday, 1980. xii, 218 pp.
Myths about and portrayals of women in ancient and medieval
Judaism are the focus of this book. Lacks, a journalist, treats
stories from Scripture and Talmud, with special attention to Eve
and Lilith. Relevant to American Judaism are her autobiographical
"Author's Note" and the concluding chapter on the views and activities of contemporary Jewish women, including those seeking
ordination as rabbis.

404 Lebeson, Anita Libman. Recall to Life: The Jewish Woman in
America. New York: A.S. Barnes & Co., 1970. 351 pp.
Lebeson seeks to "trace the continuity of Jewish faith and
life as it was manifested by committed women aware of their
ancient heritage to which they gave their undying allegiance"
(p. 39). Her narrative begins with the arrival of seventeenth-
century Sephardic Jews and culminates in the Zionist activities
of contemporary women. Portraits of notable individuals dominate
much of the book, while the origins and activities of Jewish
women's organizations dominate the chapters on the twentieth
century.

405   Lerner, Anne Lapidus. "'Who Hast Not Made Me a Man': The
       Movement for Equal Rights for Women in American Jewry." In
       American Jewish Yearbook 77 (New York: American Jewish Com-
       mittee, 1977), pp. 3-38.
            Lerner provides a thorough and judicious account of the
       activities of Jewish feminists in the early and middle 1970s and
       the responses of various segments of American Jewry. Discussed
       are challenges to Orthodox legal practices (especially on divorce);
       the ordination of women as Reform rabbis; and debates within Con-
       servative Judaism (which receives most attention) over women's
       part in rituals, public worship, ordination, and other subjects.
       Surveys of Jewish opinion on vital issues are included.

406   Lilith (1976-).
            This Jewish feminist magazine appears irregularly, but each
       issue contains a valuable collection of articles and guides to
       events and resources. Topics treated include Jewish history, law,
       education, and ritual as they relate to women; also included are
       fiction, coverage of books and media, and a regular section--"Oy
       Vey!"--which combats the stereotyping of Jewish women. An exem-
       plary issue is no. 6 (1979), which includes Reena Sigman Friedman,
       "The Politics of Ordination," and Cynthia Ozick, "Notes Toward
       Finding the Right Question (A Vindication of the Rights of Jewish
       Women)."

407   Marcus, Jacob R. The American Jewish Woman, 1654-1980. New
       York: KTAV Publishing House, 1981. xiv, 231 pp.
            Marcus calls this book an introductory monograph and recom-
       mends that it be read in conjunction with his Documentary History
       (entry 408). His survey of American Jewish women emphasizes the
       contributions of exceptionally accomplished and articulate women.
       There are sixteen pages of photographs and a lengthy bibliographi-
       cal essay.

408   Marcus, Jacob R., ed. The American Jewish Woman: A Documen-
       tary History. New York: KTAV Publishing House, 1981. xvii,
       1047 pp.
            Marcus, director of the American Jewish Archives in
       Cincinnati, has edited and provided brief introductions to 177
       documents relating to virtually all aspects of public and private
       life. The earliest is dated 1737, the latest 1980; there are 39
       photographs.

409   Mazow, Julia Wolf, ed. The Woman Who Lost Her Names: Selected
       Writings of American Jewish Women. San Francisco: Harper &
       Row, 1980. xviii, 222 pp.
            This is an anthology of short stories and excerpts from
       longer fictional and autobiographical works.

410   Pratt, Norma Fain. "Transitions in Judaism: The Jewish Amer-
       ican Woman through the 1930's." In Women in American Religion
       (entry 75), pp. 207-28.
            Pratt argues that women gained increasing prominence in the
       public aspects of American Jewish life in the 1920s and 1930s,

even though some traditional forms of exclusion persisted. Her explanation relies on a richly textured portrait of social and religious changes in American Judaism in the decades following the end of immigration and on evidence that during this period most Jewish women were committed to sustaining Jewish communal identity.

411   Preisand, Sally. Judaism and the New Woman. New York: Behrman House, Inc., 1975. xvi, 144 pp.
       Preisand, who in 1972 became the first woman to be ordained a rabbi in the United States, brings the perspectives of feminism and Reform Judaism to this general survey of women's historic oppression in Judaism and the necessity for egalitarian revisions. This short book is described in Bess Myerson's introduction as "a text for use in the formal curriculum of both religious and secular schools" (p. x).

412   Shoub, Myra. "Jewish Women's History: Development of a Critical Methodology." Conservative Judaism 35 (Winter 1982): 33-46.
       Shoub describes the methodological approaches of leading feminist historians and suggests how these might be applied to the history of Jewish women. She points to issues that need historians' attention and assesses existing books by the norms of feminist historical method.

413   Sochen, June. Consecrate Every Day: The Public Lives of Jewish American Women, 1880-1980. Albany: State University of New York Press, 1981. viii, 167 pp.
       In active lives outside the home, Sochen maintains, Jewish women have faced the dilemma of how to reconcile Judaism, personal ambition, and commitment to American secular values. Sochen thinks they have succeeded nobly, and her book praises the most accomplished among them, becoming almost a collective biography. Included are labor union leaders, radical activists (especially Emma Goldman), volunteer activists (Henrietta Szold), writers (Cynthia Ozick), entertainers, and many others. The book also contains information on the origins and activities of such organizations as the National Council of Jewish Women and Hadassah.

414   Sochen, June, ed. "American Jewish Women." American Jewish History 70 (September 1980):1-118.
       The articles included are Henry Hurwitz, "A Mother Remembered"; June Sochen, "Some Observations on the Role of American Jewish Women as Communal Volunteers"; Selma Berrol, "When Uptown Met Downtown: Julia Richman's Work in the Jewish Community of New York, 1880-1912"; Deborah Grand Golomb, "The 1983 Congress of Jewish Women: Evolution or Revolution in American Jewish Women's History?"; Norma Fain Pratt, "Culture and Radical Politics: Yiddish Women Writers, 1890-1940"; Paula E. Hyman, "Immigrant Women and Consumer Protest: The New York City Kosher Meat Boycott of 1902"; and Ellen Schiff, "What Kind of Way is that for Nice Jewish Girls to Act?: Images of Jewish Women in Modern American Drama."

415   Umansky, Ellen M. "Women in Judaism: From the Reform Movement
       to Contemporary Jewish Religious Feminism." In <u>Women of Spirit:</u>
       <u>Female Leadership in the Jewish and Christian Traditions</u> (entry
       80), pp. 333-54.
           Umansky traces the efforts of women to attain leadership
       positions in Judaism from nineteenth-century Germany through the
       Jewish feminism of the 1970s. She gives attention to the indi-
       vidual women who pioneered in seeking rabbinical education and
       leadership in the nineteenth and twentieth centuries and to the
       relevant deliberations of Jewish schools and organizations, in-
       terpreting events in the context of the changing relation of
       Judaism to modern society. Developments in the 1970s and first
       half of the 1980s are surveyed in her article "Feminism and the
       Reevaluation of Women's Roles Within American Jewish Life," in
       <u>Women, Religion, and Social Change</u> (entry 64), pp. 477-94.

416   Wagenknecht, Edward. <u>Daughters of the Covenant: Portraits of</u>
       <u>Six Jewish Women</u>. Amherst: University of Massachusetts Press,
       1983. viii, 192 pp.
           Five of the six women whose work and personalities are de-
       scribed here lived in the United States. Two of them, Emma
       Lazarus and Amy Levy, were writers; three, Rebecca Gratz, Lillian
       D. Wald, and Henrietta Szold, were Zionists; one, Emma Goldman,
       was anti-Zionist. Notes for each woman provide a brief bibliog-
       raphy of writings by and about her.

417   "Women as Rabbis." <u>Judaism: A Quarterly Journal</u> 33 (Winter
       1984):6-90.
           Twelve writers consider women as rabbis, sketching the his-
       tory of the question, analyzing the scriptures, theologizing, and
       reflecting personally on the subject.

                        IV.B. INDIVIDUAL WOMEN

Many eminent and accomplished Jewish women, treated in the works
listed above, are worthy of inclusion in such a list as the one which
follows. These four are chosen because of the availability of particularly rich sources of information on their lives.

418   <u>Ernestine Louise Siismondi Potowski Rose (1810-92)</u>
           The daughter of a Polish rabbi, Ernestine Rose early re-
       belled against the restrictions she encountered in East European
       Judaism and migrated to the United States, where she became an
       eminent mid-nineteenth-century lecturer for women's rights and
       free thought. A biography tracing her development as a reformer
       and critic of religion is Yuri Suhl, <u>Ernestine L. Rose and the</u>
       <u>Battle for Human Rights</u> (New York: Reynal & Co., 1959). See also
       the listing in <u>Notable American Women</u> (entry 35), 3:195-96.

419   <u>Elizabeth Gertrude Levin Stern (1890-1954)</u>
           In 1926, Stern published her autobiography under the
       pseudonym Leah Morton. <u>I Am Woman--and a Jew</u> (New York: J.H.
       Sears & Co.; reprint, New York: Arno Press, 1969) is a lengthy

and moving portrait of her childhood in Orthodox Judaism, her re-
jection of that tradition and her marriage to a Christian, and her
return to Jewish identity.

420   Henrietta Szold (1860-1945)
          A rabbi's daughter and the first woman to study at Jewish
Theological Seminary (1903), Szold later emigrated to Palestine.
Among her many accomplishments was that of founding Hadassah, the
women's Zionist organization which is today the largest association of Jewish women. A recent biography is Joan Dash, Summoned
to Jerusalem: The Life of Henrietta Szold (New York: Harper &
Row, 1979). See also listing in Notable American Women (entry 35),
3:417-20.

421   Anzia Yezierska (1880?-1970)
          The child of immigrants from Eastern Europe, Yezierska
usually wrote about the struggles of Jewish women like herself
with their conflicted relations to Judaism, America, and womanhood. The novel Bread Givers (1925; reprint, with introduction
by Alice Kessler-Harris, New York: George Braziller, 1975) de-
picts Jewish immigrant life on New York's Lower East Side and the
heroine's ambivalent relation to her cultural and religious heritage, symbolized by her devout and domineering father. Kessler-
Harris has also edited An Open Cage: An Anzia Yezierska Collection (New York: Persea Books, 1980). See also the semifictional
autobiography, Red Ribbon on a White Horse (1950; reprint, New
York: Persea Books, 1981), Carol Schoen's Anzia Yezierska
(Boston: G.K. Hall, 1980), and biographical listing in Notable
American Women: The Modern Period (entry 36), pp. 753-54.

          For Further Information

422   Aviva Cantor's The Jewish Woman, 1900-1980: A Bibliography
       (Rev. ed. [Fresh Meadows, N.Y.: Biblio Press, 1981], 88 pp.) is
       a guide to hundreds of sources on Jewish women in the United
       States, Israel, and other countries. Students of women in Ameri-
       can Judaism will profit from Cantor's lists of histories, memoirs,
       and imaginative literature, as well as her exhaustive list of
       sources from the contemporary Jewish feminist movement, including
       information about recent conferences and organizations. The in-
       frequent annotations are sometimes helpful. Ora Hamelsdorf and
       Sandra Adelsberg's Jewish Women and Jewish Law Bibliography (Fresh
       Meadows, N.Y.: Biblio Press, 1980), is a useful companion to
       Cantor's work, focused on "historical background and recent claims
       for change in Jewish practices toward Jewish women," including the
       question of admission to the rabbinate.

423   Fifteen syllabi from Jewish women's studies courses in the
       disciplines of history, theology, psychology, sociology, and lit-
       erature have been published in Ellen Sue Levi Elwell and Edward R.
       Levenson, The Jewish Women's Studies Guide ([Fresh Meadows, N.Y.:
       Biblio Press, 1982], 108 pp.).

424   Many of the books listed in this chapter have good bibliog-
       raphies. Of special note is the thirty-page bibliographical
       essay in The American Jewish Woman, 1654-1980 (entry 407). It is
       a richly annotated guide to archival, reference, periodical, his-
       torical, and biographical sources. Other bibliographies that con-
       tain references to women in Judaism are William W. Brickman, The
       Jewish Community in America: An Annotated and Classified Biblio-
       graphical Guide (New York: Burt Franklin & Co., 1977), and Moses
       Rischin, An Inventory of American Jewish History (Cambridge,
       Mass.: Harvard University Press, 1954). Neither Brickman nor
       Rischin indexes or explicitly treats the subject of women, but
       information on material by and about women can be found in both
       books.

425   The following periodicals are valuable resources for further
       research in this field:

       American Jewish Archives (1948-). The semiannual publication
       of the American Jewish Archives (Cincinnati, Ohio) prints his-
       torical documents with commentary. An index to vols. 1-24
       published in 1979 includes many references to women and women's
       organizations.

       American Jewish History (1892-). This quarterly publication of
       the American Jewish Historical Society (Waltham, Mass.) was
       formerly entitled Publications of the AJHS and American Jewish
       Historical Quarterly. A special issue on women's history
       (edited by June Sochen, entry 414) appeared in November 1980.
       Other issues sometimes contain information on women.

       American Jewish Yearbook (New York and Philadelphia: American
       Jewish Committee and The Jewish Publication Society of America,
       1900-). This annual publication includes statistics, articles,
       and reports on organizations of interest to students of Ameri-
       can Jewish history. See especially Anne Lapidus Lerner's arti-
       cle on women (entry 405) in the 1977 Yearbook.

       Index to Jewish Periodicals (1963-). This semiannual publica-
       tion lists English-language articles by author and subject,
       including the subject of women.

V. Afro-American Religion

426 Richardson, Marilyn. Black Women and Religion: A Bibliography.
     Boston: G.K. Hall, 1980. xxiv, 139 pp.
          This is the place to begin research into the history of
     black women in American religion. With 837 entries, indexed by
     author and title, it provides an exhaustive guide to resources,
     arranged by genres into the following chapters: books and arti-
     cles; fiction, drama, and poetry; music; art; audiovisual mate-
     rials; reference sources, theses, and dissertations; and auto-
     biographies and biographies. The most important entries are
     annotated, some of them quite extensively. In addition, Richard-
     son provides an introduction that interprets the lives and sig-
     nificance of three women--preacher Jarena Lee, lecturer and
     reformer Maria Stewart, and author Anna Julia Cooper, all active
     in the nineteenth century--as well as brief introductions to some
     chapters, several photographs, and short biographical sketches of
     17 selected black women of achievement. Therefore this book is
     more than a bibliography; readers are introduced not only to the
     sources on religious black women but also to much of the substance
     of their lives.

We hope that readers of this chapter will turn to Richardson's bibliography for guidance. It demonstrates that there are ample resources for research in this field. The books and articles that
follow are those that should be relatively easy to find and that
represent, in our judgment, some particularly important themes.

427 Blassingame, John W., ed. Slave Testimony: Two Centuries of
     Letters, Speeches, Interviews, and Autobiographies. Baton
     Rouge: Louisiana State University Press, 1977. ℓxi, 777 pp.
          This massive compilation of slaves' and ex-slaves' accounts
     of slavery includes much information about women and religion made
     accessible by an exceptionally helpful subject index.

428 Brown, Hallie W. Homespun Heroines and Other Women of Dis-
     tinction. 1926. Reprint. Freeport, N.Y.: Books for
     Libraries Press, 1971. x, 248 pp.
          Brown, president of the National Association of Colored
     Women and a prominent churchwoman, compiled this collection of

short essays on dozens of prominent black women, many of whom
were active in relgion. Pictures, poetry, and addresses are also
included.

429   Cannon, Katie Geneva. "The Emergence of Black Feminist Con-
      sciousness." In Feminist Interpretation of the Bible, edited
      by Letty M. Russell. Philadelphia: Westminster Press, 1985,
      pp. 30-40.
         Within a social context shaped by white supremacy and male
      superiority, Cannon argues, black women have "search[ed] the
      scriptures to learn how to dispel the threat of death in order to
      seize the present life" (p. 40). The article sketches how this
      was done under slavery, during Reconstruction, and in the twen-
      tieth century.

430   Daniel, Sadie Iola. Women Builders. 1931. 2d ed., rev. and
      enl. by Charles H. Wesley and Thelma D. Perry. Washington,
      D.C.: Associated Publishers, 1970. xvii, 308 pp.
         The twelve short biographies published here were intended
      partly to "satisf[y] youth's desire for hero worship" (p. iii).
      Though not scholarly, they contain much hard-to-find information,
      including that on the following religious educators: Lucy Laney,
      Mary McLeod Bethune, Nannie Burroughs, Charlotte Hawkins Brown,
      Fanny M.J. Coppin, and Hallie Quinn Brown.

431   Dodson, Jualynne. "Nineteenth-Century A.M.E. Preaching Women."
      In Women in New Worlds, vol. 1 (entry 81), pp. 276-89.
         Dozens of women who preached in the African Methodist
      Episcopal Church are named here. The article chronicles their
      achievements and their unsuccessful efforts to win the right to
      ordination, although they were granted licensure in 1888 and given
      roles as stewardesses and deaconesses.

432   Giddings, Paula. When and Where I Enter: The Impact of Black
      Women on Race and Sex in America. New York: William Morrow,
      1984. 408 pp.
         Giddings surveys the history of black women from slavery to
      the present, with emphasis upon their activities for black rights
      and women's rights and the relationship between the two movements.

433   Gilkes, Cheryl Townsend. "'Together and in Harness': Women's
      Traditions in the Sanctified Church." Signs: Journal of Women
      in Culture and Society 10 (Summer 1985):678-99.
         Gilkes assesses the strong contributions of women in black
      holiness and pentecostal churches, of which the largest is the
      Church of God in Christ. In spite of exclusion from some insti-
      tutionally structured authority (such as ordination in the COGIC),
      black women "saints" have had substantial influence, both now and
      throughout nearly a century of history. Accessible sources on
      the sanctified church--and especially on women therein--are
      scarce; this article by a sociologist with good historical sense
      is a valuable contribution.

434   Harley, Sharon, and Terborg-Penn, Rosalyn, eds. The Afro-
      American Woman: Struggles and Images. Port Washington, N.Y.:
      Kennikat Press, 1978. xiii, 137 pp.
         This collection of nine historical essays contains the fol-
      lowing that specifically treat religious subjects: "Anna J.
      Cooper: A Voice for Black Women," by Sharon Harley, and "Nannie
      Burroughs and the Education of Black Women," by Evelyn Brooks
      Barnett.

435   Humez, Jean McMahon, ed. Gifts of Power: The Writings of
      Rebecca Jackson, Black Visionary, Shaker Eldress. Amherst:
      University of Massachusetts Press, 1981. viii, 368 pp.
         The autobiographical writing of Rebecca Cox Jackson (1795-
      1871) reports both her revelatory dreams and her experiences as
      believer, preacher, and organizer in the free black community of
      Philadelphia and the network of Shaker communities. The fifty-
      page introductory essay sets Jackson in a rich context of black
      and women's history, and explanatory footnotes, bibliographical
      essay, and attention to textual complexities are also extraordi-
      narily helpful. The appendix, "Documents: Female Preaching and
      the A.M.E. Church, 1820-1852," includes a brief essay by Humez and
      autobiographical writing by several black women contemporaries of
      Jackson. A shorter treatment of this material by Humez is
      "Visionary Experience and Power: The Career of Rebecca Cox
      Jackson," in Black Apostles at Home and Abroad, edited by David W.
      Wills and Richard Newman (Boston: G.K. Hall, 1982), pp. 105-32.

436   Humez, Jean M. "'My Spirit Eye': Some Functions of Spiritual
      and Visionary Experience in the Lives of Five Black Women
      Preachers, 1810-1880." In Women and the Structure of Society,
      edited by Barbara J. Harris and JoAnn K. McNamara. Durham,
      N.C.: Duke University Press, 1984, pp. 129-43.
         The autobiographies of Elizabeth, Jarena Lee, Rebecca Cox
      Jackson, Julia A.J. Foote, and Amanda Berry Smith are the sources
      for Humez's account of their experiences of conversion and sancti-
      fication. They provide rich material for an analysis of how these
      women attained autonomy, conviction, and authority in spite of the
      surrounding context of white racism and male clerical opposition.

437   Jacobs, Sylvia M. "Their Special Mission: Afro-American Women
      as Missionaries to the Congo, 1894-1937." In Black Americans
      and the Missionary Movement in Africa, edited by Sylvia M.
      Jacobs. Westport, Conn.: Greenwood Press, 1982, pp. 155-76.
         Jacobs's account of the careers of five women who served the
      Southern Presbyterian Congo Mission recovers an important but
      little-known chapter in church history, placing them within the
      context of the Afro-American relationship to Africa and the con-
      cern of women missionaries in this period for work with women and
      children. A bibliographical essay on black American missions to
      Africa concludes this volume.

438   Jacobs, Sylvia M. "Three Afro-American Women." In Women in
      New Worlds, vol. 2 (entry 76), pp. 268-80.
         After a survey of the missionary enterprises of the African
      Methodist Episcopal Church, Jacobs gives accounts of the late
      nineteenth- to early twentieth-century missionary careers of
      Amanda Berry Smith, Sarah Gorham, and Fanny Jackson Coppin.

439   Johnson, Clifton H., ed. God Struck Me Dead: Religious Con-
      version Experiences and Autobiographies of Ex-Slaves. Phila-
      delphia: Pilgrim Press, 1969. xix, 172 pp.
         Based on interviews conducted in the 1920s, the narratives
      published here provide rich firsthand accounts of the meaning of
      religion to Southern blacks during slavery and emancipation.
      About half of the speakers are women. Introductory essays discuss
      the central themes of the narratives and describe "Negro primitive
      religious services."

440   Lawson, Ellen NicKenzie, with Marlene D. Merrill. The Three
      Sarahs: Documents of Antebellum Black College Women. New
      York: Edwin Mellen Press, 1984. 335 pp.
         Three Oberlin students of the 1840s and 1850s are the main
      subjects of this book: Sarah Margru Kinson, born in Africa, en-
      slaved, freed, and educated to return there as a missionary; Sara
      Stanley, a free-born Southerner who later was teacher to hundreds
      of newly emancipated blacks; and Sarah Jane Woodson, a free-born
      Northerner who later became prominent in religious, reform, and
      education activities. A chapter on each contains a biography and
      selected documents. Appendixes feature other black women who
      studied at Oberlin, most notably Lucy Stanton, Blanche Harris, and
      Georgiana Mitchem, as well as photos and other related documents.
      Researched in the collections of Oberlin College, this book dis-
      closes substantial achievements that are not widely known.

441   Lerner, Gerda, ed. Black Women in White America: A Documen-
      tary History (entry 23).
         Here more than 150 documents are arranged into chronological
      and topical chapters covering the range of black women's histori-
      cal experience in America, including both the accomplishments of
      leaders and the everyday lives of the unknown. Lerner's intro-
      ductions to the volume as a whole, to each chapter, and to indi-
      vidual selections weave the documents into a coherent whole; this
      book therefore serves as a general history of black women in
      America. Religion, however, receives little attention. A list of
      biographies and autobiographies of prominent black women is ap-
      pended, and a thoughtful bibliographical essay ties the study of
      black women's history to existing scholarship in related fields.

442   Loewenberg, Bert James, and Bogin, Ruth, eds. Black Women in
      Nineteenth-Century American Life: Their Words, Their Thoughts,
      Their Feelings. University Park: Pennsylvania State Univer-
      sity Press, 1976. xi, 355 pp.
         Selections from the writings of 24 women are arranged into
      chapters on family, religion, activism, and education. An intro-
      ductory essay on the history of black women, brief introductions

to the selections, and a good bibliography make this anthology a
coherent work on its topic. The selections are longer than is
usual in anthologies so that readers can here gain substantial
information on these religious figures: Elizabeth (a preacher),
Jarena Lee, Amanda Berry Smith, Ann Plato, Maria Stewart,
Sojourner Truth, Frances Ellen Watkins Harper, Ida Wells-Barnett,
Fannie Barrier Williams, Charlotte Forten Grimke, Lucy Craft
Laney, Frances Jackson Coppin, and Anna Julia Cooper.

443 Murray, Pauli. "The Liberation of the Black Woman." In Our
     American Sisters: Women in American Life and Thought (entry
     19), pp. 579-91. Also in Voices of the New Feminism, edited by
     Mary Lou Thompson. Boston: Beacon Press, 1970, pp. 88-102.
          The late Pauli Murray, an attorney whose later vocation was
     the Episcopal priesthood, documents the oppression of black women
     in history and contemporary society, arguing that human rights are
     "indivisible," calling for a movement in opposition to both racism
     and sexism. (See also entries 454 and 460.)

444 Ruether, Rosemary Radford, and Keller, Rosemary Skinner, eds.
     Women and Religion in America, vol. 1 (entry 78).
          The editors of this documentary history decided to integrate
     material on black women into the volume as a whole, so that infor-
     mation appears in the relevant topical chapters. Important fig-
     ures such as Sojourner Truth, Jarena Lee, Amanda Berry Smith, and
     Ida B. Wells-Barnett are represented in the documents, as are
     black women in revivals, missions, and utopian movements.

445 Sterling, Dorothy, ed. We Are Your Sisters: Black Women in
     the Nineteenth Century. New York: W.W. Norton, 1984. xv,
     535 pp.
          This is an anthology of personal and public documents, help-
     fully arranged in chronological sections with topical divisions
     within the sections and introduced by Sterling. Pictures occa-
     sionally enliven the text; the bibliography is fine, and notes can
     lead researchers to numerous hard-to-find sources. General
     readers will also find this a moving and fascinating way to
     encounter the history of black women in the United States.

446 Wade-Gales, Gloria. No Crystal Stair: Visions of Race and Sex
     in Black Women's Fiction. New York: Pilgrim Press, 1984.
     xxii, 280 pp.
          This study focuses on the twelve "most brilliant novels"
     written by black women between 1946 and 1976 as they address
     issues of racism and sexism. The social history of black women
     provides a context, and national media interpretations of black
     women provide contrasting images for the themes of motherhood,
     hopelessness, struggle, and emergence into wholeness that charac-
     terize the novels themselves.

447   Webb, Lillian Ashcraft. "Black Women and Religion in the
       Colonial Period." In Women and Religion in America, vol. 2
       (entry 79), pp. 233-59.
           An introductory essay discusses the African background and
       the American experiences of black women in the seventeenth and
       eighteenth centuries. Several pictures and fourteen brief selec-
       tions from historical documents are included.

448   Williams, Delores S. "Black Women's Literature and the Task
       of Feminist Theology." In Immaculate and Powerful: The Female
       in Sacred Image and Social Reality (entry 57), pp. 88-110.
       Also "Women's Oppression and Lifeline Politics in Black Women's
       Religious Narratives." Journal of Feminist Studies in Religion
       1 (Fall 1985):59-71.
           Both articles offer insightful interpretations of the tasks
       of contemporary black feminist theology, drawing on these works
       of imaginative literature as testimony of black women's expe-
       rience: Zora Neale Hurston's Jonah's Gourd Vine and Their Eyes
       Were Watching God; Margaret Walker's Jubilee; and Alice Walker's
       The Color Purple.

449   Williams, Melvin D. Community in a Black Pentecostal Church.
       Pittsburgh: University of Pittsburgh Press, 1974. xii, 202 pp.
           This ethnography, based upon three years of observation by
       anthropologist Williams, contains much information on women's
       roles in the formal and informal organization of a congregation.
       Women emerge here as powerful figures in church life; they are
       core members, church secretary, "church mother" and "missionary"
       (official positions of honor and spiritual leadership), members of
       women's organizations, and custodians of the important institu-
       tions of church dinners and picnics.

450   Wills, David W. "Womanhood and Domesticity in the A.M.E. Tra-
       dition: The Influence of Daniel Alexander Payne." In Black
       Apostles at Home and Abroad, edited by David W. Wills and
       Richard Newman. Boston: G.K. Hall, 1982, pp. 133-46.
           Wills's account of the life and thought of the great
       nineteenth-century bishop explores the sources of Payne's opposi-
       tion to women preachers (including Jarena Lee) at mid-century and
       his lifelong support of education and voluntary associations for
       African Methodist Episcopal women.

451   Wilmore, Gayraud S., and Cone, James H., eds. Black Theology:
       A Documentary History, 1966-1979. Maryknoll, N.Y.: Orbis
       Books, 1979. xi, 657 pp.
           This volume contains 57 documents and essays representing
       the development and debates of black theology. Part 5, "Black
       Theology and Black Women" (pp. 363-442), assembles several impor-
       tant statements. Cone's contributions are an introduction calling
       for a black feminist theology and an article, "New Roles in the
       Ministry: A Theological Appraisal" (pp. 389-97), which outlines
       his black theology of liberation and calls for a ministry of women
       and men based on it. Frances Beale, "Double Jeopardy: To Be
       Black and Female" (pp. 368-76; also in The Black Woman, edited by

Toni Cade [New York: Signet, 1970]), analyzes the oppression of
black women in society, but not in religion. An essay by the poet
and novelist Alice Walker, "In Search of Our Mothers' Gardens"
(pp. 434-42), a meditation on the creativity of black women, presents a nonchurchly vision of black female spirituality. Of particular interest, however, are these essays by prominent black
churchwomen:

452   Grant, Jacquelyn. "Black Theology and the Black Woman"
        (pp. 418-33).
            Grant examines the "invisibility" of black women in black
        theology and the history of women's oppression in the black
        churches and freedom movement. She argues that black
        theology must oppose both racism and sexism if it is truly
        to become "a theology of divine liberation" (p. 431).

453   Hoover, Theressa. "Black Women and the Churches: Triple
        Jeopardy" (pp. 377-88). Also in Sexist Religion and Women
        in the Church: No More Silence! (entry 65), pp. 63-76.
            Although women are the "backbone" of black churches,
        Hoover argues, their contributions are rarely recognized.
        She surveys some of these contributions in missions, women's
        organizations, and recent advocacy of civil rights and fem-
        inism, concluding with a call to black women to continue
        their struggle within the churches.

454   Murray, Pauli. "Black Theology and Feminist Theology: A
        Comparative View" (pp. 398-417). Also in Anglican Theologi-
        cal Review 60 (January 1978):3-24.
            Murray sets both black and feminist theologies in the
        international context of liberation theology and examines
        the points of commonality and tension between them, with
        emphasis upon the work of Mary Daly, Rosemary Ruether, Letty
        Russell, James Cone, J. Deotis Roberts, and Major J. Jones.

V.B. INDIVIDUAL WOMEN

The following is a selective list of black women who were prominent
in religion. Most of them are found in Notable American Women
(entry 35) and Notable American Women, The Modern Period (entry 36).
Others may be located in the first three volumes of that biographical
dictionary by consulting the "Negro Women" category in its subject
index.

455 Mary McLeod Bethune (1875-1955)
        The religious views and activities of this well-known edu-
cator and leader are explicated in Clarence G. Newsome, "Mary
McLeod Bethune as Religionist," in Women in New Worlds, vol. 1
(entry 81), pp. 102-16. For general biographies, see Rackham
Holt, Mary McLeod Bethune (Garden City, N.Y.: Doubleday, 1964);
chapter in Women Builders (entry 430), pp. 79-110; and listing in
Notable American Women: The Modern Period (entry 36), pp. 76-80.

456   Nannie Burroughs (1878-1961)
       One of the leading churchwomen of the twentieth century,
Burroughs worked with the Woman's Auxiliary of the National Baptist Convention and founded the National Training Institute for
Women and Girls (1909) during her long career of advocacy for
black women. See Evelyn Brooks Barnett, "Nannie Burroughs and the
Education of Black Women," in The Afro-American Woman: Struggles
and Images (entry 434), pp. 97-108; chapter in Women Builders
(entry 430), pp. 111-36; and listing in Notable American Women:
The Modern Period (entry 36), pp. 125-27.

457   Anna Julia Cooper (1859-1964)
       A collection of essays on black womanhood that reflects
Cooper's Christian beliefs and her reliance on themes of Christian
social feminism is A Voice from the South (1892; reprint, New
York: Negro Universities Press, 1969). Louise Daniel Hutchinson,
Anna J. Cooper: A Voice from the South (Washington, D.C.:
Smithsonian Institution Press, 1981), is a copiously illustrated
biography. Mary Grimley Mason and Carol Hurd Green, Journeys:
Autobiographical Writings by Women (entry 77), pp. 135-45, include
a biographical sketch of Cooper and her own account of her Episcopal faith. Sharon Harley, "Anna J. Cooper: A Voice for Black
Women," in The Afro-American Woman: Struggles and Images (entry
434), pp. 87-96, emphasizes Cooper's work as an educator.

458   Zora Neale Hurston (1901-1960)
       This folklorist and novelist wrote fictional and nonfictional
accounts of black religion, both Christian and hoodoo. Her work
also shows a keen concern for gender issues. The autobiography of
this daughter of a Baptist preacher comments frequently on religion; it is Dust Tracks on a Road (Philadelphia: Lippincott,
1942; reprint, New York: Arno Press, 1969). Lillie P. Howard,
Zora Neale Hurston (Boston: G.K. Hall, 1980), is a biographical
and critical assessment; Robert E. Hemenway, Zora Neale Hurston
(New Haven: Yale University Press, 1977), is a literary biography; and The Sanctified Church (Berkeley, Calif.: Turtle Island
Press, 1981) is a collection of her short pieces on religion,
edited by Alice Walker. An important interpretation of Hurston
from the perspective of contemporary black religious feminism is
Katie Geneva Cannon, "Resources for a Constructive Ethic in the
Life and Work of Zora Neale Hurston," Journal of Feminist Studies
in Religion 1 (Spring 1985):37-51. See listing in Notable American Women: The Modern Period (entry 36), pp. 361-63. For a guide
to sources, see Daryl C. Dance, "Zora Neale Hurston," in American
Women Writers: Bibliographical Essays (entry 231), pp. 321-51.

459   Jarena Lee (1783-185?)
       Lee, a preacher in the African Methodist Episcopal Church
during the early nineteenth century, published an account of her
call and experiences as a preacher, Religious Experience and
Journal of Mrs. Jarena Lee (Philadelphia: The Author, 1836). It
is republished in Early Negro Writing, 1760-1837, edited by
Dorothy Porter (Boston: Beacon Press, 1971), pp. 494-514. Excerpts

from this book are printed, with brief essays on Lee, in Journeys:
Autobiographical Writings by Women (entry 77), pp. 73-87, and
Black Women in Nineteenth-Century American Life (entry 442),
pp. 135-41.

460   Pauli Murray (1910-85)
        Lawyer, writer, and civil rights activist, Murray was also
the first black woman to be ordained an Episcopal priest (1977).
The autobiographical treatment of her family is Proud Shoes: The
Story of an American Family (New York: Harper & Row, 1965) and a
collection of her poetry is Dark Testament and Other Poems
(Norwalk, Conn.: Silvermine Publishing Co., 1970). See also
entries 443 and 454.

461   Amanda Berry Smith (1837-1915)
        An ex-slave and Methodist evangelist and foreign missionary
of the late nineteenth century, Smith wrote an autobiography, The
Story of the Lord's Dealings with Mrs. Amanda Smith, The Colored
Evangelist (Chicago: Meyer & Brother, 1893). Excerpts are
printed in Black Women in Nineteenth-Century American Life (entry
442), pp. 143-73. See also listing in Notable American Women
(entry 35), 3:304-5.

462   Maria W. Stewart (1803-79)
        Stewart gave public lectures in Boston during the 1830s on
morals, religion, and emancipation; she was probably the first
American woman to lecture publicly. Three of her lectures, including one on the religious duties of black women, are printed
in Early Negro Writing, 1760-1837, edited by Dorothy Porter
(Boston: Beacon Press, 1971), pp. 129-40, 460-71; other excerpts
from her writing are found in Black Women in Nineteenth-Century
American Life (entry 442), pp. 183-200. See also listing in
Notable American Women (entry 35), 3:377-78.

463   Sojourner Truth (1797-1883)
        An evangelical preacher and a well-known advocate of aboli-
tionism and women's rights, Truth published an autobiography
(written in the third person by the editor, Olive Gilbert), entitled Narrative of Sojourner Truth (Boston: The Author, 1850;
there are many editions; reprint of 1878 edition, New York: Arno
Press, 1968). Biographies are by Arthur H. Fauset, Sojourner
Truth: God's Faithful Pilgrim (Chapel Hill: University of North
Carolina Press, 1938; reprint, New York: Russell & Russell, 1971),
and Hertha Pauli, Her Name Was Sojourner Truth (New York:
Appleton-Century-Crofts, 1962). Excerpts from her speeches are
in Black Women in Nineteenth-Century American Life (entry 442),
pp. 235-42.

464   Alice Walker (1944-)
        A poet, novelist, and essayist, Walker often chooses to
write on religious themes, and the spiritual depth of her work has
made it a prominent source for contemporary feminist theology.
Outstanding examples include the novel The Color Purple (New York:
Harcourt Brace Jovanovich, 1982; reprint, New York: Washington

Square Press, 1983) and <u>In Search of Our Mother's Gardens: Woman-ist Prose</u> (San Diego: Harcourt Brace Jovanovich, 1983). For examples of the use of Walker's work as a source for theology, see Carter Heyward, "An Unfinished Symphony of Liberation: The Radicalization of Christian Feminism Among U.S. White Women," <u>Journal of Feminist Studies in Religion</u> 1 (Spring 1985):99-118, and the work of Delores S. Williams (entry 448).

465   Phillis Wheatley (1753-84)
        This eighteenth-century African, a slave in Boston, is known for having been the first black woman poet in America. Her col-lected work, first published in England in 1773, appeared in a number of later editions. A modern critical edition is <u>The Poems of Phillis Wheatley</u> (Chapel Hill: University of North Carolina Press, 1966), and a list of works about her is <u>Phillis Wheatley: A Bio-Bibliography</u> (Boston: G.K. Hall, 1981). See listing in <u>Notable American Women</u> (entry 35), 3:573-74, and annotation to entry 111 in this bibliography.

        For Further Information

466   General histories of black Americans provide background for the study of black women and religion. The standard narrative history is by John Hope Franklin: <u>From Slavery to Freedom: A History of Negro Americans</u>, 5th ed. (New York: Alfred A. Knopf, 1979). Mary Frances Berry and John W. Blassingame's <u>Long Memory: The Black Experience in America</u> (New York: Oxford University Press, 1982) is a general history that is arranged into topical chapters; par-ticularly relevant are chapter 3, "Family and Church: Enduring Institutions," and chapter 4, "Sex and Racism." Both books con-tain extensive bibliographies that can lead researchers to other sources in black history. Two surveys that emphasize religious themes are Gayraud S. Wilmore, <u>Black Religion and Black Radical-ism: An Interpretation of the Religious History of Afro-American People</u>, 2d ed. (Maryknoll, N.Y.: Orbis Books, 1983), and Vincent Harding, <u>There is a River: The Black Struggle for Freedom in America</u> (New York: Harcourt Brace Jovanovich, 1981).

467   American Negro slavery has been the topic of hundreds of his-torical studies that give varying degrees of attention to women and to religion. Among the recent works which are relevant to our topic are Eugene D. Genovese, <u>Roll, Jordan, Roll: The World the Slaves Made</u> (New York: Pantheon Books, 1974); Herbert G. Gutman, <u>The Black Family in Slavery and Freedom, 1750-1925</u> (New York: Vintage Books, 1976); Albert J. Raboteau, <u>Slave Religion: The "Invisible Institution" in the Antebellum South</u> (New York: Oxford University Press, 1978); and Willie Lee Rose, ed., <u>A Docu-mentary History of Slavery in North America</u> (New York: Oxford University Press, 1976).

468   Two reference works of black biography and autobiography stand out as especially helpful background information. The <u>Dictionary of American Negro Biography</u>, ed. Rayford W. Logan and Michael R. Winston (New York: W.W. Norton, 1982), is of exceptionally high

quality and includes dozens of women among hundreds of entries on persons who died before 1970. Black Americans in Autobiography: An Annotated Bibliography of Autobiographies and Autobiographical Books Written since the Civil War, by Russell C. Brigano (Durham, N.C.: Duke University Press, 1974), contains annotated entries, arranged by author and indexed by title, by "Experiences, Occupations, and Profession," and by "Geographical Locations and Educational Institutions," and also provides library locations. Many of the authors are women and/or religious figures.

469   Two resources on black women provide useful supplementary material. The Black Woman in American Society: A Selected Annotated Bibliography, by Lenwood G. Davis (Boston: G.K. Hall, 1975), contains 562 annotated entries of books and articles, as well as lists of reference works, current periodicals, occasional and government documents, library collections, national organizations, newspaper publishers and editors, and elected officials. The subject index includes religion. The Progress of Afro-American Women: A Selected Bibliography and Resource Guide, by Janet L. Sims (Westport, Conn.: Greenwood Press, 1980), is a comprehensive subject bibliography of nineteenth- and twentieth-century materials on all aspects of the life of the Afro-American woman, including a chapter on religion that contains 88 unannotated items about women and the church, many of them from black periodicals.

470   Up-to-date scholarship on blacks may be found in the annual publication Index to Periodical Articles by and about Blacks (Boston: G.K. Hall, 1973-). This revised and expanded version of an earlier similar resource (founded in 1950) lists by author, title, and subject the articles from about two dozen black-oriented journals and magazines, ranging from Jet and Ebony to Black Scholar and the Journal of Negro History.

471   An interpretive survey of black history and culture is combined with extensive information on sources in Blacks in America: Bibliographical Essays, by James M. McPherson, et al. (Garden City, N.Y.: Doubleday and Co., 1971). The authors' interests are interdisciplinary, covering literature and the arts as well as social and political history; information on women and religion is scattered throughout but is difficult to find.

472   A massive guide to primary sources is The Howard University Bibliography of African and Afro-American Religious Studies, comp. Ethel L. Williams and Clifton F. Brown (Wilmington, Del.: Scholarly Resources, 1977). Listing over 13,000 books and articles arranged by topic, chronology, and denomination or sect, this work also provides an author index but no annotations or subject index. Useful appendixes list manuscript collections and biographical and autobiographical works.

VI. Native American Religions

473 Green, Rayna. <u>Native American Women: A Contextual Bibliography.</u> Bloomington: University of Indiana Press, 1983. viii,
120 pp.

Readers seeking information about Native American women are
fortunate to have an introductory work like Green's bibliography
and should begin their research there. Green, a Cherokee, begins
with an exceedingly helpful chronological and analytical "report
on the trends and issues that characterize the literature on and
about Native North American Women" (p. 14). Frequent references
to relevant items in the annotated bibliography are incorporated
into the essay. The nearly 700-item bibliography, arranged by
author, is also noted for its evaluative comments about each work.
A date index and subject index to the bibliography are also included.

The reader discerns from Green's essay that the study of the religious beliefs of Native American women is problematic to a degree.
"Though occasional pieces have appeared on medicine women, herbal-
ists, and shamans, they generally ignored the spiritual and medical
leadership of these women," she says (p. 15). Although a partial
solution to piecemeal, inaccurate, and misleading analysis of Native
American women's religious beliefs and activity might be scholarly
work by Native American women themselves, Green says she knows of
little such systematic work being carried out. Referring to puberty
rites, for example, she notes "women may believe in them, honor them
and participate in them but, they do not, for the most part, document
them or wish to do so." Contemporary Native American women scholars
and writers, of necessity, feel that they should focus on "strategies
to address problems rather than on the descriptive analysis of problems" (p. 12).

For readers inquiring about the religious beliefs and customs of
Native American women and/or about the relationship between non-
Native American people and Native Americans, we have selected some
items of particular interest, with the guidance of Green's bibliography and supplemented by items published since compilation of her
work.

474   Albers, Patricia, and Medicine, Beatrice. "The Role of Sioux
       Women in the Production of Ceremonial Objects: The Case of the
       Star Quilt." In The Hidden Half: Studies of Plains Indian
       Women. Lanham, Md.: University Press of America, 1983,
       pp. 123-40.
            Countering the argument that women confine their artistry
       to objects made for domestic use and appreciation, the authors
       describe the symbolic and ceremonial use of the star quilt by
       women of the Sioux nation.

475   Basso, Keith H. "The Gift of Changing Woman." Bureau of
       American Ethnology Bulletin 51, no. 196 (1966):119-73.
            This article is a detailed description and analysis of the
       Apache girls' puberty rite, drawn from observation of the prep-
       arations and performance of four rites and nearly 60 interviews
       about the ceremony. Rayna Green (entry 473) describes Basso's
       work as "one of the most sensitive treatments" of the girls'
       puberty rituals (p. 25).

476   Bataille, Gretchen M., and Sands, Kathleen Mullen. American
       Indian Women Telling Their Lives. Lincoln: University of
       Nebraska Press, 1984. ix, 209 pp.
            Noting that American Indian women's autobiography has its
       roots in the oral tradition of American Indian literature as well
       as in the written tradition of Euro-American autobiography, the
       authors detail the variety of manifestations of these influences
       on this autobiographical genre through examination of a series of
       such works. A fifty-page bibliography provides additional sources
       for readers interested in the study of American women and itself
       serves as a supplement to Green's bibliography (entry 473).

477   Blanchard, Kendall. "Changing Sex Roles and Protestantism
       Among the Navajo Women in Ramah." Journal for the Scientific
       Study of Religion 14 (1975):43-50.
            Examining the position of the female in traditional Navajo
       society as seen in this western New Mexico region alongside the
       history of the Protestant mission in the area, Blanchard concludes
       that "church affiliation is simply one expression of the Navajo
       women's attempt to create sex roles commensurate with the reali-
       ties of changing cultural circumstance" (p. 43).

478   Farrer, Claire R. "Singing for Life: The Mescalero Apache
       Girls' Puberty Ceremony." In Southwestern Indian Ritual
       Drama, edited by Charlotte J. Frisbie. Albuquerque: Univer-
       sity of New Mexico Press, 1980, pp. 125-59.
            Following a full description of the ceremony, Farrer con-
       cludes that rather than being a "ritual process," the ceremony
       publicly confirms the status of the female participants as women
       and sanctifies their role. As "a reenactment of events from the
       beginning of cosmological time and a recitation of ethnohistory,"
       the ceremony has made possible the survival of the people, she
       believes, noting that the tribe began increasing in 1912 follow-
       ing a nearly 50-year U.S. government prohibition of ceremonial
       activity. In an epilogue to the anthology in which this essay

appears, its editor briefly surveys the role of women in South-
western Indian ritual drama (pp. 319-21).

479   Green, Rayna. "The Pocahontas Perplex: The Image of Indian
       Women in American Culture." Massachusetts Review 16 (1975):
       698-714.
       Green describes this piece in her bibliography (entry 473):
"a critical survey of the squaw/princess image in American folk-
lore, art, popular culture and literature--and the function of
those images." An earlier version of the introduction to her
bibliography is "Review Essay: Native American Women," Signs:
Journal of Women in Culture and Society 6 (1980):248-67.

480   Hungry Wolf, Beverly. The Ways of My Grandmothers. New York:
       William Morrow & Co., 1980. 256 pp.
       The author, a thirty-year-old member of the Blood Tribe of
the Blackfoot people, listened to stories told by her mother and
grandmother and recognized that the historical record of her people would soon be lost to the younger generation. According to
tribal custom, she says, all the old women of the past are considered one's grandmothers and so she collected the stories about
the personal lives, tribal history, legends, and myths of many
elderly women of her tribe. The book, enhanced by several dozen
remarkable photographs, addresses the religious beliefs and customs of the women in a number of the stories told here.

481   Jaskoski, Helen. "'My Heart Will Go Out': Healing Songs of
       Native American Women." International Journal of Women's
       Studies 4 (1981):118-34.
       The author has culled from secondary sources the songs and
poetry as well as description of the rituals performed by several
Native American women healers and groups of women. She notes that
such healing songs are relatively rare in published form and it is
generally believed that Native American women seldom serve as
healers, yet concludes from her research that "no generalization
about women as healers is accurate for all tribes, and contra-
dictory information sometimes comes from a single tribe" (p. 132).

482   Kent, Susan. "Hogans, Sacred Circles and Symbols--The Navaho
       Use of Space." In Navajo Religion and Culture, Selected
       Views: Papers in Honor of Leland C. Wyman, edited by David M.
       Brugge and Charlotte J. Frisbie. Santa Fe: Museum of New
       Mexico Press, 1982, pp. 128-35.
       Kent theorizes that the division of the circular hogan into
male and female areas of use occurs because the hogan, although
also utilized for secular purposes, is considered sacred space.
She concludes that "the circle represents the cosmos, and both the
hogan and the cosmos are divided into male and female areas"
(p. 135).

483   Kluckhohn, Clyde. "Navaho Women's Knowledge of Their Song
       Ceremonials." In Culture and Behavior, edited by Richard
       Kluckhohn. New York: Free Press, 1962, pp. 92-96.

This brief report of the results of a 1930s study of women the Ramah, New Mexico, area indicates an interesting divergence between the participation in theory and in practice of religious ceremonials between women and men.

484   Lurie, Nancy Oestreich, ed. Mountain Wolf Woman, Sister of Crashing Thunder: The Autobiography of a Winnebago Woman. Ann Arbor: University of Michigan Press, 1961. Reprint. 1966. xx, 142 pp.
       Transcribed and sensitively edited from oral tape interviews conducted in 1958, this full-length autobiography of a Native American woman provides both day-to-day details of her life (including religious customs and events) and an extraordinary portrayal of a very interesting personality. A number of photographs are also included.

485   Niethammer, Carolyn. Daughters of the Earth: The Lives and Legends of American Indian Women. New York: Macmillan, 1977. xvii, 281 pp.
       This collection is arranged in the chronological order of a woman's life, including narrative and a number of excerpts from anthropological sources covering childbirth and infancy to old age and death. Much information about rites, ceremonies, and religious beliefs is included within these chapters as well as in a short chapter on "religion and spirituality." A number of photographs enhance the written material and a nine-page bibliography of sources is included.

486   Peterson, Jacqueline, and Druke, Mary. "American Indian Women and Religion." In Women and Religion In America, vol. 2 (entry 79), pp. 1–41.
       The authors introduce their collection of documents by examining European attitudes toward Native American women and Native American cosmogonies and ceremonials, and the relationship between Native American women and Christianity. Nineteen original documents with brief introductions are included, one of them by a Native American woman, describing a variety of women's roles and beliefs. A brief selection of pictures enlivens the text. In addition to Peterson and Druke's chapter, others in this anthology describe the missionizing of Native American women, particularly the chapters on Spanish America (entry 348) and Colonial French America (entry 340).

487   Riley, Glenda. Women and Indians on the Frontier, 1825–1915. Albuquerque: University of New Mexico Press, 1984. xvi, 336 pp.
       The nineteenth-century white frontierswoman carried with her the same stereotypical images and preconceptions about Native Americans as did other people of her culture. Riley has found, through an extensive and close reading of the diaries, journals, letters, memoirs, and reminiscences of these women, that two factors effected a change in their opinions as the women moved westward. As they "discover[ed] their own resilience in the face of the harsh demands imposed on them by the western environment" and

actually experienced personal contact with Native Americans, they
"began to reject such stereotypes in favor of a more authentic
relationship between themselves and Indians" (p. xiv)--a change
in attitude that did not usually occur among white men. The
reader might wish to question Riley's undocumented observation
that missionary women "frequently held deeply ingrained and
fairly inflexible perceptions of American Indians peculiar to
their own sense of mission" (p. xv), but she has presented a
provocative thesis based on interesting data and modeled a new
approach to studies about the West.

488   Sekaquaptewa, Helen. Me and Mine: The Life Story of Helen
      Sekaquaptewa. Tucson: University of Arizona Press, 1969.
      262 pp.
         Born in 1898 to very traditional Hopi parents in Arizona,
      Sekaquaptewa was highly influenced by the incursion of white
      culture into the native one. She married and gave birth to ten
      children before converting to the Church of Jesus Christ of
      Latter Day Saints when in her early fifties. This autobiography,
      as told to Louise Udall, is of particular interest for its depic-
      tion of the interaction of two cultures and religions in the life
      of one woman and her family.

489   Sheridan, Mary Ann E., and Sheridan, Daniel P. "Changing Woman
      and the Dis-ease of the Navaho Psychological and Historical
      Perspective." Anima 6 (1980):84-95.
         Analyzing the feminine figures and symbolism that charac-
      terized Navajo myth, religion, and culture during three phases of
      Navaho history from the earliest hunter period to the mid-
      nineteenth century, the authors conclude that the evolution of an
      integrative female archetype "was prematurely slowed down by the
      catastrophic contact with American culture and guns in the later
      nineteenth century" (p. 85).

490   Shimony, Annemarie. "Women of Influence and Prestige Among
      the Native American Iroquois." In Unspoken Worlds: Women's
      Religious Lives in Non-Western Cultures, edited by Nancy A.
      Falk and Rita M. Gross. New York: Harper & Row, 1980,
      pp. 243-59.
         In the larger context of a selection of pieces designed to
      illustrate that the diversity and richness of women's religious
      lives in non-Judaic and non-Christian cultures has never been
      fully appreciated, Shimony contributes her description of the
      Iroquois women's religious role and relationship with the men in
      their culture.

491   Stone, Merlin. "To Walk the Trail of Beauty: Native Ameri-
      cans of North America." In Ancient Mirrors of Womanhood: A
      Treasury of Goddess and Heroine Lore from Around the World.
      Boston: Beacon Press, 1979, pp. 284-312.
         A brief survey of Native American history precedes a collec-
      tion of female creation stories and legends about female deities
      in Native American tradition.

492   Voegelin, C.F.   The Shawnee Female Deity.   Yale University
      Publications in Anthropology, no. 10.   New Haven: Yale Uni-
      versity Press, 1936.   Reprint.   1970.
          This anthropological description of the dominant member--she
      is called "Our Grandmother"--of a small pantheon of Gods is based
      on field notes taken during the first decades of the twentieth
      century from observation of three bands of Shawnee Indians in
      Oklahoma.   The focus on this female deity, on what she does and
      her influence on the lives of the people, is highly unusual in
      the anthropological literature of that period.

493   Young, Mary E.   "Women, Civilization, and the Indian Question."
      In Clio Was a Woman: Studies in the History of American Women,
      edited by Mabel E. Deutrich and Virginia C. Purdy.   Washington,
      D.C.:   Howard University Press, 1980, pp. 98-110.
          Young illustrates the ways in which government agents and
      missionaries focused on the education of girls in order to induce
      "change in family structure, family life, and the division of
      labor between the sexes" (p. 99) as part of their efforts to con-
      vert Native Americans to a "Christian, civilized" life-style.

      For Further Information

494   Bea Medicine, Native American anthropologist, compiled the
      first bibliography on Native American women: "The Role of Women
      in Native American Societies: A Bibliography," Indian Historian
      8 (1975):50-53.   It contains mostly ethnographic sources that re-
      flect not only her scholarly interests but what was available at
      the time.   One of the most recent contributions among many of hers
      on Native Americans is "Contemporary Literature on Indian Women:
      A Review Essay," Frontiers 6 (1982):122-25, which discusses two
      recent works on Indian women.

495   Dwight L. Smith has edited two volumes of bibliography entitled
      Indians of the United States and Canada: A Bibliography (Santa
      Barbara, Calif.:   ABC-CLIO, 1974-82).   They are drawn from the
      data base that produces America: History and Life (entry 1) and
      cover the years 1954 to 1978.   These two volumes and subsequent
      volumes of America: History and Life provide excellent guidance
      to contemporary literature on many aspects of Native American life
      and history.

496   A lengthy, though unannotated, bibliography on Native American
      women is Lyle Koehler's "Native Women of the Americas: A Bibliog-
      raphy," Frontiers 6 (1982):73-101.   There is no specifically
      "religious" category, but the completeness of the bibliography
      makes it of use for detailed study of Native American women.

497   For a listing of the biographies of Native American women in-
      cluded in the volumes of Notable American Women (entry 35), see
      number 312 in Rayna Green's bibliography (entry 473) or footnote
      2 in her "Review Essay: Native American Women" (entry 479).

VII. Utopian, Communitarian, Millenarian, and Other Alternative Religious Movements

498   Bednarowski, Mary Farrell. "Outside the Mainstream: Women's
      Religion and Women Religious Leaders in Nineteenth-Century
      America." Journal of the American Academy of Religion 48
      (1980):207-31.
          Asserting that the beliefs of mainstream religious groups
      about the nature of the divine, human nature, the function of the
      clergy, and the nature of marriage are tied to the absence of fe-
      male leadership in these groups, Bednarowski analyzes four mar-
      ginal groups that have a positive opinion about leadership roles
      for women. Examining Shakerism, Spiritualism, Christian Science,
      and Theosophy, she shows how their views deemphasize the mascu-
      line, temper or deny the doctrine of the Fall, reject the tradi-
      tional ordained clergy, and do not hold marriage and motherhood
      as the only acceptable roles for women.

499   Ellwood, Robert S., Jr. Alternative Altars: Unconventional
      and Eastern Spirituality in America. Chicago: University of
      Chicago Press, 1979. xvi, 192 pp.
          In contrast to established, mainline religion where ritual
      reinforces social roles and activities, Ellwood holds that the so-
      called "new" religions--where people on spiritual pilgrimage seek
      alternate realities--have existed throughout time. He supports
      his arguments with historical examples, prominently including
      movements led by women: Ann Lee's Shakerism and Madame Helena
      Blavatsky's Theosophy.

500   Klein, Janice. "Ann Lee and Mary Baker Eddy: The Parenting of
      New Religions." Journal of Psychohistory 6 (1979):361-75.
          Using a psychohistorical approach, Klein focuses on the per-
      sonal lives of the two religious founders and the relationship of
      their experiences to the theology of the religions they founded.

501   Maniha, John K., and Maniha, Barbara B. "A Comparison of
      Psychohistorical Differences Among Some Female Religious and
      Secular Leaders." Journal of Psychohistory 5 (1978):523-49.
          Postulating that women who became religious leaders were
      more likely to have received traditional sex-role training than

did women who became leaders in the secular world, the authors
compare the upbringing of religious leaders such as Helena
Blavatsky, Mary Baker Eddy, Aimee Semple McPherson, and Jemima
Wilkinson with that of secular leaders such as Carry Nation,
Margaret Sanger, Lucretia Mott, and Elizabeth Cady Stanton to
support their thesis.

502   Ruether, Rosemary Radford. "Women in Utopian Movements." In
      Women and Religion in America, vol. 1 (entry 78), pp. 46-100.
      Also Ruether and Catherine M. Prelinger, "Women in Sectarian
      and Utopian Groups." In Women and Religion in America, vol. 2
      (entry 79), pp. 260-315.
         In vol. 2, focusing on seventeenth- and eighteenth-century
      descendants of European radical, anabaptist, and mystical Protes-
      tant groups, the author-editors provide introduction to and repre-
      sentative documents of Quakers, the Ephrata Cloister and Moravian
      sectarians in Pennsylvania, and the movements led by two "female
      Messiahs in the revolutionary war era"--Ann Lee and Jemima
      Wilkinson. Interesting photographs enliven the texts and exten-
      sive footnotes lead the reader to further resources. In vol. 1,
      Ruether covers several nineteenth-century groups by examining
      themes of concern to this movement: "The Androgynous God and the
      New Humanity," "The Marriage Question," "Patterns of Female
      Leadership," and "Utopianism and Feminism."

503   Tyler, Alice Felt. Freedom's Ferment: Phases of American
      Social History from the Colonial Period to the Outbreak of the
      Civil War. New York: Harper & Row, 1944. Reprint. 1962.
      608 pp.
         Nearly a third of this compendium is devoted to cults and
      utopias and to women's participation in them. Among the groups
      and individuals treated are Margaret Fuller, the Fox sisters,
      Mormons, the Ephrata Cloister, Jemima Wilkinson, Mother Ann Lee,
      and Frances Wright's Nashoba.

504   Zikmund, Barbara Brown. "The Feminist Thrust of Sectarian
      Christianity." In Women of Spirit: Female Leadership in the
      Jewish and Christian Traditions (entry 80), pp. 205-24.
         Zikmund supports her thesis that there was a correlation
      between feminism and sectarianism in the nineteenth century by
      examining the concepts of God, life-style, reform, and female
      leadership in a variety of sectarian groups.

      VII.B. CHURCH OF JESUS CHRIST OF LATTER DAY SAINTS

505   Arrington, Leonard J. "Blessed Damozels: Women in Mormon
      History." Dialogue 6 (1971):22-31. "Persons for All Seasons:
      Women in Mormon History." Brigham Young University Studies 20
      (1979):39-58.
         Well-known Mormon historian addresses women's contributions
      to Mormon history.

506   Beecher, Maureen Ursenbach. "The 'Leading Sisters': A Female
       Hierarchy in Nineteenth Century Mormon Society." Journal of
       Mormon History 9 (1982):25-39. "Under the Sunbonnets: Mormon
       Women with Faces." Brigham Young University Studies 16 (1976):
       471-84. "All Things Move in Order in the City: The Nauvoo
       Diary of Zina Diantha Huntington Jacobs." Brigham Young Uni-
       versity Studies 19 (1979):285-320. "The Eliza Enigma: The
       Life and Legend of Eliza R. Snow." In Essays on the American
       West, edited by Thomas G. Alexander. Provo: Brigham Young
       University Press, 1976, pp. 29-46. "Three Women and the Life
       of the Mind." Utah Historical Quarterly 43 (1975):26-40.
           A selection of the articles written by Beecher, a Mormon
       historian, editor, and educator.

507   Best, Christy. Guide to Sources for Studies of Mormon Women in
       the Church Archives, The Church of Jesus Christ of Latter Day
       Saints. Salt Lake City: Church of Jesus Christ of Latter-Day
       Saints, Historical Department, 1976. 44 pp.
           This finding-aid of the library-archives provides listing
       and brief description of the diaries, autobiographies, letters,
       and oral histories of about 300 Mormon women.

508   Bitton, Davis, and Bunker, Gary L. "Double Jeopardy: Visual
       Images of Mormon Women to 1914." Utah Historical Quarterly 46
       (1978):184-202.
           The authors here describe the stereotypical portrayal of
       Mormon women in visual images in an article that is part of a
       larger project dealing with pictorial images of Mormonism between
       1830 and 1914. A somewhat revised version of this article appears
       in their The Mormon Graphic Image, 1834-1914: Cartoons, Carica-
       tures, and Illustrations (Bunker is listed as first author) (Salt
       Lake City, University of Utah Press, 1983), pp. 123-36.

509   Bushman, Claudia L., ed. Mormon Sisters: Women in Early Utah.
       Cambridge, Mass.: Emmeline Press; Salt Lake City: Olympus
       Pub. Co., 1976. xxxii, 283 pp.
           The essays in this collection describe the sacramental func-
       tioning of early Mormon women, their movement into the practice of
       medicine and midwifery, response to plural marriage, activism, and
       the imagery of women in Mormon historical novels. Also included
       is a comparative chronology of events in the secular world,
       women's history, Mormon history, and Mormon women's history.

510   Dialogue: A Journal of Mormon Thought 14 (1981).
           This special issue includes Laurel Thatcher Ulrich, "The
       Pink Dialogue and Beyond"; Carol Cornwall Madsen, "Mormon Women
       and the Struggle for Definition"; Nadine Hansen, "Women and
       Priesthood"; and Lavinia Fielding Anderson, "Mary Fielding Smith:
       Her Ox Goes Marching On."

511   Embry, Jessie L. "Effects of Polygamy on Mormon Women."
       Frontiers 7 (1984):56-64.
           Basing her work on numerous oral history interviews with
       children of polygamous families, Embry pays particular attention

to Mormonism's religious commitment to polygamy and the women's
"adaptation of western traditions derived from the monogamous
family [in order] to define their relationships within the plural
households" (p. 56).

512   Foster, Lawrence. "A New and Everlasting Covenant of Marriage:
        Joseph Smith and the Origins of Mormon Polygamy, 1831-1844" and
        "'Puritan Polygamy': Brigham Young and the Institutionaliza-
        tion of Mormon Polygamy, 1844-1852." In Religion and Sexuality
        (entry 559), pp. 123-225.
            Writing from an anthropological-sociological perspective and
        utilizing extensive research into Mormon archives, Foster provides
        a history and analysis of the Mormon response to social upheaval
        in the nineteenth century.

513   Godfrey, Kenneth W.; Godfrey, Audrey M.; and Derr, Jill Mulvay.
        Women's Voices: An Untold History of the Latter-day Saints,
        1830-1900. Salt Lake City: Deseret Book Co., 1982. viii,
        448 pp.
            Chronologically arranged, this collection of personal writ-
        ings by Mormon women provides not only excerpts from primary
        sources but helpful introductory historical essays and notes. No
        controversial or unflattering materials are included, reflecting
        the editors' personal preference for the Mormon faith, but the
        book makes widely available useful historical data and the writ-
        ings of otherwise obscure diarists.

514   Iversen, Joan. "Feminist Implications of Mormon Polygyny."
        Dunfey, Julie. "'Living the Principle' of Plural Marriage:
        Mormon Women, Utopia, and Female Sexuality in the Nineteenth
        Century." Feminist Studies 10 (1984):504-36.
            Iversen's article, written from an explicitly twentieth-
        century feminist perspective, and Dunfey's, carefully examining
        the same subject from within its own historical context, both
        illustrate "how women persistently adapt and adjust the sexual
        codes and marriage arrangement of their time" (p. 504).

515   Jeffrey, Julie Roy. "If Polygamy is the Lord's Order, We Must
        Carry it Out." In Frontier Women: The Trans-Mississippi West,
        1840-1880 (entry 183), pp. 147-78.
            In this thorough and balanced survey of the Mormon utopian
        frontier, Jeffrey discusses the theological, sociological, and
        political aspects of the women's experience. Although there are
        no footnotes, a bibliographical essay (pp. 221-24) provides in-
        formation about primary and secondary sources on Mormonism and
        Mormon women.

516   Johnson, Sonia. From Housewife to Heretic. Garden City, N.Y.:
        Doubleday, 1981. 406 pp.
            Johnson tells the story of her evolution from deeply com-
        mitted Mormon to radical feminist through her struggles with the
        church over support of the Equal Rights Amendment. During the
        period of time in which this story took place (1976-80), she was
        divorced by her husband and excommunicated by the church.

517   Journal of Mormon History 6 (1979):1-145.
      This issue includes several articles on Mormon women:
Lawrence Foster, "From Frontier Activism to Neo-Victorian Domes-
ticity: Mormon Women in the Nineteenth and Twentieth Centuries";
Linda K. Newell and Valeen T. Avery, "New Light on the Sun: Emma
Smith and the New York Sun Letter"; Nancy Hiles Isihawa, "Alice
Smith Edwards: The Little Princess"; Malcolm R. Thorp, "Winifred
Graham and the Mormon Image"; and Carol Cornwall Madsen and David
J. Whittaker, "History's Sequel: A Source Essay on Women in
Mormon History."

518   Kern, Louis J. "Celestial Marriage: Mormon Sexuality and Sex
      Roles in Ideology and Practice." In An Ordered Love (entry
      560), pp. 137-204.
      Using psychohistorical and Freudian categories, Kern ana-
lyzes the reorganization of sex roles and sexual expression in the
Mormon religious movement.

519   Newell, Linda King, and Avery, Valeen Tippetts. Mormon Enigma:
      Emma Hale Smith: Prophet's Wife, "Elect Lady," Polygamy's Foe,
      1804-1879. Garden City, N.Y.: Doubleday, 1984. xiii, 394 pp.
      This thoroughly researched and documented biography of the
wife of the founding prophet of Mormonism chronicles Emma Hale
Smith's story from the time of her elopement with Joseph Smith in
1827 to her death in 1879. Smith's opposition to the plural marriages of her husband and the promulgation of the practice among
the Mormons led her, after Joseph Smith's murder, to stay in
Illinois when Brigham Young led the Saints west to Utah. Those
who remained behind founded the Reorganized Church of Jesus Christ
of Latter Day Saints, of which Emma's son Joseph Smith III became
prophet and president in 1860. At that time she was received as
a member of the group. In their article "The Lion and the Lady:
Brigham Young and Emma Smith" (Utah Historical Quarterly 48
[1980]:81-97), Avery and Newell focus on the period after Joseph
Smith's death in 1844. A brief biographical treatment of Emma
Hale Smith appears in Notable American Women (entry 35), 3:311-12.

520   Pace, D. Gene. "Wives of Nineteenth-Century Mormon Bishops:
      A Quantitative Analysis." Journal of the West 11 (1982):49-57.
      Utilizing a sample of 835 wives of Mormon bishops, Pace de-
scribes the impact of polygamy on their lives by discussing their
religious beliefs, the extent of polygamy among them, their ages,
the number of sisters involved in plural marriages, childbearing,
intermarriage patterns, and the impact of the Federal government's
antipolygamy crusade on bishops' wives. A bibliographical essay
concludes the article.

521   Warenski, Marilyn. Patriarchs and Politics: The Plight of the
      Mormon Woman. New York: McGraw-Hill, 1978. xvi, 332 pp.
      Warenski's thesis is that nineteenth-century Mormon women
were as much under the authority of the church's patriarchal
authorities as are today's anti-Equal Rights Mormon women and that
the Mormon hierarchy has a great stake in maintaining that situation. She supports her thesis by describing church doctrine and

recording political and economic manipulation of Mormon women. A comparison of their treatment with that of women by Roman Catholic and fundamentalist Protestant hierarchies is also included.

522   White, Jean Bickmore. "Woman's Place Is in the Constitution:
      The Struggle for Equal Rights in Utah in 1895." In Essays on
      the American West, 1974-1975, edited by Thomas G. Alexander.
      Provo: Brigham Young University Press, 1976, pp. 81-104.
          Addressing the struggle for inclusion of a provision for
      equal rights in the Utah constitution, White views it in the con-
      text of Mormon-gentile conflict in Utah territorial politics and
      looks at division in Mormon leadership over the issue as well as
      the work of prominent Mormon women for equal rights.

523   White, William Griffin, Jr. "The Feminist Campaign for the
      Exclusion of Brigham Henry Roberts from the Fifty-Sixth Con-
      gress." Journal of the West 17 (1978):45-52.
          The concerted efforts of Presbyterian and other church women
      throughout the country were successful in forcing the exclusion of
      Roberts, a polygamist elected to the U.S. House of Representatives
      from Utah, from being seated in 1900 when his fellow congressmen
      were sworn in.

      For Further Information

524   For current periodical resources on Morman women, see Women and
      Religion: A Bibliography Selected from the ATLA Religion Database
      (entry 15) and the periodical indexes from which it was compiled;
      America: History and Life (entry 1); and articles from Dialogue:
      A Journal of Mormon Thought, Brigham Young University Studies,
      Journal of Mormon History, and Utah Historical Quarterly.

VII.C.   MILLENARIAN GROUPS

525   Beach, John G. Notable Women of Spirit: The Historical Role
      of Women in the Seventh-day Adventist Church. Nashville:
      Southern Publishing Association, 1976. 125 pp.
          This popularly written survey of the history of women in the
      Seventh-Day tradition from Ellen G. White to the 1960s also in-
      cludes a listing of significant women with their dates and very
      brief description of their contributions and short bibliography.

526   Harrison, Barbara Grizzuti. Visions of Glory: A History and
      a Memory of Jehovah's Witnesses. New York: Simon & Schuster,
      1978. 413 pp.
          A member of the Jehovah's Witnesses from the age of nine
      until she left at age twenty-one, Harrison interlaces a descrip-
      tion of the sect's history and ideology throughout an engrossing
      narrative of her personal involvement with the sect and growing
      disenchantment with its oppressive and authoritarian features.

527   Numbers, Ronald L. Prophetess of Health: A Study of Ellen G.
       White. New York: Harper & Row, 1976. xiv, 271 pp.
       This well-researched and readable treatise on the co-founder
(1827-1915) of the Seventh-Day Adventist Church written by a
church member is nevertheless a balanced treatment of its subject,
providing very helpful information on the health reform movement
of the nineteenth century. A review article prompted by publication of this book is Henry D. Shapiro, "Getting Back-and-Down-To
Basics," Reviews in American History 5 (1977):242-48. A recent
analysis of Ellen G. White and her church is "Ministries of Healing: Mary Baker Eddy, Ellen G. White, and the Religion of Health"
(entry 535), and biographical information on this important
nineteenth-century religious figure is found in Notable American
Women (entry 35), 3:585-88. Helpful background on Adventism was
gathered by Edwin Scott Gaustad in a collection of essays by
American religious historians: The Rise of Adventism: Religion
and Society in Mid-Nineteenth-Century America (New York: Harper &
Row, 1975).

528   Theobald, Robin. "The Role of Charisma in the Development of
       Social Movements: Ellen G. White and the Emergence of Seventh-
       Day Adventism." Archives de Sciences Sociales des Religions
       (France) 49 (1980):83-100.
       Theobald traces the influence of Ellen G. White on Adventism
from her visionary prophetic pronouncements in 1848 to the late
nineteenth-century challenges to her power and the decline of her
authority.

       VII.D. NEW THOUGHT, CHRISTIAN SCIENCE, AND UNITY

529   Ahlstrom, Sydney. "Mary Baker Eddy." In Notable American
       Women (entry 35), 1:551-61.
       Ahlstrom's biographical treatment of Mary Baker Eddy (1821-
1910) amounts to a major and important essay about her and her
career in the context of its nineteenth-century milieu. A comprehensive bibliographical essay covers works by and about Mary Baker
Eddy published through the mid-1960s and may be supplemented by
works listed in this bibliography.

530   Bednarowski, Mary Farrell. "Outside the Mainstream: Women's
       Religion and Women Religious Leaders in Nineteenth-Century
       America" (entry 498).
       Mary Baker Eddy, founder of Christian Science, is one of the
figures analyzed in Bednarowski's article.

531   Beebe, Tom. Who's Who in New Thought: Biographical Dictionary
       of New Thought: Personnel, Centers, and Authors' Publications.
       Lakemont, Ga.: C.S.A. Press, 1977. 318 pp.
       Although not a scholarly publication, this compilation sup-
plies in one volume brief biographies of New Thought leaders past
and present with their publications and listings of contemporary
New Thought churches, centers, and educational institutions.

532   Fox, Margery. "Protest in Piety: Christian Science Revisited."
       International Journal of Women's Studies 1 (1978):401-16.
           In contrast to former interpretations of Mary Baker Eddy's
       therapeutic religion, Fox proposes that Christian Science was an
       unconscious protest movement directed specifically against women's
       social disabilities in the late nineteenth century. Eddy, like
       many middle-class Victorian women who at times resorted to illness
       to escape the narrow confines of the female stereotype, found the
       resolution to her personal conflicts in developing Christian
       Science and assuming an extraordinary power role therein. At the
       same time, she provided many other women the opportunities to
       develop leadership abilities and elevate their social status.

533   Klein, Janice. "Ann Lee and Mary Baker Eddy: The Parenting of
       New Religions." Journal of Psychohistory 6 (1979):361-75.
           Examining the personal lives of two religious founders,
       Klein posits their influence on the theologies of the religions
       founded by Lee and Eddy.

534   Lindley, Susan Hill. "The Ambiguous Feminism of Mary Baker
       Eddy." Journal of Religion 64 (1984):318-31.
           Lindley surveys Eddy's ideas about women and religion,
       assessing them both in the context of nineteenth-century views and
       in comparison to contemporary feminist theology. Her finding of
       deep ambiguity on both counts contrasts to other pro- and anti-
       Eddy scholarship, to which this article also provides a brief
       reliable guide.

535   Numbers, Ronald L., and Schoepflin, Rennie B. "Ministries of
       Healing: Mary Baker Eddy, Ellen G. White, and the Religion of
       Health." In Women and Health in America: Historical Readings,
       edited by Judith Walzer Leavitt. Madison: University of
       Wisconsin Press, 1984, pp. 376-89.
           Despite a trend toward secularization of medical theory and
       professionalization of medical practice, a continuing interaction
       between religion and medicine in the nineteenth century is illus-
       trated by the appearance of two new churches that "actively inte-
       grated physical and spiritual concerns" (p. 376), according to the
       authors. Their essay focuses on the lives and similar personal
       experiences of the women who founded those sects.

536   Parker, Gail Thain. Mind-Cure in New England: From the Civil
       War to World War I. Hanover, N.H.: University Press of New
       England, 1973. xi, 197 pp.
           In her study of the movement that spoke to the social pres-
       sures brought about by the American industrial revolution by
       focusing attention on health and mental status, Parker includes
       an early ground-breaking feminist analysis. See also her article
       "Mary Baker Eddy and Sentimental Womanhood" (New England Quarterly
       43 [1970]:3-18) for a briefer version of her work.

537   Peel, Robert. Mary Baker Eddy. Vol. 1, The Years of Dis-
       covery; vol. 2, The Years of Trial; vol. 3, The Years of

Authority. New York: Holt, Rinehart & Winston, 1966-77. xi,
372 pp.; vii, 391 pp.; xii, 528 pp.

In his three-volume biographical treatment of Mary Baker
Eddy, Christian Science practitioner Peel attempts (fairly suc-
cessfully) to provide a view of her that steers a course between
"the yellow journalism [and] the denominational hagiography of her
day" (3:365), although his apologetic stance is apparent. The
work is thorough, based on unrestricted access to the archives
of the Mother Church.

538   Silberger, Julius, Jr. <u>Mary Baker Eddy: An Interpretive
Biography of the Founder of Christian Science</u>. Boston:
Little, Brown & Co., 1980. x, 274 pp.

Secular psychiatrist Silberger, finding Baker "a woman of
great historical and psychological interest" (p. 11), details how
she used her own internal struggles and intuition about the world
around her to "discover a solution that would offer hope for the
amelioration of the everyday problems that burdened so many of her
contemporaries" (p. 246). Although purporting not to provide a
diagnosis of Eddy, Silberger pays a great deal of attention to the
disappointing relationships with the men in her life.

539   Stein, Stephen J. "Retrospection and Introspection: The
Gospel According to Mary Baker Eddy." <u>Harvard Theological
Review</u> 75 (1982):97-116.

Countering biographer Robert Peel's assessment of Eddy's
autobiography as being more concerned with Christian Science than
with personal self-revelation, Stein examines the content and
structure of the text in order to shed light on Eddy's "self-
conception as the discoverer and founder of Christian Science"
(p. 97.).

540   Witherspoon, Thomas E. <u>Myrtle Fillmore: Mother of Unity</u>.
Unity Village, Mo.: Unity Books, 1977. viii, 306 pp.

This popularly written biography published by the church's
publishing house contains many photographs but no footnotes or
bibliography. A briefer--and scholarly--treatment appears in
<u>Notable American Women</u> (entry 35), 1:617-19.

VII.E. THE SHAKERS

541   Campbell, D'Ann. "Women's Life in Utopia: The Shaker Experiment in Sexual Equality Reappraised--1810 to 1860." <u>New
England Quarterly</u> 51 (1978):23-38.

Believing that an examination of the role of women in communitarian experiments may yield essential information not only on
the experiments themselves but on the "internal stress of the
larger American society" (p. 23), Campbell sets forth such an
analysis. Her concise treatment of the subject from a feminist
perspective identifies a multitude of issues and suggests areas
for further research.

542   Foster, Lawrence. "They Neither Marry Nor Are Given in Mar-
      riage: The Origins and Early Development of Celibate Shaker
      Communities." In Religion and Sexuality (entry 559),
      pp. 21-71.
            Within an anthropological framework, Foster provides a
      history and analysis of the development of the Shaker response to
      cultural upheaval in the late eighteenth and early nineteenth cen-
      turies.

543   Kern, Louis J. "Hymenius Bound: Shaker Sexuality in Ideology
      and Practice." In An Ordered Love (entry 560), pp. 71-134.
            Dismissing religious ideology as a basis for Shaker utopian-
      ism, Kern uses psychohistorical and Freudian categories to explore
      Shaker response to sexual ambiguity in the nineteenth-century
      historical setting.

544   Humez, Jean McMahon, ed. Gifts of Power: The Writings of
      Rebecca Jackson, Black Visionary, Shaker Eldress (entry 435).
            In her painstaking contextual introduction to the auto-
      biographical writing of Rebecca Cox Jackson (1795-1871) as well
      as her expository footnotes and bibliographical essay, Humez has
      provided an invaluable resource on women and nineteenth-century
      religion. The reader may wish to consult Richard E. Williams's
      Called and Chosen: The Story of Mother Rebecca Jackson and the
      Philadelphia Shakers (Metuchen, N.J.: Scarecrow Press, 1981) for
      its very complete treatment of Jackson's Shaker career.

545   Procter-Smith, Marjorie. Women in Shaker Community and Wor-
      ship: A Feminist Analysis of the Uses of Religious Symbolism.
      Lewiston, N.Y.: Edwin Mellen Press, 1985. xvii, 253 pp.
            Calling this a "historic study of ideology," Procter-Smith
      examines the Shaker development and use of female God-language in
      worship and theology and its relationship to the actual status of
      women in the Shaker communities.

546   Whitson, Robley Edward. "God: Father and Mother." In The
      Shakers: Two Centuries of Spiritual Reflection. New York:
      Paulist Press, 1983, pp. 207-57.
            This chapter of Whitson's collection of theological docu-
      ments with introductions focuses on feminine spirituality and,
      with the rest of the collection, provides a very useful companion
      for the historical study of the Shakers.

      For Further Information

547   Notable American Women (entry 35) should be consulted for bio-
      graphical treatment of the Shaker founder Ann Lee (2:385-87) and
      leaders Anna White (3:583-84) and Lucy Wright (3:681-82).

      VII.F.   SPIRITUALISM AND THEOSOPHY

548   Bednarowski, Mary Farrell. "Women in Occult America." In The
      Occult in America: New Historical Perspectives (entry 554),
      pp. 177-95.

Providing a comparative study of women in spiritualism, Theosophy, and feminist witchcraft, Bednarowski sees three themes: an indictment of male-dominated Western society; a call for the healing of the Cartesian split in the universe; and an affirmation of women's nature. These movements explicitly addressed woman's position in the institutional church, protested the prevailing structures, and created alternate realities that were more affirming of woman's sexuality and spirituality. Bednarowski, in "Spiritualism in Wisconsin in the Nineteenth Century" (Wisconsin Magazine of History 59 [1975]:2-19), treats a local manifestation of spiritualism in some depth, including describing the contributions of several prominent women.

549   Brandon, Ruth. The Spiritualists: The Passion for the Occult in the Nineteenth and Twentieth Centuries. New York: Knopf, 1983. Reprint. Buffalo, N.Y.: Prometheus Books, 1984. xiii, 315 pp.
        In telling the history of the spiritualist movement Brandon focuses on the response by a number of well-known enthusiasts, the skepticism and hostility of the scientific community, and the evidence that proves the falsity of the phenomenon.

550   Braude, Ann D. "Spirits Defend the Rights of Women: Spiritualism and Changing Sex Roles in Nineteenth-Century America." In Women, Religion, and Social Change (entry 64), pp. 419-31.
        Braude here contributes to the growing body of scholarship on women and spiritualism an intriguing analysis of the interaction between the movements of spiritualism and women's rights in mid-nineteenth-century America.

551   Campbell, Bruce F. Ancient Wisdom Revived: A History of the Theosophical Movement. Berkeley: University of California Press, 1980. x, 249 pp.
        In this most comprehensive treatment of the Theosophical movement, Campbell provides both historical narrative and contemporary assessment. Information about Helena Blavatsky (1831-91), Annie Besant (1847-1933), and Katherine Tingley (1847-1929) is included along with a fifteen-page bibliography. Although her career was spent entirely in England and India, the importance of Annie Besant to the Theosophical movement (and the Indian Independence movement) should be noted. Extensive biographical treatment of her is found in Arthur H. Nethercot's The First Five Lives of Annie Besant and The Last Four Lives of Annie Besant (Chicago: University of Chicago Press, 1960, 1963). For further information on Blavatsky, see entry 555; on Tingley, see entry 552.

552   Greenwalt, Emmett A. The Point Loma Community in California, 1897-1942: A Theosophical Experiment. Berkeley: University of California Press, 1955. 236 pp. Several reprints. Rev. ed. San Diego: Point Loma Publications, 1978 (as California Utopia: Point Loma 1897-1942).
        The author tells the story of one of the largest and most architecturally unusual of the late nineteenth-century Utopian

communities and its Theosophist founder, Katherine A.W. Tingley.
More biographical information about Tingley, also a philanthropist
and social reformer, may be found in Notable American Women
(entry 35), 3:466-68 and entry 551.

553   Isaacs, Ernest. "The Fox Sisters and American Spiritualism."
       In The Occult in America (entry 554), pp. 79-110.
           The spiritualist experiences in 1848 of the three Fox sis-
       ters mark the beginning of the extensive American spiritualist
       movement of the nineteenth century. Isaacs here provides a nar-
       rative account of the movement in which Ann Leah (1818?-92),
       Margaret (1833?-93), and Catherine (1839?-92) Fox played such an
       important part. He also wrote the biographical treatment of them
       that appears in Notable American Women (entry 35), 1:655-57, as
       well as that of Mary Fenn Davis (1824-86), spiritualist lecturer
       and reformer (1:441-42).

554   Kerr, Howard, and Crow, Charles L., eds. The Occult in America:
       New Historical Perspectives. Urbana: University of Illinois
       Press, 1983. 246 pp.
           This collection of essays on an old subject written from a
       modern perspective includes several of interest to our topic.
       "The Fox Sisters and American Spiritualism" by Ernest Isaacs
       (entry 553) and "The American Theosophical Synthesis" by Robert S.
       Ellwood, Jr. (pp. 111-34) are historical surveys, while "Women in
       Occult America" by Mary Farrell Bednarowski (entry 548) is ana-
       lytical in its treatment. Other articles in the book supply help-
       ful background, notably "The Occult Connection? Mormonism,
       Christian Science, and Spiritualism" by R. Lawrence Moore
       (pp. 135-61).

555   Meade, Marion. Madame Blavatsky: The Woman Behind the Myth.
       New York: G.P. Putnam's Sons, 1980. 528 pp.
           This is the most current and extensive biography of Helena
       Petrovna Blavatsky (1831-91), the principal founder of the Theo-
       sophical Society. A thirteen-page bibliography is included.
       Other resources on Blavatsky are Richard A. Hutch, "Helena
       Blavatsky Unveiled," Journal of Religious History 11 (1980):
       320-41; Bruce F. Campbell, Ancient Wisdom Revisited (entry 551);
       Robert S. Ellwood, Jr., Alternative Altars (entry 499); John K.
       Maniha and Robert B. Maniha, "A Comparison of Psychohistorical
       Differences Among Some Female Religious and Secular Leaders"
       (entry 501); and Notable American Women (entry 35), 1:174-77.

556   Moore, R. Laurence. "The Medium and Her Message: A Case of
       Female Professionalism." In In Search of White Crows: Spiri-
       tualism, Parapsychology, and American Culture. New York:
       Oxford University Press, 1977, pp. 102-29.
           Moore demonstrates how nineteenth-century female spiritual-
       ists achieved upward mobility and gained self-esteem and satis-
       faction from helping others by means of the practice of their
       profession. Women who had been weak and sickly were able to
       travel, achieve financial independence, gain respect from male
       colleagues, and have a sense of sexual freedom through their

work. (This is a lightly revised version of an earlier article, "The Spiritualist Medium: A Study of Female Professionalism in Victorian America," in Women's Experience in America: An Historical Anthology [entry 20], pp. 145-68.)

VII.G. UTOPIAN AND COMMUNAL GROUPS

557 Eckhardt, Celia M. Fanny Wright: Rebel in America. Cambridge, Mass.: Harvard University Press, 1984. xii, 337 pp.
    Frances Wright (1795-1852) was the founder, in 1825, of a radical community at Nashoba, Tennessee, where slaves could work to free themselves from bondage. She also gave voice to a feminist criticism of organized religion and clericalism in American society. Eckhardt's narrative biography pays little attention to Wright's religious views, which are best approached through her own writings. Helpful excerpts may be found in The Feminist Papers: From Adams to de Beauvoir (entry 226), pp. 86-117. See also Notable American Women (entry 35), 3:675-80.

558 Fogarty, Robert S. Dictionary of American Communal and Utopian History. Westport, Conn.: Greenwood Press, 1980. xxvi, 271 pp.
    Fogarty has collected here much useful information about communal and utopian groups: biographical sketches of more than 140 people prominent in these movements, descriptions of nearly 60 communities, annotated chronology of societies established between 1787 and 1919, a bibliographical essay on communal history in America, and a seven-page bibliography. Sources are also included following each of the biographies and community descriptions.

559 Foster, Lawrence. Religion and Sexuality: Three American Communal Experiments of the Nineteenth Century. New York: Oxford University Press, 1981. xi, 363 pp. Reprint as Religion and Sexuality: The Shakers, the Mormons, and the Oneida Community. Urbana: University of Illinois Press, 1984.
    Viewing the adherents of three communal experiments not as marginal fanatics but as men and women "acutely sensitive . . . to the anguish of their transitional age," Foster draws on anthropological theory in rendering the unconventional religious and sexual practices of his subjects remarkably comprehensible. Extensive research in archival resources--notably those of the Mormons--lays the groundwork for rich case studies in each group, while the book also provides comparative analysis. The radical character of millenial religion, the religious importance of family structure, and the access of women to religious and social power are among the themes illuminated by this thorough and insightful study.

560 Kern, Louis J. An Ordered Love: Sex Roles and Sexuality in Victorian Utopias--the Shakers, the Mormons, and the Oneida Community. Chapel Hill: University of North Carolina Press, 1981. xiii, 430 pp.

Holding that sexuality--not religion--was the organizing
principle of these three societies, Kern provides a Freudian-
psychobiographical approach while also attempting to evaluate each
group from a contemporary feminist viewpoint. His treatment of
Mormons is uneven and he misses the changes each group underwent,
but he provides interesting data on these communitarian groups.
This book should be read with Foster's Religion and Sexuality
(entry 559) for Foster's emphasis on the millenial religious beliefs of these societies and thorough treatment of the Mormons.

561   Rohrlich, Ruby, and Baruch, Elaine Hoffman, eds. Women in
       Search of Utopia: Mavericks and Mythmakers. New York:
       Schocken Books, 1984. xxvii, 325 pp.
       This cross-cultural anthology describes utopias from the
ancient past, the recent past, and the present, as well as crit-
ically examining utopian fiction, poetry, drama, and science fiction. In the section on the recent past are found essays about
the nineteenth-century Shaker communities, Frances Wright's
Nashoba, the Owenite Socialist communities, and the Belton Texas
Woman's Commonwealth.

562   Ruether, Rosemary Radford. "Women in Utopian Movements" and
       (with Catherine M. Prelinger) "Women in Sectarian and Utopian
       Groups" (entry 502).
       The authors survey these topics in the colonial and revolu-
tionary periods and the nineteenth century, providing substantive
discussions about the various groups and topical issues of concern
relating to these movements as well as selections of relevant
documents and photographs. See fuller annotation under entry 502.

563   Wisbey, Herbert, Jr. Pioneer Prophetess: Jemima Wilkinson,
       The Publick Universal Friend. Ithaca, N.Y.: Cornell Univer-
       sity Press, 1964. xiv, 232 pp.
       Using microfilms of original sources now lost and other con-
temporary accounts, Wisbey provides the only full-length biographical treatment of the Revolutionary War era (1752-1819) controversial itinerant preacher and prophet. The briefer biographical
sketch in Notable American Women (entry 35), 3:609-10, is also by
Wisbey. Further biographical information along with excerpts from
her writings and contemporary descriptions of her appears in Women
and Religion in America, vol. 2 (entry 79), pp. 267-70 and 312-15,
as well as in Freedom's Ferment (entry 145), pp. 115-20.

       For Further Information

564   The only modern account of the life of Barbara Heinemann (1795-
       1883), spiritual leader of the Amana Societies, is the brief bio-
       graphical treatment by Marcus Bach in Notable American Women
       (entry 35), 2:175-77.

565   A preliminary look at women in the four communal societies of
       the Amish, Hutterites, Chassidic Jewish groups, and the Kibbutz is
       Freida Shoenberg Rozen's "The Permanent First-Floor Tenant: Women
       and the Gemeinschaft," Mennonite Quarterly Review 51 (1977):
       319-28.

VII.H. HOLINESS AND PENTECOSTAL MOVEMENTS

566   Buckingham, Jamie. <u>Daughter of Destiny: Kathryn Kuhlman, Her
      Story</u>. Plainfield, N.J.: Logos International, 1976. ix,
      309 pp.
           Kathryn Kuhlman, famed preacher and faith healer, is
      treated sympathetically in this commissioned biography, which
      provides an intriguing view into her religious and social context.

567   Setta, Susan M. "Patriarchy and Feminism in Conflict: The
      Life and Thought of Aimee Semple McPherson." <u>Anima</u> 9 (Fall
      1983):128-37.
           This consideration of the pentecostal preacher who founded
      the International Church of the Foursquare Gospel provides a use-
      ful introduction to her ministry. See also the biographical
      treatment in <u>Notable American Women</u> (entry 35), 2:477-80, and the
      material collected in <u>This is That: Personal Experiences, Ser-
      mons and Writings of Aimee Semple McPherson</u> (Los Angeles: Echo
      Park Evangelistic Association, 1923). An assessment of the tra-
      dition to which McPherson belonged is Charles H. Barfoot and
      Gerald T. Sheppard, "Prophetic vs. Priestly Religion: The Chang-
      ing Role of Women Clergy in Classical Pentecostal Churches,"
      <u>Review of Religious Research</u> 22 (September 1980):2-10.

568   Wisbey, Herbert, Jr. "Evangeline Cory Booth" and "Maud
      Ballington Booth." In <u>Notable American Women</u> (entry 35),
      1:204-7, 208-10.
           Wisbey provides modern biographical accounts of the lives of
      two of the Booth women most active in the United States branch of
      the Salvation Army. Evangeline (1865-1950), daughter of the
      founders of the Salvation Army in England, William and Catherine
      Mumford Booth, served as national commander in the United States
      and later as general of the entire Army. Maud (1865-1948), whose
      husband was a brother of Evangeline, served with her husband as
      supervisor of the work in the United States before they founded
      the Volunteers of America in 1896. Wisbey's bibliographical
      entries for both women provide further information, which may be
      supplemented by consulting Edward H. McKinley's <u>Marching to Glory:
      The History of the Salvation Army, 1880-1980</u> (San Francisco:
      Harper & Row, 1980) and works about Catherine Mumford Booth
      (1829-90), for example, Norman H. Murdoch, "Female Ministry in the
      Thought and Work of Catherine Booth," <u>Church History</u> 53 (1984):
      348-62.

Index

The numbers below refer to entry numbers, not to page numbers.